Magda Dolińska-Rydzek

The Antichrist in Post-Soviet Russia:
Transformations of an Ideomyth

Literatur und Kultur im mittleren und östlichen Europa

herausgegeben von Reinhard Ibler

ISSN 2195-1497

14   *Alexander Lell*
        Studien zum erzählerischen Schaffen Vsevolod M. Garšins
        Zur Betrachtung des Unrechts in seinen Werken aus der Willensperspektive
        Arthur Schopenhauers
        ISBN 978-3-8382-1042-1

15   *Dmitry Shlapentokh*
        The Mongol Conquests in the Novels of Vasily Yan
        An Intellectual Biography
        ISBN 978-3-8382-1017-9

16   *Katharina Bauer*
        Liebe – Glaube – Russland:
        Russlandkonzeptionen im Schaffen Aleksej N. Tolstojs
        ISBN 978-3-8382-1182-4

17   *Magdalena Baran-Szołtys, Monika Glosowitz,*
        Aleksandra Konarzewska (eds.)
        Imagined Geographies
        Central European Spatial Narratives between 1984 and 2014
        ISBN 978-3-8382-1225-8

18   *Adam Jarosz*
        Der Spiegel und die Spiegelungen
        Über Geschlecht und Seele im Werk von Stanisław Przybyszewski
        ISBN 978-3-8382-1246-3

19   *Šárka Sladovníková*
        The Holocaust in Czechoslovak
        and Czech Feature Films
        ISBN 978-3-8382-1196-1

20   *Julia Spanberger*
        Grenzen und Grenzerfahrungen in den Texten Viktor Pelevins
        Eine Analyse seiner frühen Prosa
        ISBN 978-3-8382-1460-3

Magda Dolińska-Rydzek

THE ANTICHRIST IN POST-SOVIET RUSSIA:
TRANSFORMATIONS OF AN IDEOMYTH

Bibliografische Information der Deutschen Nationalbibliothek
Die Deutsche Nationalbibliothek verzeichnet diese Publikation in der Deutschen Nationalbibliografie; detaillierte bibliografische Daten sind im Internet über http://dnb.d-nb.de abrufbar.

Bibliographic information published by the Deutsche Nationalbibliothek
Die Deutsche Nationalbibliothek lists this publication in the Deutsche Nationalbibliografie; detailed bibliographic data are available in the Internet at http://dnb.d-nb.de.

ISBN-13: 978-3-8382-1545-7
© *ibidem*-Verlag, Stuttgart 2021
Alle Rechte vorbehalten

Das Werk einschließlich aller seiner Teile ist urheberrechtlich geschützt. Jede Verwertung außerhalb der engen Grenzen des Urheberrechtsgesetzes ist ohne Zustimmung des Verlages unzulässig und strafbar. Dies gilt insbesondere für Vervielfältigungen, Übersetzungen, Mikroverfilmungen und elektronische Speicherformen sowie die Einspeicherung und Verarbeitung in elektronischen Systemen.

All rights reserved. No part of this publication may be reproduced, stored in or introduced into a retrieval system, or transmitted, in any form, or by any means (electronic, mechanical, photocopying, recording or otherwise) without the prior written permission of the publisher. Any person who does any unauthorized act in relation to this publication may be liable to criminal prosecution and civil claims for damages.

Printed in the EU

Table of Contents

Acknowledgements 7

Introduction 9

I. Is the Antichrist a Russian Ideomyth? 23
    I.1.   The Russian Idea and the Antichrist 24
    I.2.   Ideomyth as an Analytical Tool 36

II. Who is the Antichrist? More than Two Millennia of Antichrist Developments 45
    II.1.   The Antichrist in Western Christianity 46
    II.2.   Imminent Apocalypse: Russia and the Antichrist 57

III. The Antichrist and His Plot Against Russia 75
    III.1. (D)evils of Postmodernism: Gradual Apostasy and the Mystery of Lawlessness 76
    III.2. Antisemitism and Eschatology: The New World Order and Invisible Khazaria 104

IV. "Without Doubt, the Antichrist is a Real Political Possibility of Our Times": Russia, the Antichrist, and Political Theology 117
    IV.1. The Antichrist: Image of a Political Enemy 118
    IV.2. Sacral Geography and the Kingdom of the Antichrist 136

V. The Antichrist: New Incarnations 153
    V.1.   I, the Antichrist or the Antichrist in Me 155
    V.2.   (Not Only) Postmodern Variations: From Scientist and Serial Killer to Politician and Trickster 166

VI. Ultimate Fight: Orthodox Russia Against the Antichrist 183
    VI.1. The Role of Russia in the Endtime Drama: The Katechon or Not? 185
    VI.2. Apocalypse Now! 196

Conclusions 205

Bibliography 217

Acknowledgements

This book is based on my dissertation, defended at Fachbereich 5 of the Justus-Liebig University Gießen in November 2018. It would have not come to existence if it were not for the engagement of many people and institutions. First and foremost, I would like to express my gratitude to my research advisor, Professor Reinhard Ibler, for his insightful comments and support. Another person without whom this book would not have been written is Professor Alexander Panchenko. He, above all, provided me with the in-depth knowledge of the Russian culture and saved me from taking intellectual shortcuts. I would also like to express my special thanks to John Crust. Due to his efforts, this book is much more enjoyable to read.

I would also like to thank all the colleagues and professors from the Graduate Centre for the Study of Culture, the Institute for Slavic Studies, and the Department of Eastern European History at the Justus-Liebig University in Giessen. I had the pleasure to engage in numerous debates with them and received insightful comments and constructive criticism. Also, I direct my appreciation to DAAD (German Agency for Academic Exchange), which provided me with the financial support to carry out my research in Germany and Russia.

I am deeply grateful to my family and friends, and, above all, Xru, who with great patience and love, endured with me all stages of working on this book. We made it!

Introduction

At first glance, they are virtually indistinguishable. Two handsome men with long hair, eyes wide open, and tightened lips concealed in bushy beards. The enigmatic twins on the red background are portrayed as on old Russian icons. Only after a while, the discrepancies between them become evident. As we can see, one of the twins has calm blue eyes and his head is surrounded by a bright nimbus with a cross inscribed in it. The other twin, in turn, has a slightly longer chin and darker complexion. His dark brown, almost black, eyes, gaze thoughtfully and somewhat tensely. Instead of a halo, his head is surrounded by a black circle into which a five-pointed star with three sixes is inscribed. The 666 is the symbolic number of the Beast from St. John's Apocalypse, and the pentagram is often associated with Freemasonry, black magic, and Satanism. All of a sudden, it becomes clear that one of the twins symbolises good and holiness and that the other is the personification of evil.

This is how Ilya Glazunov (1930-2017), believed to be the most popular contemporary Russian painter, imagined Christ and the Antichrist in his painting *Christ and Antichrist* (1999). Portraying the Antichrist as a mirror reflection and evil twin of Christ has its roots in ambiguity embedded in the very word "antichrist", in which the prefix ἀντί means both "against" and "in opposition to", as well as "instead of". In this context, the Antichrist can be understood both as the antithesis and the ultimate enemy of Christ, as well as his evil twin and usurper, who presents himself as the Saviour, and only after winning people's trust and power over the world, he will reveal his true nature. Just like the biblical wolf in a lamb's skin, the Antichrist is the personification of evil disguised as good and, thus, practically impossible to recognise.

What such a representation of Christ and the Antichrist communicates is that in today's complicated world, it is increasingly difficult for people to distinguish between good and evil. The reason for this is both a departure from traditional religious values and the growing importance of postmodernist ideas that disperse grand narratives and claim that everything is relative. This way of interpreting Ilya Glazunov's painting resonated, above all, among Russian Orthodox and conservative circles. Similar doubts regarding the mysterious entanglement of Christ and the Antichrist as virtually indistinguishable twins can be found in the writings and utterances of numerous post-Soviet Russian public figures related to the right side of the political scene, such as Metropolitan of Saint Petersburg and Ladoga Ioann Snychev; a political scientist, historian, and academic, Alexander Dugin; and a writer and editor, known for his monarchist and antisemitic views, Mikhail Nazarov. Even though they have different backgrounds and represent different worldviews, what unites them are frequent references to Christian eschatology and, primarily, the use of the Antichrist figure in various contexts, both religious and secular.

This study's basic assumption is that the Antichrist figure, alluded to by numerous post-Soviet authors, is an essential part of Russian cultural imagery. Throughout the years, not only has it been a significant part of historiosophic conceptions, such as Moscow the Third Rome or the Holy Rus', but it also has served as a constitutive Other and the final enemy against whom Russian national identity has been constructed. In other words, this book attempts to demonstrate how the Antichrist figure encapsulates the most important features of Russian culture. Moreover, it sets out to explain in what contexts it serves as the constitutive part of Russian auto-stereotypes and a response to social, political, and cultural changes. I believe that addressing the subject of the Antichrist, by combining various theoretical perspectives, including the history of ideas, literary studies, religious studies, and political sciences, will significantly contribute to contemporary Russian studies.

Overall, by employing the theoretical notion of ideomyth, this study addresses the following questions: How is the Antichrist ideomyth constructed within the Post-Soviet Russian semiosphere? How and why is it employed in political and geopolitical discourses, conspiracy theories, and literary works? What is the meaning of this ideomyth for contemporary Russian culture? How does this apocalyptic narrative intermingle with a range of post-Soviet anti-Western, antisemitic, and messianic discourses? How do various post-Soviet discourses, employing the Antichrist ideomyth, refer to Russian history and cultural traditions? Finally, is the Antichrist ideomyth only an image of the archenemy or is it rather a "word on the intersection of discourses" which, depending on the context, conveys different messages and meanings?

Imagining the Antichrist in Russia and Beyond

As suggested, the Antichrist did not appear in post-Soviet Russian discourses out of the blue. Instead, being an essential part of what Nikolai Berdyaev, a Russian religious thinker and philosopher, recognises as the Russian "eschatological myth", the Antichrist in Russia has undergone numerous historical and semantic transformations throughout the centuries. He was viewed not only as a false Messiah, the enemy of God, and grand deceiver, but also as a usurper of the Tsar's power, religious dissenter and the embodiment of evil forces. The Antichrist has also been recognised in historical figures such as Ivan the Terrible, Peter the Great, Napoleon, and Adolf Hitler, as well as political and social systems such as Russian autocracy, the Bolshevik regime, and liberal democracy (Isupov 1995). In short, as claimed by Vardan Bagdasaryan (2004), "each epoch of Russian historiosophy created its own Antichrist, who has little in common with the Beast from the Revelation of John". This study indicates that post-Soviet Russia is no exception. As I will demonstrate, in the last two and a half decades, the Antichrist figure has been central to numerous speculations within various, sometimes surprising, contexts.

Ilya Glazunov's painting *Christ and Antichrist*, which was completed in 1999, serves as an excellent example of how persistent the Antichrist ideomyth is in Russia. Also, by imagining Christ and the Antichrist as almost identical twins, the painting makes use of one of the most canonical ways of representing Christ and his evil adversary in art. It is important to note, however, that the physical appearance of the Antichrist has significantly evolved. In the medieval iconography, the Antichrist was usually portrayed as the apocalyptic "beast from the abyss" – a four-legged monster with many horns and protruding fangs. This way of imagining the Antichrist was also characteristic for the so-called Old Believers who, after the 17th century, developed quite rich iconography illustrating this apocalyptic beast (Sulikowska 2014).

With time, the Antichrist began to be portrayed as less demonic and more human. In this iconographic tradition, he was imagined either as a handsome man, behind whose back a horned Satan is whispering in his ear, or as a person with a "double face" – one handsome and pleasant, and the other satanic and wicked, symbolising his dual and deceptive nature. Following theological tradition, according to which the Antichrist will be the mirror reflection of Christ, numerous images depicting the Antichrist and Christ as identical twins have been produced. In this context, the evil nature of the Antichrist has been indicated only by symbols and figures associated with his demonic nature (Derevenskiy 2007). Ilya Glazunov's painting is an example of the contemporary continuation of this iconographic tradition. Portraying the Antichrist as someone who will come instead of Christ and deceive humanity went beyond iconographic representations and penetrated other fields of art, especially literature. In the Russian context, the canonical literary example of a wicked individual, who claims to be the Saviour of humanity, but, in fact, is the embodiment of evil and the enemy of Christianity, is the Grand Inquisitor from Fyodor Dostoyevsky's novel *The Brothers Karamazov* (1880). In the parable told by Ivan Karamazov to his younger brother Alyosha in a tavern, we are taken back to 16th-century Seville ruled by a compassionate and merciful cardinal – the Grand Inquisitor. When Christ finally arrives in the earthly world after one and a half centuries after his death and resurrection, he remains unrecognised by people. Only the Grand Inquisitor identifies him as the Messiah and, threatened by his power, orders him to be arrested.

In his extended monologue, the Grand Inquisitor accuses Christ of leaving people in confusion and agony. Also, believing that people are too weak to value the freedom offered them by Jesus, the cardinal decides to improve God's work and provides humanity with what it needs the most: he replaces heavenly bread with earthly bread. The only price humanity has to pay is abandoning freedom and surrendering to the authoritarian power of the Grand Inquisitor, based on the three temptations of Satan: a miracle, a mystery, and authority, all of which were rejected by Jesus in the desert. Even though the very word "antichrist" is never used in the parable, it is evident that the power of the Grand Inquisitor is of devilish origin. Situating himself in opposition to Christ, the cardinal preaches values detached from God. He turns out to be a false Messiah and the antithesis of Christ. Since Glazunov was very interested in Dostoyevsky's work and authored illustrations for new editions of his books, one can assume that the Grand Inquisitor was an important inspiration for the painting *Christ and Antichrist*.

Another image of an imposter Messiah, who tries to seduce humanity with false miracles and values detached from God, is Apollon from Vladimir Solovyov's

The Short Tale about the Antichrist (1899-1900). First portrayed as a thirty-three-year-old pacifist, philanthropist, and humanist, he becomes the ecumenical leader of a universal state that unifies all the nations. Only then Apollon is revealed as a false Messiah who wants to seize unlimited power over the world and even replace God. Interestingly, due to its prophetic acuity, Solovyov's parable is in many ways consistent with Dostoyevsky's Grand Inquisitor. The image of Apollon as an autocratic ruler preaching progressive, humanistic ideals under the guise of Christian values not only alludes to Dostoevsky's vision, but also situates the Antichrist figure in a historical context – it is not a mere religious concept nor a rhetorical figure anymore. Instead, in Solovyov's view, the adversary of Christ becomes a real historical threat (Walicki 1979).

Antichrist-like figures created by Dostoyevsky and Solovyov have significantly influenced Russian interpretations of who the adversary of Christ is and how he will attempt to seduce humanity. Nevertheless, this was not the only way of portraying this apocalyptic figure. As I demonstrate in this book, from the very beginning, the Antichrist figure eludes straightforward and unambiguous interpretations. Neither in the Scriptures nor other early-Christian eschatological narratives, such as the writings of Church Fathers and subsequent prophecies about the end of the world, was it possible to clearly determine whether the Antichrist would be spiritual or tangible, if he will be an individual, a duo, or a collective, and, finally, when and where he would be born and how long he would rule before the ultimate Apocalypse.

Analogous speculations have been present in various Russian discourses, especially as a result of turbulent historical, political, and social change that, as historian Aleksey Beglov (2014) argues, triggered "waves of eschatological expectations". Among events that led to the acceleration of apocalyptic fears in Russia, Beglov mentions the schism, also known as the *Raskol*, in the Russian Orthodox Church that took place in the 17th century, the rapid changes in the Russian Empire at the turn of the 19th and the 20th centuries, the Bolshevik Revolution, both world wars, and the dissolution of the Soviet Union. Taking that all into consideration, one can argue that the Antichrist figure, employed particularly willingly in times of turmoil and uncertainty, still remains complex, ambiguous, and polysemic.

Features of an Ideomyth: Theoretical Framework

To thoroughly scrutinise the multifaceted the Antichrist figure in various post-Soviet Russian discourses, the category of ideomyth is used. I hope that this analytical tool will enable me to grasp all semiotic implications of this multidimensional apocalyptic figure. I derive the concept of ideomyth from Konstantin Isupov's introduction to his book *Antichrist: Anthology* (1994) and Vardan Bagdasaryan's article "The Image of the Antichrist in the Russian Historiosophic Thought" (2004). Since neither of them defines this notion, I took a liberty to put forth my own definition and to approach ideomyth as an analytical tool combining critical perspectives embedded both in the concepts of the "Russian idea" and "myth". In this context, the Russian idea is viewed as a traditional category of self-knowledge and a reservoir of Russian cultural myths. Myth, in turn, is understood as an ideologically driven narrative which mirrors thoughts, words, and values underlying a given culture (Liszka 1989, Barthes 1957, Veraksa 2013).

In short, I define ideomyth as a culture-mirroring and culture-forming narrative, adjusting its objectives to the contexts in which it is employed. This theoretical perspective allows me to look at the post-Soviet variant of the legend of the Antichrist as a transforming ideomyth which not only reflects, but also constitutes, Russian culture. Furthermore, the category of ideomyth enables me to reveal implicit intentions undermining the appropriations of this notion in various religious and secular contexts in post-Soviet Russia.

Glazunov and Others: Sources

A characteristic feature of the discourses analysed in this study is the belief that we are living in the Endtime and that the final battle between the forces of good and evil, represented by Christ and the Antichrist, will soon take place. This belief is typical, specifically for post-Soviet Russian Orthodox and conservative communities, the representatives of which eagerly use the eschatological motifs and update them according to their needs. In this context, the painting of Ilya Glazunov, who in his oeuvre often employs eschatological motifs, including the Antichrist, serves as a starting point for my study of the role and shape taken by the Antichrist ideomyth in post-Soviet Russian discourses.

Glazunov, who survived the siege of Leningrad during the Second World War, came from an intelligentsia family, and was quite a personality. He was a respected artist, educator, and writer, whose art attracted a lot of attention, both in Russia and abroad. Not only were his works exhibited in numerous Western European cities, but he was also awarded the UNESCO Picasso Golden Medal for contribution to world culture, regardless that his worldview is rather contradictory to the values promoted by this institution. Indeed, Glazunov is well known not only for his conservative, nationalistic, and antisemitic views, but also for being an anti-liberal and anti-democratic supporter of the idea of introducing the Orthodox monarchy in Russia. Glazunov expressed his views in detail in a monumental two-volume autobiographical treaty entitled *Crucified Russia*, published first in 2004. In this work, not only did he tell the story of his life, but also tackled a wide range of subjects, including Russian history, political philosophy, literature, art, and religion. Like his writings, Glazunov's paintings employ themes from Russian history, often mixed with apocalyptic motifs and the obsession with a Judeo-Masonic conspiracy aimed at destroying Russia.

A dissident during the Soviet era, when his works were considered not socialist enough, Glazunov gained remarkable recognition in post-Soviet Russia. According to Michael Hagemeister (2004), Glazunov's works owe their popularity to numerous reproductions distributed not only through professional art albums, but also calendars, posters, magazines, and cheap brochures. In addition, Glazunov reached people with his books, movies, TV appearances, and public speeches. While critics argue that Glazunov's art is nothing more than kitsch and he is more of a politician than an artist, his admirers, including prominent political and religious figures such as Vladimir Putin and Patriarch Kirill, perceive his works as an antidote to anti-values promoted by the West. Meanwhile, Glazunov, an ardent advocate and supporter of the annexation of Crimea, believes that in a world permeated with forces of the Antichrist, Orthodox Russia is the last hope for humanity.

In this study, I analyse numerous writings and texts authored by post-Soviet public figures whose views coincide with those of Glazunov. Among the adherents of the belief that the Antichrist is approaching and Russia will play an important role in the apocalyptic drama, one should mention prominent post-Soviet Russian public figures such as Ioann Snychev, Alexander Dugin, Mikhail Nazarov, Oleg Platonov, Konstantin Dushenov, Olga Chetverikova, Tatyana Gracheva, Vladimir Osipov, Julia Voznesenskaya, and Alexander Prokhanov. Taking into account that they are political scientists, journalists, writers, ecclesiastics, and academics, who have many possibilities to reach their audience through utterances, publications, and media presence, one can assume that they shape to a large extent the public debate in post-Soviet Russia.

What also connects these authors is the fact that the majority of them is related to religious and conservative milieus and, as Alexander Verkhovsky (2004: 129) asserts, they can be recognised as "Russian Orthodox nationalists". Their intellectual lives revolve around right-wing journals such as Oleg Platonov's *Russkiy Vestnik* and Alexander Prokhanov's *Zavtra*; TV channels such as *Spas* and the internet-TV channel *Den*, run by Andrey Fefelov, the son of Alexander Prokhanov; internet portals like Logoslovo.ru and Pravaya.ru; and the analytical information agency Russkaya Narodnaya Linya, which is a continuation of Konstantin Dushenov's journal *Rus' Pravoslavnaya* and prohibited in 2010, when Dushenov was sentenced to prison for inciting hatred and enmity, as well as humiliating the dignity of a group of people on the grounds of nationality, origin, attitude to religion. Although the authors have different backgrounds and their views differ on many issues, what interests me the most are the intersections and similarities in the selected narratives and, above all, how they utilise the Antichrist ideomyth.

To explore dominant rhetorical and narrative strategies employed by the above-mentioned authors, I analyse philosophical and historical books, novels, political conceptions, ecclesiastical writings, scientific, as well as quasi-scientific[1], texts published in the Russian Federation after the collapse of the Soviet Union. What connects all of the analysed discourses is a tendency to employ eschatological

---

[1] Quasi-scientific discourse is one which, by employing a specific language and method, pretends to be scientific. In this context, I follow the claim by Mariya Akhmetova, who argues that quasi-scientific discourse is often used not "to solve scientific problems, but to confirm religious ideas". In other words, not only is it used to explain religious concepts with the help of scientific terminology, but also to analyse "scientific problems from a religious point of view" (Akhmetova 2008: 3). Quasi-science can also be called "pseudo-science" (Shermer 1997).

motifs, specifically the Antichrist figure. Even though some of them may seem marginal and odd, I consider them relevant since, as Viktor Shnirelman (2017) argues, what was once marginal can very quickly become mainstream. In this context, *The Protocols of Elders of Zion* serves as an adequate example. It is especially relevant in the context of the resurgence of radical ideologies in Europe and beyond. Indeed, in recent years, in countries such as the United States, Brazil, Germany, France, Poland, Hungary, Croatia, among others, we have witnessed an increase of the political significance of right-wing and populist parties. By exploiting a crisis of democratic values, many politicians have gained power by pushing anti-modernist, anti-liberal, and anti-globalist ideas. Interestingly, as Anton Shekhovtsov (2018) claims, the Russian Federation plays a significant role in this process by influencing the Western far-right both financially and ideologically.

It is important to emphasise that the analysed texts are used here as a synecdoche. Being only a part of all post-Soviet discourses referring to the Antichrist figure, they are used in order to synecdochically represent prevailing tendencies and potential motivations behind them. I believe that they adequately demonstrate the complexity of interpretations of the Antichrist figure in post-Soviet Russia in a sufficiently profound and extensive way. Furthermore, they show various transformations this ideomyth undergoes, depending on cultural, social, and political needs it has to fulfil. Even though many texts discussed in this study could be the subject of a separate monograph, in this context, they are used as examples, showing the richness of how the Antichrist figure can be employed and interpreted. In short, this study aims to capture the semiotic ambiguity of the post-Soviet Antichrist, as well as to demonstrate the diversity of voices, discourses, problems, and functions related to this ideomyth.

Although this study focuses on a religious concept, it is not theological. Instead, I look at the ecclesiastical writings in a broader socio-political context. I am interested not in the texts developed within the Russian Orthodox Church, but in their influence on other discourses, namely, historical, political, and literary ones. Moreover, this book attempts to investigate how purely religious images and motifs penetrate secular discourses. I focus on Orthodoxy, as the dominant religion in Russia, often considered one of the most important determinants of Russian culture (Fedotov 1960).² Thus, in my work, I do not analyse eschatological discourses established in other Russian traditional religions (Judaism, Islam, Buddhism, Catholicism, and Protestantism), nor in the new religious movements, which flourished as the Soviet Union was dismantled, such as the Church of the Last Testament, the White Brotherhood, and the Vissarion community (Panchenko 2004, Akhmetova 2010). Furthermore, as my study is focused on the discursive representations of the Antichrist ideomyth, I discuss iconographic images only to a very limited extent.

Literature Review

Throughout the centuries, the Antichrist figure received a lot of attention. It was the subject of numerous monographs, articles, and book chapters. Nevertheless, none of the existing works has tackled the multifaceted and complex problem of how and why the apocalyptic image of the Antichrist transforms across diverse discourses in post-Soviet Russia. Hence, based on the assumption that Antichrist figure serves as a culture-specific ideomyth in Russia, in my study, not only do I track the genealogy of the concept of the Antichrist, but I also analyse its meaning in contemporary Russian culture.

The history of how the images of the Antichrist have developed over the centuries, especially in the context of Western Christianity, has been well chronicled. For instance, it is the topic of the seminal book by Bernard McGinn, *The Antichrist: Two Thousand Years of the Human Fascination with Evil* (1994), in which the author provides a detailed analysis of the transformations of the Antichrist figure from its biblical origin to the present day. Other essential works tackling the developments of the Antichrist are Richard Emmerson's *The Antichrist in the Middle Ages: A Study of Medieval Apocalypticism, Art, and Literature* (1981) and the collection of articles edited by Wolfram Brandes and Felicitas Schmieder entitled *The Antichrist: Constructing the Enemy* (2010). The Antichrist was also a subject of the book written by a Polish priest, Stefan Ewertowski, entitled *The Idea of The*

---

² In recent years, one may observe the falling number of believers of the Russian Orthodox Church. Nevertheless, according to the survey carried out by the Levada Centre in January, 2020, 65% of Russians consider themselves Orthodox. Hence, Orthodoxy remains the dominant religion in the Russian Federation (Levada.ru 2020).

Antichrist in Contemporary Culture: A Theological Study in the Interdisciplinary Dimension (2010). All these works discuss various stages of the development of the idea of the Antichrist in different cultures, focusing primarily on the Western Christian context.

There are also numerous studies exploring what can be called the "Russian Antichrist". The most important examples include Konstantin Isupov's *Antichrist: Anthology* (1995) and the two books by Boris Derevenskiy: *The Teaching About the Antichrist in Antiquity and the Middle Ages* (2000) and *The Book About the Antichrist* (2007). Other important works that should be mentioned here are *The Old Believers & The World of Antichrist: The Vyg Community and the Russian State 1694-1855* (1970) by Robert Crummey and *In the Shadow of the Antichrist: Old Believers' Ideas in the 17th Century* (1999) by Elżbieta Przybył. They focus on how the legend of the Antichrist was developed within a complex historiosophy put forth by the Old Believers after the schism within the Russian Orthodox Church in the 17th century.

Even though the Antichrist figure was analysed in numerous works, surprisingly little attention has been given to its post-Soviet interpretations. Nevertheless, it is important to mention the following works: "Where Does the Antichrist Come From?" (2004) by Andrzej de Lazari; Michael Hagemeister's "*The Protocols of the Elders of Zion*: Between History and Fiction" (2008) and "Trilogy of the Apocalypse. Vladimir Solovyov, Seraphim of Sarov and Sergey Nilus on the Coming of the Antichrist and the End of World's History" (2010) as well as Viktor Shnirelman's book scrutinising the relationship between post-Soviet eschatological discourses and antisemitism, *The Tribe of Dan: Eschatology and Antisemitism in Contemporary Russia* (2017).

All of these publications serve as a point of departure of this study, which attempts to demonstrate that despite the passing of time and numerous changes – historical, political, and social – the Antichrist ideomyth has not lost its actuality. On the contrary, being actualised and reinterpreted in various post-Soviet discourses, it has acquired a range of new dimensions.

Structure of the Study

This book comprises six chapters preceded by the introduction and followed by general conclusions. In the first chapter, "Is the Antichrist a Russian Ideomyth?", I introduce the theoretical framework of my analysis and explain why I consider the concept of the ideomyth to be the most useful analytical tool to analyse the transformations of the Antichrist figure in various discourses. This chapter is followed by "Who is the Antichrist? More than Two Millennia of Antichrist Developments", which tracks the historical developments of the Antichrist figure in Western and Russian contexts. It highlights the most important moments in the semantic history of the Antichrist – early-Christian eschatological narratives and writings by Church Fathers, who were the most influential ancient Christian theologians, including Irenaeus of Lyons, Origen of Alexandria, John Chrysostom, Tertullian, and Augustine of Hippo, to the art of the *fin de siècle* and the tragic events of the 20th century interpreted in the apocalyptic key. Notably, when discussing Russian transformations of the Antichrist ideomyth, I focus on the historical moments when eschatological moods reached their momentum: the *Raskol* within the Orthodox Church in the 17th century, the Bolshevik Revolution, and the collapse of the Soviet Union.

The collapse of the Soviet Union and suspicions that it was caused not by the historical contingency, but by a conspiracy of mysterious yet mighty forces, is the starting point of the third chapter of this study, "The Antichrist and His Plot Against Russia". It focuses on post-Soviet discourses portraying the Antichrist as the mastermind behind evil plans aimed at destroying Russia. Permeated with antisemitic and anti-Western prejudices, texts analysed in this chapter tend to depict certain groups such as Jews, Communists, and sexual minorities as servants of the Antichrist, who will pave his way to power over the world. In this context, all misfortunes Russia has experienced throughout its history are interpreted in the light of a wicked conspiracy, the final event of which will be the ultimate fight with the Antichrist. For me, these discourses, indeed, serve as a pretext for an in-depth look into conspiracy theories as alternate ways of comprehending reality.

The title of the following chapter, "'Without Doubt, the Antichrist is a Real Political Possibility of Our Times': Russia, the Antichrist, and Political Theology", is partly a quote from the article "The Mystery of Lawlessness" (1992) written by

Ioann Snychev, the Metropolitan of the Eparchy of Saint Petersburg and Ladoga (1990-1995), and, thus, one of the most influential figures in the Russian Orthodox Church of that time. In his article, he depicts the reality of post-Soviet Russia as the Endtime characterised not only by the collapse of what he identifies as moral values, but also by insecurity, turmoil, and anarchy. In this chapter, collating Snychev's writings with works by authors such as Aleksandr Dugin, Mikhail Nazarov, Oleg Platonov, Olga Chetverikova et al., I demonstrate how and why contemporary political events are inscribed into the apocalyptic context by means of political theology. The most important difference between discourses analysed in this and the next chapter is the presence, or absence, of the belief that a given political situation is the result of a conspiracy. The theories discussed in Chapter Four, though involving the same authors as those discussed in Chapter Three, do not refer to conspiratorial imagery.

In Chapter Five, "The Antichrist: New Incarnations?", *I* tackle new interpretations of the Antichrist ideomyth in post-Soviet writings, both religious and secular. Focusing predominantly on contemporary Russian literature, I discuss here to what extent the selected authors rely on old interpretations of this figure, and what new dimensions and meanings they might add to it. In this context, the Antichrist is portrayed not only in a traditional way as a false Messiah, who will turn out to be a ruthless apocalyptic tyrant, but also as a serial killer or a trickster, who turns the existing world upside down. In this context, I rely on the figure of a trickster, characteristic in folklore and popular culture, which symbolises an archetypal joker-deity. Being the "boundary-crosser", a trickster is always believed to oppose dictated norms, and act against conventions (Hyde 2017, Lipovetsky 2010). As I argue, like the Antichrist, a trickster changes his form, lies, cheats, and always gets away with it.

Finally, in the last chapter, "The Ultimate Fight: Orthodox Russia Against the Antichrist", I discuss diverse discourses describing the ultimate fight between Orthodox Russia and the Antichrist. Referring to the concept of the Katechon (Engström 2014), the majority of writings analysed in this chapter portray Russia as the only force capable of destroying the Antichrist. The necessary condition to succeed in this struggle is the return to Russia's Orthodox heritage and traditional conservative values. Only then Russia will become the Third Rome and will complete its historical mission, which is to save the world from total destruction and the rule of the Antichrist. However, there exists also the other side of the belief that Russia has a crucial role to play in the Endtime: the conviction that the Antichrist will be born in Russia. Even though this belief is less popular than the belief that Russia is the Katechon, it is deeply rooted in Russian culture, and in the writings by religious and conservative thinkers of the 19th century, such as Seraphim of Sarov and Konstantin Leontiev. In this chapter, utilising their conceptions as well as the idea of the Katechon, not only do I analyse Post-Soviet Russian messianism, but also elucidate apocalyptic motifs embedded in it. Finally, I discuss a range of popular post-Soviet ideas about the end of the world and the final fight between good and evil, that is between Christ and the Antichrist.

Throughout this study, for the spelling of Russian words, I rely on the BGN/PCGN transliteration system unless there is another convention (i.e. Dostoyevsky instead Dostoyevskiy). Also, I decided to use only English translations of titles of works cited and analysed in the text. The original titles can be found in the bibliography at the end of the book. If not stated otherwise, all translations from Russian, Polish, and German are mine.

I. Is the Antichrist a Russian Ideomyth?

"Each epoch of Russian historiosophy created its own Antichrist, who has little in common with the Beast from the Revelation of John", argues a Russian historian, Vardan Bagdasaryan (2004). Throughout the centuries, the image of the Antichrist in Russia has undergone numerous transformations: he has been portrayed as a false Messiah, an enemy of God, a usurper of the Tsar's power, an embodiment of evil forces, as well as an individual who interprets Christian values detached from God. Moreover, Russian historiosophy has seen the Antichrist not only in historical figures such as Ivan the Terrible, Peter the Great, and Lenin, but also in political and social systems, e.g. Russian autocracy, the Bolshevik regime, and liberal democracy. Furthermore, a multifaceted and ambiguous Antichrist figure has been an essential part of the Russian collective imagery. Representing the demonic Other it has been an essential element of the Russian idea and its constitutive elements, such as the idea of the Holy Rus' and the conception of Moscow the Third Rome.

As Bagdasaryan suggests, the Antichrist figure has not only been very important for the Russian culture so far, but it will also shape its future developments, especially in the 21st century. Two decades into this new century, one can undoubtedly say that Bagdasaryan was right. His view can be confirmed by numerous post-Soviet discourses that have continued to recontextualise and reinterpret the apocalyptic Antichrist figure. As a result, the image of the Antichrist in Russia has gained new dimensions – it has served not only as a historiosophic or literary image, but also as an image of a real political enemy, whose intention is to destroy Orthodox Russia. In other words, the Russian the Antichrist ideomyth has become a kind of a "mythological image" which, by being used in different, often secular, contexts, has grown out from its original, religious meaning.

Taking into account the complexity of the apocalyptic Antichrist figure, which I discuss in 2.1. and 2.2., as well as the fact that it tends to elude simple definitions and rigid interpretations, it is necessary to find a methodology that will bring out the whole richness of this concept. Therefore, the analytical tool I chose for my analysis is the category of the ideomyth, taken from two articles discussing transformations of the image of the Antichrist in the context of Russian culture – Vardan Bagdasaryan's "The Image of Antichrist in Russian Historiosophic Thought" (2004) and Konstantin Isupov's introduction to the book *The Antichrist: Anthology* (1995). Since neither of these works defines this concept, I took the liberty of carrying out an "intellectual experiment" and putting forth my own definition. In this chapter, I elaborate on how and why the notion of ideomyth can be applied to elucidate the Antichrist figure in various post-Soviet Russian contexts, including political conceptions, conspiracy theories, and literature. Also, I explain how this category, being a combination of the concept of the Russian idea and the notion of myth, can be used as an analytical tool.

I.1. The Russian Idea and the Antichrist

A Method.
To understand Russia, one has to loosen up. Take off the pants.
Wear a warm bathrobe. Lie down on the sofa. Fall asleep (Yerofeyev 1999).

Russia has always been a riddle, both on its own and for the rest of the world. Even though this statement might sound somewhat essentialist, the problem of solving the so-called "Russian mystery" has for centuries been absorbing the minds of prominent thinkers, writers, and philosophers from Russia and beyond. In the Russian context, the continuous queries about its self-identity, Russian relationship towards the West, Russian destiny, and its mission in the world, significantly contributed to the development of the category of the Russian idea, which has the fundamental meaning for Russian culture. The complex and equivocal category of the Russian idea is, however, a riddle itself – there is no exhaustive and unambiguous definition of this concept. Thus, there arises a question: is solving the Russian riddle and defining the Russian idea possible at all? Is it enough, post-Soviet Russian writer Victor Yerofeyev suggests in the epigraph, to loosen up, undress, and fall asleep on the sofa? Will it enable us to comprehend Russia? This chapter does not aspire to provide any definite answers to these questions. Rather, it aims at clarifying the concept of the Russian idea, its history, and implications it has for Russian culture and philosophy, as well as discussing the role of the Antichrist figure within it.

Many Russian authors claim that understanding Russia is particularly difficult, if not impossible, from a Western perspective. Fyodor Dostoyevsky (1861) used to argue that the West would sooner discover the Perpetuum Mobile or the elixir of life than apprehend the Russian character. His words, based on a belief that Russian uniqueness cannot be comprehended from outside, were reaffirmed in 1866 by Fyodor Tyutchev, a Russian poet, who famously stated that "Russia cannot be grasped by the mind (...) in Russia one can only believe". In other words, both Dostoyevsky and Tyutchev believe that Russia is, in fact, an incomprehensible world in itself and untranslatable reality, whose secrets cannot be reached from the outside world. Interestingly, many Western theoreticians have fallen into the trap of this cognitive model and, tempted by essentialism and oversimplification, often described Russia in terms of "holy, orthodox, romantic, national, popular, imperial, autocratic and eschatological" (Williams 1999: xi-xvi).

However, since there exists no single and homogenous "West" when discussing Western representations of Russia, it is impossible to talk about one "Western attitude" towards Russia as well. According to Martin Malia (2000:8), the fluctuating images of Russia in various Western discourses are reflections of numerous conflicting perspectives: those of the left and the right, the romantics and rationalists, and, finally, those of the English, the French, the German, and the Polish, who perceive Russia in many different ways. On the other hand, some predominant patterns within Western discourses about Russia may be observed. Deriving from a specific mixture of hopes and aspirations combined with fears and frustrations, they tend to oscillate between a positive approach and positioning Russia as the threatening Other, or even the "dark double".

What is more, Western perceptions of Russia are dominated by memes many of which have their roots in ideologically-driven approaches based on a narrative of inevitable democratisation of Russia after the collapse of the Soviet Union (Sanders 2013). Indeed, the majority of Western leaders expected that Russia would follow the path of Western-style liberal democracy. When it did not happen, Western institutions not only started to blame Russian leaders for the lack of desire to cooperate with them, but also pointed to structural incompatibilities and geopolitical rivalry between Russia and the West. As a consequence, the image of

Russia in the majority of Western discourses remained strongly stereotyped and dominated by "clichéd codes".
Where do these clichéd codes come from? In a search for reasons why Russia has been stereotyped within Western discourses, scholars tend to point out a notion of Orientalism, defined by Edward Said as a mode of discourse through which European culture managed and produced its Other on political, sociological, ideological, and imaginative levels (Wolff 1994, Neumann 1996, 1999). However, applying this framework to Russia may not be entirely correct for two reasons. First, by "mimicking" the West and complex processes of "self-semiotisation", numerous Russian poets, thinkers, and politicians tended to orientalise Russia along with Western patterns. Second, through "internal colonisation", Russia has cultivated its own "secondary Orientalism", especially towards the Caucasus, Central Asia, and Siberia (Tolstanova 2008, Etkind 2011, Tolz 2011).

An example of how Russian thinkers constructed what they call "the Russianness" by turning to alternate values to those they considered represent the West could be accurately articulated by Dmitry Merezhkovsky, a Russian writer, poet, and religious thinker. In his 1914 article, "Not Peace, But a Sword", he wrote:

> We resemble you like the left hand resembles the right one: the right-hand does not coincide with the left one, it is necessary to turn one of them so that they fit together. What you have, we have as well, but inversely: we are you inside out. In the Kantian language, your realm is phenomenological, ours – transcendental; in Nietzschean language – you have Apollo, we have Dionysus; your genius is the limit, ours – the extremity... You love the middle, we love extremes. You are sober, we are drunk; you are rational, we are malfeasant (...) For you, politics equals knowledge; for us it is religion. Not in the reason and the sense, in which we frequently reach the perfect negation and nihilism – but in our inmost freedom, we are the mystics (Merezhkovsky 1914).

Merezhkovsky's words illustrated the two tendencies characteristic for various Russian discourses: portraying the West as "ideological antipodes" of Russia and portraying Russia as mystical and ambiguous, in the spirit of Tyutchev's renowned quatrain. In this romanticised picture, Russia is viewed as transcendent and genuine, contrary to the phenomenological and rational West.

What is more, the negative characterisation of the West, implicit in the Merezhkovsky text, shows that Orientalist discourse was used in both directions.

Russia, often serving as the Western Other and perceived as a second-class Europe, has established its own Orientalism – a specific "Orientalism *à rebours*", in which all negative aspects attributed to Russia, emphasised in Western discourses, have been "transubstantiated" into positive values. As a result, various Russian discourses have depicted the West not only as an important benchmark of civilisational development, but also as the Other in relation to whom Russian self-knowledge and identity have been established and negotiated, frequently based on the outright contradiction (Zamaleev 2010). Moreover, such a cognitive pattern applied in numerous Russian discourses about the West have become the exact inversion of Western Orientalist practices: being the object of orientalisation, Russia orientalises the West. Also, as Valeriy Achkasov (1997) insists, since Russian attitudes towards the West may be viewed as a mirror reflection of Russia's attitudes towards itself; each crisis of Russian identity has in a way corresponded with a crisis in Russian-Western relations.

Mutual stereotypes and prejudices between Russia and the West were consolidated during the Cold War. Moreover, the dissolution of the Soviet Union and the end of the bipolar geopolitical order did not end these mutual animosities. In the first years after the collapse of the Soviet Union, for Russians, the West became the embodiment of "progress, freedom, democracy, civil society, normality, and a nation-state"; nevertheless, disillusion over reforms in the 1990s, along with the frustration and resentment towards the West, began to grow (Duncan 2005: 277). Consequently, Russians started to believe that democratic and liberal values promoted by the United States and Western Europe were alien to original Russian culture. It resulted in portraying the West as the antagonistic Other again (Gudkov 1997).

The roots of portraying the West as the Other in Russian discourses go back deep into the past. Indeed, from a historical perspective, the relationships between Russia and the West have always been complicated and ambiguous. One of the first ideological discrepancies occurred in the 11th century and led to the East-West Schism in 1054. It was a split within Christianity over ecclesiastical differences, such as the origin of the Holy Spirit, the existence of purgatory, the number of sacraments, and the form of the Eucharist. As a result, the Eastern and the Western

Churches mutually cursed each other, and some of the Orthodox milieus perceived the "Latinism" as a "blasphemous parody of genuine Christianity" (Lotman and Uspensky 1985: 40).
Another event that rendered Russian perception of the West even more complicated was the transformation under Peter the Great. The innovatory Western-inspired reforms enforced by the Tsar resulted in two prevailing attitudes among Russian society: on the one hand, they were perceived positively as a new stimulus, triggering "rapid cultural progress" and, on the other hand, they were viewed as an attempt to destroy national individuality. Furthermore, whereas the Petrine Reforms led to a feeling of secondariness in relation to the West among some Russian intellectuals, others have seen them as an opportunity for their country to develop beyond old and "spiritually dead" Europe. Marian Broda (2011), a Polish specialist in Russian philosophy, argues that such a perception of Russian-Western relations has continued not only in the debate between Slavophiles and Westernizers that began in the 19th century, but also in discussions about the future of Russia after the dissolution of the Soviet Union.
The 19th-century debate about Russia's place in world history, which has continued to the present day, was triggered by Pyotr Chaadayev's *First Philosophical Letter*, published in 1836. In this publication, Chaadayev argued that Russia is a country without a past and a future, and that it had made no contribution to global culture. Such a bold assertion irritated the Russian authorities. Subsequently, Chaadayev was declared "clinically insane", placed under house arrest, and subjected to compulsory treatment. Interestingly, a year later, Chaadayev drastically changed his views. In another work, *Apology of the Madman* (1837), he deemed that the civilisational latency of Russia is, in fact, an asset – and thanks to that, Russia had a chance for much faster development, and it can make a significant contribution to building Christian civilisation. Chaadayev's ideas initiated two of the most important currents of Russian philosophical thought in the 19th century: the Slavophiles and the Westernizers.
The Slavophiles were a relatively homogenous group of romantic intellectuals who believed in the fundamental historical mission of Orthodox Russia and its development independent of the West. The Westernizers, in turn, were a much more diverse group unified by the idea that the historical development of the West

should serve as an example for Russia. Another issue that disunited these ongoing currents was the approach to reforms introduced by Peter the Great. Whereas Slavophiles rejected them, claiming that they were an attempt to destroy the core of Russian identity, Westernizers glorified Peter the Great. They argued that he had brought Western civilisation to Russia and pushed it towards modernisation (Billington 1966, Walicki 1979).

Yuri Lotman and Boris Uspensky, the two most famous representatives of the Moscow-Tartu Semiotic School, provide an interesting perspective on the repercussions of the reforms introduced by Peter the Great and post-Petrine Russian culture in general. According to these authors, contrary to widespread belief, post-Petrine culture was much more traditional than it is commonly thought: compared to underlying traditionally Russian forms of socio-political order, Western influences turned out to be only superficial (Lotman and Uspensky 1985: 52-54). Consequently, Russian society, as well as its intelligentsia, were torn between native old-Russian tradition and European norms and values. The tension experienced by Russian intellectuals led to a polarisation of their attitudes and aspirations: whereas Slavophiles preached a return to the original old-Russian culture, liberated from Western influences, Westernizers claimed that Russia should follow the Western course of development. Both conceptions, even though seemingly antagonistic, were paradoxically analogous, and should be approached as reactions to the apparent inconsistency of Russian and Western hierarchies of values.

Many scholars researching Russian culture argue that ideological discord between Slavophiles and Westernizers is a result of "binary models", which are a prevailing cognitive paradigm shaping Russian culture. This perception derives from a relatively essentialist conception put forth by Lotman and Uspensky. They claim that the traditional Russian cognitive paradigm is based on "sharp divisions lacking the axiologically neutral sphere". In other words, they believe that within Russian culture, the reality is comprehended through bipolar divisions of cultural values: ideological, political, and religious. As a result, nothing is perceived as neutral, and the world is viewed in the paradigm "either/or": either holy or diabolical; either good or bad; either Christian or anti-Christian (Lotman and Uspensky 1985: 30-66). Even though this theory may seem simplified in many respects, it partially explains the polarised attitudes towards the West, as well as diverse ideas about the Russian future that divide Russian society to this day. Also, it explains why the Christ/Antichrist duo is so willingly employed to describe reality, primarily among religious and conservative milieus. In their view, the world is based on extreme opposites, and what is not Orthodox is automatically considered hostile and categorically alien to Russian culture. Such a worldview, as well as its implications for post-Soviet Russian culture, will often be invoked throughout this study.

Whether the debate between Slavophiles and Westernizers has its source in "binary models" shaping Russian culture or not, it has undoubtedly determined the development of the Russian idea. Notably, even though it has been discussed in disciplines such as philosophy, history, cultural studies, and political science, no consensus on the final conceptualisation of the Russian idea has been reached so far. No matter whether it is perceived as a political category, fuelling the ideology of Russian imperialism or as a cultural concept, derived from Russian Orthodoxy, the Russian idea remains vague and ambiguous. Nevertheless, the majority of scholars and thinkers tackling this concept agree on one issue: no matter how differently the Russian idea is approached in Russian discourses – whether it is from the religious, nationalist, or patriotic perspective – it is predominantly viewed as an ideal image of Russia, past, present, and future. In other words, the Russian idea is, above all, a Russian category of self-knowledge.

The very notion of the Russian idea made its debut relatively late, in 1861. Fyodor Dostoyevsky introduced the term in the journal *Vremya*. He argued:

> We know that we cannot be separated now from humanity by means of the Chinese Wall. We anticipate that the nature of our future activity should be sublimely pan-human, that Russian idea may become the synthesis of all the ideas, which with such obstinacy, with such a bravery Europe develops in different nations; that it is possible that contradictions of these ideas will find their solution and the further development in Russian nationality... (Dostoyevsky 1981).

Dostoyevsky viewed the Russian idea as the final synthesis of all national ideas that had emerged in the 19th century. He believes that only the Russian nation has been capable of overcoming contradictions embedded in other national ideas and, thus, it could fulfil its historical role. In other words, Dostoevsky perceived the

Russian idea in political terms as a specific mission that only the Russian nation, thanks to its unique attributes, might accomplish.

After twenty-seven years, the notion of the Russian idea appeared again in a speech delivered in Paris by Vladimir Solovyov, another Russian philosopher of that time. Contrary to Dostoevsky, Solovyov emphasised the religious character of the Russian idea. Seeking to prove that the Russian nation is the only one capable of intermediating between human and divine dimensions, Solovyov combined the Russian idea with the conception of Moscow being the Third Rome – the kingdom, where a drama of the Apocalypse will take place, and the Antichrist will be defeated. In that way, he suggested that the mission of Russia is to lead the world to its final chapter, and the establishment of the Kingdom of God. To achieve this, Russia has to renounce its egoism and its particular interests, and to make the Russian idea ecumenical, he argued. In Solovyov's view, only in that way, Russia could fulfil a "faithful image of the Holy Trinity" in the world. Even though he focused predominantly on the religious character of the Russian idea, like Dostoyevsky, he argued Russia had a unique destiny which cannot be fulfilled by any other nation.

Dostoevsky and Solovyov were not the only embracers of the Russian idea. At the close of the 19th century, the Russian idea had been, in fact, one of the most important topics tackled by numerous Russian philosophers and thinkers. Although authors such as Vasily Rozanov, Vladimir Lossky, and Pavel Florensky cannot be overlooked, it was Nikolai Berdyaev who provided the most complex and interesting definition of this category (Gulyga 2003). In his book *The Russian Idea*, published in France in 1948, Berdyaev argued that the 19th century was not only the century when Russian philosophy emerged, but also the time when the Russian idea – the "mental image of Russia", as he calls it – was truly developed. For him, the Russian idea should be understood as the "eschatological idea of the Kingdom of God". In other words, deeply embedded in Orthodox Christianity, which significantly shaped Russian mentality, the Russian idea is a messianic concept that combines the past, the present, and the future of the Russian state.

Berdyaev's *The Russian Idea* outlined the development of the Russian idea as a socio-political category and the basis for an alternate state ideology to Marxism. What is interesting, the book was not only an account of characteristics making up of what he considered genuine Russianness, but it was also a history of the Russian intelligentsia. In describing the Russian intelligentsia, Berdyaev saw it as being rootless, an eschatological way of thinking, and longing for a better reality, essentially a mirror of all of Russian society. As he saw it, the history of the Russian intelligentsia was a pretext in telling Russian history. More importantly, Berdyaev differentiated between Russia the nation and Russia the state. Whereas he perceived Russia the nation as a bearer of the icon of God, Russia the state was for him, a source of all of Russia's misfortunes. By equating Russia the state with a mythological figure of Leviathan, which symbolises the oppressive and demonic state apparatus, Berdyaev stood up to the Bolshevik regime.

Overall, the Russian idea as discussed by Dostoyevsky, Solovyov, Berdyaev, among other authors, can be considered a set of various ideas and signs, which, to a certain extent, serves as a foundation for Russian national ideology (Nöth 2004). It not only defines the Russian national mission, establishes frontiers for the Russian national identity, and reassures values that bind the community, but also provides an ideological underpinning for various political concepts. Thus, despite its ambiguous character, throughout the centuries, the Russian idea has provided some enduring concepts and values considered to constitute a genuine Russianness. Furthermore, the primary function of the Russian idea has been justifying and legitimising the existing socio-political order.

What is more, as a specific category of self-knowledge and self-identification, the Russian idea, like each identity discourse, manifests features similar to those attributed to myths. According to Alexander Petrov (1997), although myth is often considered an obsolete category and an expression of an archaic mode of thinking, in many cases it turns out to be the only exhaustive way to grasp reality. Petrov insists that in Russia, myth has not only shaped the people's consciousness throughout the centuries, but also helped people to explain troublesome and complicated historical phenomena and events. In his view, myth in Russia has repeatedly been useful in the face of sudden changes and crises, including the dismantling of the USSR. Indeed, after the fall of the Soviet Union, when all traditional social structures had been disrupted, the myth was the last ideological resort that helped Russian society avoid the dissolution of community. In other words, in post-Soviet Russia, myth was one of a few cognitive schemata that enabled people to comprehend complex phenomena and ongoing processes in their country, especially that the rational explanations were often not sufficient at the time (Akhmetova 2010). Thus, since the Russian idea has for centuries provided Russians with a repertoire of categories, concepts, and features comprising Russian self-image, it can be deemed a specific political myth that enhances a political and social coherence.

Sergey Kocherov (2003), a Russian scholar and philosopher, provides another perspective on the entanglement of the Russian idea and myth. For him, the Russian idea, even though in some respects similar to myth, is a different form of consciousness. Whereas myth tends to generalise and may be described as "miraculous", the Russian idea is not miraculous at all – it is an empirical phenomenon, a meta-language of Russian historiosophic discourse. For this reason, he argues, the Russian idea is not, and cannot be, considered as a mere myth. Instead, it should be viewed as a reservoir of narratives shaping Russian self-knowledge and a contingent conglomerate of different concepts and values. The Russian idea is, for him, a miscellaneous cluster of Russian cultural myths.

Indeed, based on the conviction about Russian uniqueness and its cultural and spiritual distinctness from both the East and the West, throughout the centuries, the Russian idea has been a reservoir of cultural narratives and concepts. The two perceptions are especially significant when discussing the place of the Antichrist figure in Russian culture – the idea of the Holy Rus' and the notion of Moscow the Third Rome, as noted earlier. The concept of the Holy Rus' first appeared in the 1570s, in a letter written by the Prince Andrey Kurbsky to Ivan the Terrible. He stated that the Tsar had betrayed the "divine mission of Russia" and turned it into the antithesis of the Holy Orthodox Rus' – the kingdom permeated by evil influences (Suslov 2013, Duncan 2000). Kurbsky portrayed Russia as a sacred space, where there should be no division between *sacrum* and *profanum* and secular and religious powers. In this context, the Tsar was expected to ensure the Orthodoxy and purity of faith in Russia. Also, he was seen as the representative of God and the icon of Christ on Earth. However, any deviation from the strict rules of Orthodoxy, or the break from the symphony between secular and religious powers, was to risk losing Russia's divine status. Consequently, it was feared the Holy Rus' would be turned into the diabolic Kingdom of the Antichrist, and the

Tsar was losing the legitimacy of his power and was considered the Antichrist or his servant (Uspiensky and Zhivov 2018).

The initial view of Moscow as the Third Rome is, in turn, an example of an idea which was the original affirmation of Orthodox Christianity in opposition to the "heretic West"; over time it grew out of its religious context and became an influential political concept. This view first appeared in 1511, in a letter written by the monk Philotheus of Pskov to the Grand Prince of Moscow, Vasili III Ivanovich. Referring to the idea of four kingdoms, the last of which will be the eternal Kingdom of God, derived from the biblical Book of Daniel, Philotheus reassured the Tsar that after heresy and the betrayal of Christianity allegedly led to the downfall of the Roman and Byzantine empires, Orthodox Russia became the last bulwark of Christianity. Moscow was believed to be the eschatological empire, where the Endtime drama will take place, and the forces of the Antichrist will be defeated (Billington 1966).

The concept of Moscow the Third Rome is based on the idea of *translatio imperii*, derived from Daniel's prophecy about the subsequent kingdoms that, as a supreme power embedded in a ruler, inherit the status of *emperium* (Empire) (Daniel 7:21). Since, according to Philotheus, the two Romes failed, and there was no fourth Rome, Russia was the last world empire where the Antichrist will be defeated. Different Christian states were supposed to inherit the status of the Katechon. Based on the teachings of the Second Epistle of St. Paul to the Thessalonians, the Katechon can be translated as "that which withholds" and "the one that restrains". In his letter, the apostle warns one of the early Christian communities that "the mystery of lawlessness is already at work" and "only he who now restrains it" can prevent the arrival of the Antichrist (2 Thess 2: 7-8). Once the "withholding" will be removed, the mystery of lawlessness will prevail, and the Son of Perdition will come to the temporal world. However, as long as the Katechon exists, the drama of the Apocalypse is hindered. Even though St. Paul does not identify the Katechon explicitly, in the Christian tradition the "one that withholds" the advent of the Antichrist has for centuries been interpreted as the "apocalyptic space of politics". This interpretation is based not only on St. Paul's Epistles, but also on patristic writings. Whereas Tertullian identified the Katechon as the Roman Empire, St. John Chrysostom argued that it is the Emperor and his authority that restrain Anomia, which he perceived as socio-political chaos equated with the Antichrist (Hell 2009, Engström 2014).

The concept of the Katechon, as well as the precepts of the Holy Rus' and Moscow the Third Rome, emphasise the significant role of Russia in the Endtime drama and, thus, are deeply rooted in Russian messianic tradition. According to researcher Peter Duncan (2000), Russian messianism has its roots in the 15th century, shortly before Philotheus formulated his ideas in a letter to the Tsar. The emergence of Russian messianism coincided with the fall of the Byzantine Empire. It contributed to the claim that Russia remained the only genuinely Orthodox state, appointed to serve a redemptive role in the history of humanity. Moreover, many Russian and Western scholars often fall into essentialism and oversimplification. They argue that Russian messianism is characterised by apocalyptic yearnings, imperial tendencies, as well as emphasising the uniqueness of historical developments in Russia. However, since messianism is a broad set of ideas, including religious conceptions, social utopias, and political projects, it is impossible to limit it to one nation, one religion, or one historical era.[3]

In this discussion, it is important to note the place that will be occupied by the Antichrist figure. Indeed, both the idea of the Holy Rus' and the concept of Moscow the Third Rome, being a specific fusion of Russian messianism, anti-Western sentiments, and apocalyptic visions, are modelled on oppositions between good and evil, Orthodox and blasphemy, Christ and the anti-Christ. In this context, the Antichrist is portrayed not only as a false Messiah and usurper striving to supersede the Tsar as the icon of God on Earth, but also as the embodiment of evil forces unleashed in the world. The Antichrist, representing everything that Russia is not, serves as a canonical image of the enemy that threatens the land. It is both

---

[3] To read more on Russian messianism, see: Duncan, P.J.S. (2000). *Russian Messianism: Third Rome, Holy Revolution, Communism and After*. London, New York: Routledge; Bouveng K. R. (2010). *The Role of Messianism in Contemporary Russian Identity and Statecraft*. Durham theses, Durham University. Available at: http://etheses.dur.ac.uk/438/ [Accessed 31 August 2020]; Baehr S.L. (1991). *The Paradise Myth in 18th-Century Russia*. Stanford: Stanford University Press; Engström, M. (2014). Contemporary Russian Messianism and New Russian Foreign Policy, *Contemporary Security Policy*, 35 (3): 356-379; and Siljak A. (2016). Nikolay Berdyaev and the Origin of Russian Messianism, *The Journal of Modern History*, 88(4): 737-763.

the image of Russia's constitutive Other and demonic doppelganger (Kantor 2012). However, as stated, in the context of Russian culture, the apocalyptic Antichrist figure is even more ambiguous and fluid. Throughout Russian history, the Antichrist has been associated with various cultural phenomena and historical events, including the *Raskol*[4], the Bolshevik Revolution, and the collapse of the Soviet Union; it, in a sense, reflects the ambivalence of the historical development of Russia (Isupov 1995).

Overall, being the essential component of conceptions constituting the Russian idea such as the Holy Rus' and Moscow the Third Rome, the apocalyptic Antichrist figure is deeply anchored in Russian culture. Since transformations of the Antichrist in various post-Soviet contexts are the subject of this study, to better understand this complex picture, in the following paragraphs I will attempt to explain how the Antichrist figure became an ideomyth, which combines the analytical features of the Russian idea viewed as a category of self-knowledge and myth understood as a cultural narrative. Also, I will attempt to show that serving different purposes in different discourses, the Antichrist figure in post-Soviet discourses performs a role of "a culture-mirroring and culture-forming narrative, adjusting its objectives to the context in which it is employed".

I.2. Ideomyth as an Analytical Tool

> Society is held together by our need; we bind it together with legend, myth, coercion, fearing that without it we will be hurled into that void, within which, like the earth, before the Word was spoken, the foundations of society are hidden
>
> (Baldwin 1955: 20-21).

As author James Baldwin argued in the epigraph, what binds society against the void and chaos of the unspoken is an act of creation embedded in "legend, myth and coercion". According to Baldwin, these three types of cultural practises not only unconsciously manifest a dominant ideology, but also determine collective behaviours. This assessment follows Ernest Cassirer's view of myth as a narrative derived from a symbolic character of the language. In his work *The Myth of the*

---

[4] The schism within the Russian Orthodox Church was triggered by reforms introduced by Patriarch Nikon in the 17th century. I will discuss its causes and consequences, as well as the meaning of the Antichrist figure in Old Believers' historiosophy, in the next chapter.

State, the German philosopher accentuated an important, yet often overlooked, aspect of myth – its great potential in the realm of politics. Also, Cassirer (1946: 296) suggested that it is a great mistake to perceive myths and symbols as "fantastic and ludicrous" and, thus, ignoring their undeniable importance in constructing communities. Cassirer, in analysing Germany before and during World War II, concluded, contrary to common belief, that myths not only characterise so-called primitive cultures, but also what may be deemed more advanced societies. Hence, in his view, myths are not so much a rudimentary form of consciousness, but empirical phenomena which come to power in the time of crisis when rational thinking fails.

The German philosopher was later criticised for basing too much of his theory on the traditional division of *mythos* and *logos* as perpetuated by the philosophy of the Enlightenment. As many scholars argue, before the strict division of *mythos* and *logos* was imposed by modern philosophy, both categories were not perceived as counterparts. The semantic scope of the ancient Greek notion of myth, meaning "word, speech, utterance", not only corresponded to the field that was later covered by the term *logos*, but also there were no implications of the truth or falsehood attributed to its content (Bottici 2007: 22-43, van Binsbergen 2009). Interestingly, as Bruce Lincoln (1999) demonstrates in his detailed analysis of the origin of the concept of myth, whereas *mythos* was initially understood as "an assertive discourse of power and authority", *logos* was associated with a "soft, delightful and charming" speech of women, the weak, and the young.

The purpose of this chapter, however, is not to yield an exhaustive analysis of the role of myth in contemporary politics, nor to provide a detailed overview of how the definitions of myth have changed across the centuries and disciplines.[5] Instead, I intend to demonstrate why, in many contexts, especially socio-political

---

[5] There exists an extensive number of works dealing with the category of myth and in the context of philosophy, history, anthropology, psychology, literature, and politics. See, for instance, seminal works on myth by Lévi-Strauss C. (1955). The Structural Study of Myth, *The Journal of American Folklore,* 68 (270): 428-444; Lévi-Strauss C. (1979). *Myth and Meaning.* New York: Schocken Books; Eliade M. (1998) *Myth and Reality.* Long Grove: Waveland Press; Lévy-Bruhl L. (1983). *Primitive Mythology: The Mythic World of the Australian and Papuan Natives.* St. Lucia: University of Queensland Press; Malinowski B. (1971). *Myth in Primitive Psychology.* Westport, Conn: Negro Universities Press; Lyosev

ones, myth can serve as both a cultural narrative and an analytical tool. Also, I aim to demonstrate that analytical features embedded in categories of myth and the Russian idea form a coherent category of ideomyth, which enables an in-depth analysis of the ambiguous and complex Antichrist figure, ways in which it is employed in various post-Soviet discourses. Moreover, rather than confining a study to interpretative frameworks imposed in the Enlightenment, I prefer to approach it as a category beyond a dialectic division of rationality and counter-rationality. Thus, breaking with the strict division between *mythos* and *logos*, I understand myth as a "mental construct" and a cultural narrative that not only imposes meaning and order on reality, but also undergoes constant metamorphoses and transformations. Essentially, I view myth as a concept "at work", which continuously changes and, on each occasion, is re-appropriated by different needs and exigencies (Bottici 2007).

The Work on Myth (1985) is a book by Hans Blumenberg, a German philosopher and historian, in which he puts forth a hermeneutic model based on constructing myths both by reproduction and reception. According to Blumenberg, since myths are told from the perspective of the present, they are often revised and reinterpreted within political narratives and adjusted to the ideological needs of a current political situation. Hence, myths and symbols are never simply invented, and their meaning is never permanently determined. Rather, they gain meaning as a result of continual "work on myth", which is a response to the human need for symbolic mediation of continually changing and dynamic circumstances. In other words, myths maintain their irrepressibility only through constant processes of actualisation and transformation.

A. (2003). *Dialectics of Myth*. London; New York: Routledge; Meletinsky Y. (2014) *The Poetics of Myth*. Hoboken: Taylor and Francis. There are also works attempting to trace the history of myth as well as those discussing it in more contemporary contexts: Doty W. G. (2004). *Myth: A Handbook*. Westport: Greenwood Press; Armstrong, K. (2005). *A Short History of Myth*. Edinburgh; New York: Canongate; Segal R. (Ed.). *Myth: Critical Concepts in Literary and Cultural Studies*. Vol. I-III. Routledge: New York; Stråth B. (Ed.). *Myth and Memory in the Construction of Community: Historical Patterns in Europe and Beyond*. Bruxelles, Bern, Berlin, Frankfurt/M, New York, Wien: Peter Lang; Von Hendy A. (2001). *The Modern Construction of Myth*. Bloomington: Indiana University Press; Murray H. (1960). *Myth and Mythmaking*. New York: G. Brazillers; Midgley M. (2003). *The Myths We Live By*. London, New York: Routledge, and many others.

By constant re-telling and reinterpreting the stories of origin, rebirth, and renewal, as well as heroic and eschatological legends, political myths not only render reality meaningful and set strong boundaries within collectives, but, also, in a sense, serve as secular prophecies. Such an approach to myth has its source in philosopher Baruch Spinoza's 1670 critical interpretation of the Bible. Spinoza argued that ancient prophecies, symbolically reinterpreting the ongoing events and adjusting the teachings of God to ideological needs in a given historical situation, operate similarly to myths. In this context, both prophecies and myths not only serve as specific bridges between past, present, and future events, but also seek to impose certain values on members of society and to bind the collective together. Hence, in certain situations, prophecies about the future serve as political myths, which not only provide the "ultimate meaning and unique truth", but also enhance political and social coherence (Bottici 2007: 259).

Myths, undergoing numerous metamorphoses and transformations over time, have developed not only their histories, but also their geographies. According to French semiotician Roland Barthes (1957: 151), although it is impossible to delimit a precise "social geography of myth", it is possible to draw the lines limiting its social outreach. In this context, the social outreach of myth is a distinct, limited semiosphere, in which meanings are negotiated. Yuri Lotman, the prominent semiotician and one of the founders of the Tartu-Moscow Semiotic School, noted earlier, explored the notion of the semiosphere in his book *On the Semiophere* (2005). He defined the semiosphere as a hierarchical sphere, where "semiotic substructures", such as human personalities, memory images, and individual texts, are interconnected with each other.

A semiosphere, however, does not exist in a void. Other semiospheres surround it and, together with them, it is a part of a broader semiotic continuum. According to Lotman, the borders between semiospheres are places where two important processes occur: the process of translation from one semiotic system to the other and the process of creating meanings. Even though a sign can exist simultaneously in various semiospheres, its meaning may differ across them as it is deeply anchored in specificities of language and culture shaping a given semiosphere. The Antichrist figure may serve as an example here – being a sign existing in various cultures-semiospheres, it acquires different meanings in different cultures.

As noted, in the Russian semiosphere, the Antichrist figure has an idiosyncratic meaning. Not only is it an important component of the Russian idea, but also, in many situations, it has served as a myth consolidating the community in the face of crisis. Furthermore, just like myth, it has been multidimensional, complicated, and obscure. To decipher all levels of meanings embedded in the Antichrist figure in post-Soviet Russian contexts, it is crucial not only to look at it as an element of Russian culture, but also to acknowledge a broader context in which it is used. It is also important to look at ideological motives behind invoking such a powerful apocalyptic motif. In combining analytical prospects of the Russian idea and myth, a compliant, multidimensional, and interdisciplinary tool of the ideomyth emerges. As such, it endows exposing how and why the Antichrist figure has been employed in diverse Post-Soviet Russian discourses, such as political and religious writings, conspiracy theories, and literary texts.

For purposes of this study, I define ideomyth as a culture-mirroring and culture-forming narrative, adjusting its objectives to the context in which it is employed. As stated, I understand the Russian idea as a category of self-knowledge and self-identification. Myth, in turn, is approached from a semiotic perspective as an ideologically driven narrative, which mirrors thoughts, words, and values, underlying a given culture. Addressing myth as something more than a mere representation of the existing reality, I make use of a theory put forth by Jan Jakub Liszka, who, in his book *The Semiotic of Myth: A Critical Study of the Symbol*, argues:

> ... myths are not merely a passive representation of cultural life; rather, they are reflexive, in the sense that the cultural participants view their own culture through the spectacles of myth. They are therefore not just ideological representations of rules which inform a culture; they take part in the in-formation of culture; they are not always guided formations, but, in many senses, steering mechanisms as well (Liszka 1989: 15).

In this perspective, myth performs a significant culture-forming role. It is "the most elementary form of the narrative" in all types of societies, including traditional and (post)modern ones. Appealing to the emotional human need of living in a collective, myth – together with rite and ceremony – justifies social laws, conveys universal values, and strengthens traditions. Furthermore, providing community members with narratives, myth plays an important role in the processes of identification, as well as reconciles "the individual consciousness with the universal will" (Lincoln 1999: 140). Especially in the realm of politics, myth, which tends to appeal to emotions, not only can provoke certain actions, but also satisfies two primary needs of social groups: a need for belonging and a need for stability and consistency. By establishing common frames of reference, it legitimises a given political system, and forges and underpins shared identities. Thus, by stabilising discourse, myth situates an individual in a particular socio-political context (Wöll and Wydra 2008).

In addition, myth is inextricably intertwined with ideology, understood in this context in the Barthian spirit as a secondary message hidden behind specific images and ideas. As Roland Barthes argues in *Mythologies* (1957), since myth is a "second-order semiological system", it not only is subordinated to language, but also may serve as a specific "lens" that enables us to see complex cultural phenomena in a new light. Barthes builds up his theory of myth on the Saussurean conception of a sign as a semiotic system consisting of two integral components: *the signified* (a word, a sound, an image) and *the signifier* (the concept). For Barthes, myth is a "global sign" – it is a metalanguage, based on an existing semiological chain. In this context, Barthes argues, a signifier in myth should be approached from two perspectives: as the final term of a linguistic system in which the signifier and meaning are the same, and the first term of the mythical system in which the signifier becomes a *form* containing meaning.

In the process of turning the signifier into a form, some information hitherto embedded in the *signifier* is conveyed to the signified and a new meaning emerges – a meaning that shapes a world-view of the recipients of myth. Consequently, not only is a whole new history "implanted in the myth", but also "the knowledge contained in the mythical concept is confused". By turning from semiology to ideology, intentions behind myth become far more important than its literal meaning (Barthes 1957). Here, political myths serve as vessels conveying certain ideologies and consolidating the desirable state of affair. As a result, while analysing cultural constructs, one should always be looking at, and at the same time, through myth.

Another role of myth, especially important in the context of this study, is enabling individuals to overcome anxiety and deal with the uncertainties of life. Through the processes of narrativisation, myths help to explain extreme situations of social disaster and devastation. Also, they preserve coherence within the community in a time of transition or crisis and portray reality as a coherent entity. Myths become important meditative instruments, especially when other means fail. As with the Russian idea, which is not only a category of self-knowledge, but also an identity discourse enhancing a political and social coherence, myth provides an essential "cognitive schemata" for comprehending the world (Bottici 2007:179, Flood 1996).

In the same vein, Alexander Veraksa (2013), a researcher and vice president of the Russian Psychological Society, asserts that when external features are known, but the internal structure is hidden, language becomes "an efficient tool of orientation (…) at the very moment of cognising the unknown when a sign had yet to gain power". Even though, for him, the analytical tool enabling interpreting and understanding various cultural phenomena should be a symbol, since myth is an essential element of the "symbolic consciousness", as suggested by Cassirer (1955), it may perform the same function. And it often does. Not without reason, myth and mythical narratives tend to be revoked in times of crises to interpret complex processes, especially when rational explanations turn out to be insufficient. As mentioned, this strategy was employed, for instance, after the dissolution of the Soviet Union, which resulted in a sudden economic, political, and social upheaval. Society in the Russian Federation started to look for reliable interpretations of existing reality. Therefore, people not only adopted mythical thinking, but they also searched for compensation in a romanticised glorious past or a promising future. Furthermore, they established an image of the enemy, to whom they shifted responsibility for all the country's failures (Achkasov 1997: 23, Akhmetova 2010). From this perspective, the Antichrist has served as the personification of a collective enemy demonised to the very extreme.

Nevertheless, in post-Soviet Russian discourses, the Antichrist figure is evoked not only as an image of the enemy. With roots in the Scriptures, ancient prophecies, and their subsequent interpretations, as well as secular ideologies and political myths, the Antichrist ideomyth has a vast semantic field. It denotes not only the forthcoming global Apocalypse and the decay of the West, but also the complexity of Russian-Western relations and Russian supremacy as the only genuinely Orthodox power. What is more, the Antichrist represents phenomena such as globalisation, ecumenism, new technologies, and anti-Russian plots. Transforming across various post-Soviet Russian discourses, this ideomyth is never a product given once and for all. On the contrary, it is a result of unceasing processes of re-interpreting and re-working of apocalyptic and eschatological narratives, and aligning them to existing reality. Consequently, the Antichrist figure not only changes according to different contexts, but also maintains a whole cluster of meanings. When the Antichrist ideomyth is evoked, much more than Christ's adversary figure is at stake.

Given this background, I draw upon a semiotic perspective on culture that recognises the multiplicity, diversity, and inter-correlation of signs within a given system. I analyse the Antichrist in post-Soviet discourses as an ideological narrative, which simultaneously reflects and constitutes Russian culture. The concept of ideomyth allows me to study the Russian variant of the Antichrist legend, which also serves as a specific lens shedding light on the complexity of Russian culture as a whole. By looking at the ideomyth itself and, at the same time, through it, I intend to unmask meanings. Such a perspective enables me to reveal implicit intentions undermining the appropriations of the Antichrist ideomyth in post-Soviet Russian literary, ecclesiastic, and socio-political discourses, among others.

II. Who is the Antichrist? More than Two Millennia of Antichrist Developments

Who is the Antichrist? Is he an antithesis of Christ or his opponent? Is he the false Messiah or the Endtime tyrant? Human or Beast? An individual or a collective? Is the Antichrist the final enemy of humanity or the embodiment of evil dormant in each of us? What signs will precede his coming? How long will he rule? Will he be the forerunner of the Parousia or the Last Judgment? And, finally, is he already in the world or yet to emerge? These and many other questions concerning the Antichrist have been bothering theologians, philosophers, artists, and everyday people since early Christianity. Indeed, even though the Antichrist does not belong to the pantheon of great ideas that shaped the history of nations, for more than two millennia, it has been fuelling apocalyptic images all over the world.

Attempts to grasp the essence of the Antichrist apocalyptic figure have been problematic for two reasons. First, the name "antichrist" appears in the Scriptures explicitly only in plural form in the Epistles of St. John. There are, nevertheless, many Antichrist-like figures, hidden under different names and avatars in both the Old and the New Testaments. The figures most frequently associated with the Antichrist are the Beast(s) from the Book of Revelation, King Antiochus IV Epiphanes from the Book of Daniel, as well as the Man of Sin from the Second Epistle of St. Paul to the Thessalonians. The very word "antichrist" invokes a certain ambiguity: it derives from the ancient Greek, in which the prefix $\dot{\alpha}\nu\tau\acute{\iota}$ means "against", "in opposition to", and "instead". Subsequently, the Antichrist can be understood not only as the ultimate adversary of Christ, but also a false prophet who wants to replace the true Messiah.

Another difficulty with unequivocally pinning down the meaning of the word "antichrist" is that, throughout the centuries, it has been a subject to constant changes and metamorphoses. It has been mostly evoked in ideological disputes, as well as during specific historical events. As a result, the term "antichrist" drifted from its religious roots and diffused to various secular discourses, including those of mass culture and politics. In other words, often used in non-eschatological contexts and deprived of its apocalyptic significance, the Antichrist came to represent not only malicious individuals, including Nero, Hitler, Stalin, and Saddam Hussein, but also various phenomena such as a loss of faith, broadly understood evil – both on individual and collective levels – along with various social, religious, and ethnic groups excluded from a community. Overall, the Antichrist figure was – and remains – the subject of numerous, and not necessarily theologian, speculations.

In this chapter, taking into account that the existing literature on the Antichrist is almost limitless, I demonstrate dominant narrative patterns and rhetorical strategies used in portraying the Antichrist figure since early Christianity. In the first part of this chapter, I discuss the different ways the Antichrist has been interpreted in Western Christianity. It is followed by a discussion of how the ideomyth has developed in Russian discourses since the 17th century, marked by the schism within the Russian Orthodox Church, to the dissolution of the Soviet Union, undoubtedly one of the most important events of the 20th century.

II.1. The Antichrist in Western Christianity

Imagine a giant meatball with limbs made of spaghetti. This creature has an unrestrained appetite and wants you to satisfy it. That is the apocalyptic Beast, which you have to appease with food to avoid the ultimate catastrophe. To do so, you impersonate one of the funny animal chefs and, as fast as you can, prepare vegetable soup, burgers, and pizza. However, it is not an easy task. Many things are hindering your endeavours: fiery meteorites, ghosts that move tables and ovens, and even ordinary passers-by. It is getting harder and harder to prepare dishes demanded by the greedy Beast, the Antichrist. Will you succeed to feed it and stop the end of the world or will the Kingdom of the Onion be ultimately destroyed? It all depends on how well you cooperate with other players.

This is the humorous plot of *Overcooked*, the hit independent video game by Ghost Town Games released in 2017. Impersonating the valiant chefs whose task is to feed the beast and save the world is, indeed, only one of many scenarios of the Apocalypse created by modern pop culture. Images of wars, technological catastrophes, plagues, and ecological cataclysms that erupt when the world ends are paramount themes of countless novels, comics, movies, TV series, and video games. Of course, no imagination of the Endtime can go without the Antichrist.

In the majority of pop culture narratives, especially in the United States, the Antichrist is portrayed as the human son of Satan. Such an image has been perpetuated by iconic movies such as *Rosemary's Baby* (1968) and the Omen trilogy (*The Omen* [1976], *Damien* [1978], and *The Final Conflict* [1981]). Even though this way of portraying the Antichrist is quite one-dimensional, it prevails in our popular consciousness due to the universality of mass culture, which nowadays seems to be the primary source of knowledge about the Apocalypse.

The popularity of fantasies about how the world will end go much deeper in history. According to British historian Norman Cohn (1993), even though discourses about the Endtime are mostly associated with Jewish and Christian cultures, they have their roots in ancient mythologies developed by Egyptians, Sumerians, Babylonians, Indo-Iranians, and pre-exile Israelites. Christianity, with remarkable durability of prophecies evoked in the Book of Revelation, has particularly been preoccupied with the final events of human history. The ultimate destruction of the world as we know it, resurrection from death, and the afterlife have not only fuelled the Christian apocalyptic imagination for centuries, but have also been subject to numerous eschatological speculations. As a matter of fact, eschatology, the name of which derives from the Greek word ἔσχατος, meaning "the last", has been one of the most significant branches of Christian theology.

It is important to emphasise that Christian eschatology, contrary to the images served by pop culture, does not interpret the end of the world exclusively as ultimate doom and catastrophe. In many narratives, the Apocalypse serves as a horizon of history which ends a specific epoch and, at the same time, is already beyond it. In the millenarian perspective, for instance, it is believed that the end of the world will give rise to the Kingdom of God on Earth, which will last for at least a thousand years – a millennium. Although terrifying and dangerous, the Apocalypse is an inevitable end of the old order and the promise of a new and better reality. Throughout the centuries, the millenarian beliefs have not only been one of the most important subjects of traditional Christian theology, but also gave rise to various religious movements, including those that emerged in Russia after the *Raskol* among the Old Believers, as well as the new religious movements that appeared in the Soviet and post-Soviet periods. The hope that the end of the world as we know it can be the beginning of a new, better reality, also characterised the end of the 1980s and the start of the 1990s, when the Soviet Union was dismantled.

The millenarian hope that the end of the current world will be the beginning of a new and better reality is only one of the reasons why eschatology has accompanied humanity for the last millennia. According to Dariusz Czaja (2015: 13), a Polish cultural anthropologist, the fascination with the end is a natural feature of human culture. As he argues in *Scenarios of the End*, a collection of essays about the Endtime, "we are living on the ruins of unfulfilled prophecies, carrying in the mental baggage the 'ends of the world', which – though many times announced and passionately awaited – have never happened". In his view, the durability of "apocalyptic patterns" in human thinking is the result of the tension between "already fulfilled" and "not yet consummated" that characterises Christian eschatology. In this perspective, it is believed that the Eschaton has already been inaugurated by the death and the resurrection of Christ, but not yet accomplished as the Parousia and the Last Judgment have yet to happen, preceded by the arrival of the Antichrist (Cullman 1967: 172).

Another reason for people's tendency to employ eschatological discourses is that they provide a cognitive schemata enabling society to interpret the complex reality. Neal DeRoo and John P. Manoussakis, two contemporary philosophers, argue in their book *Phenomenology and Eschatology: Not Yet in the Now* (2009: 2) that "Christian eschatology is not solely futural, but works retroactively to condition the present and the past". In other words, apocalyptic narratives tend to interpret history from a perspective of its end. History, prefigured by prophecies, is viewed not so much as a contingent set of events, but as a continual transcendent struggle between good and evil, which will be finalised with the ultimate fight between Christ and the Antichrist, and followed by establishing the Kingdom of God. Adding the metaphysical dimension to the earthly whereabouts not only enables people to grasp the changeability and fragmentation of existence from the perspective of eternity, but also "imposes a structure on the existential flux, chaos, and fragmentation of daily life" (Brown et al. 1996: 5).

Furthermore, since in apocalyptic thinking there is no room for moral ambiguity, it provides relatively uncomplicated, determined structures of meaning that help people to deal with "eschatological moments" such as wars, catastrophes, revolutions, and crises. In this regard, as Lynne Viola (1990) suggests, apocalyptic discourses are a universal social phenomenon, rather than a national or cultural attribute, characteristic for a specific moment in time. Indeed, they alleviate the fear of the unknown, help to deal with the unexpected, and console the community confronted with "the threat or the reality of oppression" (Cohn 1970: 19). The threat may be represented by non-human and human factors, including droughts, famine, and plagues, as well as hostile external and internal enemies, or a tyrannical ruler. Eschatological narratives give hope that times of chaos, uncertainty, oppression, and despair will finally end; that good will conquer evil, and the world will be transformed and purified. Thus, throughout the years, such texts have been especially tenacious among marginalised and oppressed communities with early Christians persecuted during the reign of Nero being a prime example.

It was the persecuted early Christian community that gave the world the most canonical apocalyptic narration, which for millennia has fuelled eschatological imagery: the Book of Revelation, also known as the Apocalypse of St. John. Written in the 1st century, it was not only an answer to the maltreatment of Christians in the Roman Empire, but also a continuation of the rich Judeo-Christian apocalyptic tradition, both written and unwritten (Jenks 1991, Barr 2003). Even though, as stated, the word "apocalypse" is associated today with end-of-the-world disasters, embedded in social consciousness by images from Hollywood blockbusters, it derives from the ancient Greek and denotes "unveiling what is hidden". In this regard, the Book of Revelation, which forewarns of what will come, serves as an example of "a genre of revelatory literature with a narrative framework, in which a revelation is mediated by an otherworldly being to a human recipient" (Collins 1979: 9). By disclosing the reality hidden from the eyes of an average person, the Book of Revelation is an attempt to transcend the present, earthly circumstances, and interpret them in the light of God's intentions. Historical events, concealed within multileveled and complex metaphors, acquire universal characters. Subsequently, what is described in the Apocalypse of St. John can be arbitrarily interpreted according to specific historical and political needs (Frye and Macpherson 2004).

In his apocalyptic prophecy, St. John unveils what he considers the truth about the Last Days, which will be crowned by the Second Coming of Christ. In his vision, the end of the world is inaugurated by opening the seven seals protecting the Book of Life. The opening of the seventh seal results in the roar of the seven trumpets and the arrival of the Four Horsemen of the Apocalypse, named Death, Famine, War, and Conquest, symbolising all misfortunes that will fall on people. Then there will be a fight between Archangel Michael and the Dragon, who will pass his power to the Beast, or rather to two beasts, one of which is named 666. After the triumph of the Beast and its rule for three and a half years, the Lamb will come and defeat it. As a result, Great Babylon will fall, and, after the Second Coming of Christ and the Last Judgment, the Kingdom of God will be established (Barr 2003).

Written in a mystical and symbolic language, nearly two millennia after its composition, the Book of Revelation remains the most puzzling and controversial book of the New Testament. Almost every aspect of this prophecy has stimulated numerous analyses, debates, and interpretations. A subject of controversy was not only the date of its creation and the historical circumstances it emerged in, but also the authorship[6] and the meaning of opaque symbols and eerie images it is suffused with. In the book *Naming the Antichrist: The History of an American Obsession* (1995), author Robert Fuller explores the interpretive difficulties, as well as the psychedelic character, of John's vision, and humorously states that anyone who has attempted to read the Revelation may relate to playwright and critic Bernard Shaw's claim that it is, in fact, "a curious record of the vision of the drug addict". This statement, obviously a bit of an exaggeration, nevertheless, carries a grain of truth: John's use of images and symbols, discussed at length through the centuries by countless exegetes and scholars, to this day remain vague and ambiguous. The Antichrist figure is, in this regard, no exception.

The Antichrist figure has been mostly associated with the Beast from the Book of Revelation, believed to appear on the eve of the end of the world and "lead the forces of Satan in one last desperate battle against the forces of God" (Fuller 1995:

---

[6] Although the author calls himself John, biblical scholars have reached no agreement whether he really was one of Christ's Apostles (McGinn 1994, Barr 2006).

3). This interpretation is, however, highly problematic. First, the very word "antichrist" never appears in the Book of Revelation. Second, as indicated, there are two beasts: the beast from the sea and the beast from the earth. Whereas the beast from the sea receives power from the dragon and rules over humanity for forty-two months (three and a half years), the beast from the earth is a false prophet performing miracles on its behalf. According to Bernard McGinn (1994: 54), this doubleness has significantly influenced subsequent interpretations of the Antichrist as both the Endtime tyrant and the false Messiah. Depending on the context, the Antichrist has been viewed either as an individual embodying these two personas at once or as two separate beings, one preceding the other. Also, McGinn insists that this vision of the two beasts alludes to Jewish speculations about the Leviathan (the monster of the sea) and the Behemoth[7] (the monster of the land), which appear in the Old Testament, in the Book of Job. However, whereas the Leviathan, like both beasts from the Book of Revelation, is believed to belong to the realm of evil, the Behemoth is depicted as his opponent, not an ally.

The Book of Revelation, though quite influential, is not the only biblical text that inspired subsequent interpretations of the Antichrist. In the Scriptures, there are numerous Antichrist-like figures, hidden under different names and avatars, such as the evil King Antiochus IV Epiphanes from the Book of Daniel (Daniel 11:20-25) and the Man of Wickedness, mentioned by St. Paul in his Second Letter to the Thessalonians (2 Thess: 2:1-12). According to literary critic Northrop Frye (2004), all biblical demonic figures and images representing evil are mere types. Through the use of metaphor, anti-Christian rulers, monsters, and demons are spiritually identical and interchangeable. In other words, the Antichrist, the Beast, the Leviathan, Nero the Emperor, and the city of Babylon, are all equal embodiments of evil in a single chain of identifications.

What connects the Antichrist-like figures "scattered" throughout the Scriptures is their anthropomorphic character. Interestingly, even though the Book of Revelation is traditionally believed to indicate that the Antichrist will be the Beast, it hints also to his human nature. At some point, St. John reveals the name of the

---

[7] The word "Behemoth" is, in fact, a plural form and means "beasts". In the exegesis of the Scriptures, however, it is interpreted as a single mythological creature represented by animals such as the hippopotamus, the elephant, or the buffalo.

second beast as "six hundred sixty-six" – "the number of the beast, for it is the number of a man" (Rev 13:18). Since the "number of the beast" is synonymous to the "number of a man", it becomes clear that the second beast will appear in the world as a human being, the author of the Apocalypse seems to suggest. Even though no conclusive explanation of the number 666 has been established, numerous interpreters, leaning on gematria[8], insist that it stands for "Nero the Emperor". According to them, St. John used the number to secretly speak against the emperor known for the bloody persecutions of Christians, whom he accused of setting fire to Rome. However, not all exegetes agreed with this view. For instance, a Church Father and influential thinker of early Christianity, Irenaeus of Lyon (ca. 130-200), insisted that Nero could not have been the Antichrist since the Antichrist is a future emperor, who will rebuild the Temple in Jerusalem and rule from there for three and a half years as foretold in the Apocalypse. The futural character of an image of the Antichrist suggested by Irenaeus and continued by other Christian commentators turned out to be a useful discursive tool. Over the centuries, the "number of a man" has been ascribed to numerous autocratic rulers and tyrants, including, Napoleon, Lenin, and Hitler.

Irenaeus of Lyon was one of the first early Christian thinkers to acknowledge the alleged Jewish origin of the Antichrist. In his treaty *Against Heresies,* Irenaeus identified the Antichrist as the Man of Sin, who appears in Paul's Epistles to the Thessalonians, the Little Horn from the Book of Daniel, and the Beast from the Revelation. Also, he insisted that since Christ was born in the Tribe of Judah, the Antichrist would come from the Tribe of Dan, one of the few tribes mentioned in the Old Testament, in the Book of Jeremiah (8:16), which does not appear among the "sealed tribes" listed by John in the Revelation. Consequently, Irenaeus' claim that the Antichrist will come from the Tribe of Dan has often been deemed a source of antisemitic mythology, reproduced through a variety of commentators, all the way up to Thomas Aquinas (McGinn 1994).

It is important to emphasise that this discourse has not been limited to theological speculation. Over the centuries, appearing in numerous secular writings, including

---

[8] Gematria is an ancient system of numerology in which each word, name, and phrase in Hebrew has a certain number assigned to it (McGinn 1994: 53).

philosophical and political treaties, it has fuelled antisemitic attitudes and provided a justification for the mistreatment of Jews. Ironically, many of those who willingly referred to Irenaeus' argument and blamed Jews for giving the Antichrist to the world tended to forget that Christ himself was Jewish. In the Christian tradition, Christ's adversary has been portrayed not only as an eschatological tyrant, but also a deceitful Messiah and a false prophet. The aspect of the fraudulent nature of the Antichrist appears, for instance, in numerous early Christian patristic writings, including the works of John Chrysostom (ca. 349-407), Cyril of Jerusalem (c. 325-386), and Efrem the Syrian (ca. 306-373). According to these exegetes, the Antichrist will come to the world, presenting himself as the Saviour and the Messiah, and only after gaining absolute power over humanity will he reveal his true, evil nature. In essence, the Antichrist will gain power by using deception and devilry. For this reason, he will not be a legitimate ruler, but a usurper. Since the Antichrist will present himself as the Messiah, distinguishing him from Christ will be practically impossible, at least until he reveals his true, evil nature. The Antichrist will be Christ's evil twin as suggested, for instance, by Ilya Glazunov in his painting *Christ and Antichrist*.

Although the Antichrist was commonly perceived as an individual, the term "antichrist" is explicitly evoked in the Scriptures in plural form only. It appears in the Epistles of John, which, most likely written by another John than the author of the Apocalypse[9], and is an example of a correspondence between various early Christian groups facing a split within the Christian community over the interpretations of the teachings about Christ. The author of the Epistles warns other Christians about the arrival of multiple antichrists who deny that Jesus is the Son of God and the Messiah:

> Children, it is the last hour, and as you have heard that the antichrist is coming, so now many antichrists have come. Therefore we know that it is the last hour. They went out from us, but they were not of us; for if they had been of us, they would have continued

---

[9] There are contradictory opinions who the author of the Epistles was. The majority of scholars agree that, due to significant differences in language, narrative patterns, and structure, it is very unlikely that the Epistles and the Apocalypse were written by the same person. The same relates to the Gospel of John – whereas some researchers argue that the Gospel and the Epistles were written by the same author, others emphasise differences between the two texts (Betz et al. 2007).

with us. But they went out, that it might become plain that they all are not of us. But you have been anointed by the Holy One, and you all have knowledge. I write to you, not because you do not know the truth, but because you know it, and because no lie is of the truth. Who is the liar but he who denies that Jesus is the Christ? This is the antichrist, he who denies the Father and the Son (1 John 2:18-22).

In his letters, John warns this fellow Christians of the last hour marked by the coming of the Antichrist – or, rather, "antichrists" – to the mundane world. For him, those who do not recognise Jesus as the only Messiah, are antichrists and deceivers of true faith. He portrays them as people who not only contradict Christ and his teachings, but also pretend to be Christian and preach false and distorted values. The denial of the God-like nature of Christ is viewed both as heresy and an attempt to destroy the Church.

The author of the Epistles insists that the antichrists "went out from us, but they were not of us". John suggests that the threat to Christianity comes from within. The antichrists are traitors who belonged to the community, but betrayed its values and stood out against it. Interestingly, the Epistles of John adds a new dimension to the Antichrist figure: he is viewed not only as a demonic and supernatural beast or an omnipotent ruler, but as an everyday person, whose sin is the rejection of Christian teachings. Also, since John uses the word "antichrist" in the plural form, it can represent a collective believed to be against Christian doctrine. Such a strategy has been employed throughout the centuries, not only to denote heretics, religious dissenters, and non-believers, but also as a plea for hostility towards certain ethnic and religious groups viewed as a threat to Christianity.

The Johannine Epistles were an inspiration for another interpretation of the Antichrist's nature. Contrary to perceiving the Antichrist as an individual or a collective hostile to Christianity, Origen of Alexandria (ca. 185-253) draws attention to the presence of the anti-Christian evil present in each human. In his view, until the illumination by the Word of God, in every human soul, there is false wisdom and lies. Hence, each person who turns down God's teaching, essentially, rejects Christ as the Messiah and goes over to the side of the Antichrist. A similar view is echoed by one of the greatest thinkers of early Christianity, St. Augustine (ca. 354-430). In his classic *The City of God*, Augustine argues that "whatsoever is contrary to the Word of God is in Antichrist" (as quoted in Emmerson 1981: 64).

Thereby he views the Antichrist not as a "supernatural agent who would appear outside the political and social borders of Christianity", but as a permanent struggle between good and evil, both in terms of the Church and the individual human soul (Fuller 1995: 32). In subsequent centuries, the internalised understanding of the Antichrist, as suggested by Origen of Alexandria and St. Augustine, has inspired numerous thinkers, philosophers, and writers, including Friedrich Nietzsche and Fyodor Dostoyevsky.

As illustrated, the Scriptures, and especially the Book of Revelation, have initiated heated debates about the nature of the Antichrist. For more than two millennia, the questions have persisted: whether there will be one Antichrist, two, or many; whether he will be a beast or a human being; whether he will come in the flesh or be represented by unseen evil powers as illuminated by numerous theologians, philosophers, artists, and everyday people. Even though the great thinkers dealing with the Antichrist issue did not reach a consensus on the final interpretation of his nature and whereabouts, we may observe some dominant motifs in the exegesis of this figure: portraying the Antichrist as a hypocrite and a wolf disguised as a lamb; seeing him as the Endtime wicked ruler, who will rebuild the Temple in Jerusalem and persecute true believers; and, finally, viewing the Antichrist as an individual or a collective that will reject the teachings of Christ and preach heresy. The notion the "antichrist" has been used to denote the Other, especially in the context of religious and political conflicts. As a result, it has lost its apocalyptic overtone and became synonymous to heretics, reformers, and popes, as well as political figures and intellectual adversaries. According to art historian Richard Emmerson (1981), the climax of this phenomenon was reached during the Reformation and years that followed. When, in 1530, Martin Luther decided to break from the Roman Catholic Church, he argued in the Augsburg Confession that the Pope was the embodiment of the Antichrist. For Luther, the fundamental principle governing the world was a constant struggle between good and evil; he perceived his opponents as the "partisans" of the ultimate evil (Fuller 1995: 36-39). He charged the tyranny and corruption of the papacy and Roman Catholicism were tied to the work of the Antichrist, an accusation adopted by other leaders of the Reformation, including John Wycliffe and Jan Hus. Of course, the Catholic Church countercharged it was really the Reformers who were each an Antichrist.

In the 19th century, the notion of the Antichrist underwent an important semantic shift: from a word mostly used to condemn religious and political enemies, it became an umbrella term for a critique of Christianity. This shift came to be when Ernest Renan, a French historian and philosopher, profoundly examined the Bible and came to the conclusion that it is a mere myth, based on superstitions and falsifications. In his book *The Antichrist* (1890), the fourth volume of a series called *Origins of Christianity*, Renan described the persecutions of early Christianity by Nero, whose name had been traditionally associated with the Beast from the Revelation. However, it was Friedrich Nietzsche's *The Antichrist* (1888) that forever changed the understanding of the notion of the Antichrist. Nietzsche, leaning more toward the ambiguous meaning of the German *der Antichrist*, which means both an apocalyptic figure and everything that turns against Christianity, took up a polemic riding Renan's interpretation, but also lambasted Christianity as a spiritless religion based on a false "slave morality". Nietzsche radically criticised pseudo-humanistic Christian values, the hypocrisy, and the petrified dogmas of the Church, arguing that it was hostile to all forms of life, including scientific progress.

In his book, *The Antichrist: Two Thousand Years of the Human Fascination with Evil*, Bernard McGinn suggests (1994: 225-231) that "juggling" with the word "antichrist" has led to the devaluation of its rhetorical power. Nevertheless, it has still been employed as a reaction to major social and political changes. In this regard, the 20th century turned out to be fertile ground for new interpretations of the Antichrist. Horrors afflicted by the two world wars, the sudden end of the Cold War, and the approaching end of the second millennium, were increasingly interpreted in the context of the Apocalypse, which, again, was not a distant and abstract event, but rather an imminent historical possibility. What is more, as Michael Barkun argues in his book *A Culture of Conspiracy: Apocalyptic Visions in Contemporary America* (2003: 44), the dynamic development of new technologies and digital media "appeared to equip the Antichrist with hitherto unavailable capacities for misrepresentation and domination". I discuss such an apocalyptic approach to the new technologies, as well as conspiracy theories related to it, in the following chapter.

The majority of interpretations of the Antichrist that emerged in the 20th century did not add new dimensions to this figure. Nevertheless, leaning on the old narratives, they enmeshed the concept of the Antichrist in a complexity of interrelated ideas, stretching through diverse, sometimes surprisingly distant, contexts. As a result, it has been used not only as a popular bugaboo when it came to discussing politics, new technologies, and global economy, but also as a haunting image in literature and art, and especially mass culture. As noted with the independent video game *Overcooked*, the Antichrist has penetrated numerous fields of contemporary culture and entertainment, including computer games, fantasy and science fiction, comics, cinematography, as well as punk and rock music. However, as it became a universal, and sometimes even playful, symbol of evil, it has lost much of its philosophical depth.

II.2. Imminent Apocalypse: Russia and the Antichrist

> A rule of Russian literature is that each story must contain at least one reference to the Apocalypse. But by convention, references to horses may do (Chudo 2000: 30).

As Alicia Chudo, an alter ego of Slavist and literary critic Gary Saul Morson, humorously states in the quotation above, the Apocalypse has always been one of the most recurring themes of Russian literature. Although this statement is an ironic exaggeration, apocalyptic themes and tropes have been persistent, not only in Russian literature, but also in Russian culture in general, especially in times of chaos and uncertainty. Major political, economic, and social upheavals, such as the schism within the Russian Orthodox Church in the 17th century, reforms introduced by Peter the Great, and the Bolshevik Revolution, led to a noticeable proliferation of eschatological fears. For many Russians, these events were not only a traumatic and often unacceptable change, but also proof that the Apocalypse is happening here and now. Along with perceiving historical events as being transcendental, and inscribed in the eschatological historiosophy, in many Russian discourses, the Antichrist has appeared both as an embodiment of evil and as an actual individual.

According to Catholic theologian Bernard McGinn (1991: 231), after the Reformation, neither significant historical changes nor great ideological and political conflicts contributed to particularly new developments of the Antichrist figure in

Western Christianity. In this regard, Russia has been an exception. Russia is the place where the most powerful and creative interpretations of the Antichrist were developed, especially since the 16th century. Approached first as a purely religious idea, deeply immersed in Christian Orthodox tradition, with time the Antichrist diffused to other Russian discourses, including philosophical, literary, and political narratives, all of which added new dimensions to this figure. As a result, the Russian Antichrist has grown into a complex, diverse, and heterogeneous ideomyth (Isupov 1995).

The development of the Antichrist ideomyth in Russia reached its momentum in the 17th century. It was a result of the schism within the Russian Orthodox Church, the *Raskol*. However, it is important to emphasise that the schism was not a single event. Rather, it was a gradual descent within the Russian Orthodox Church, triggered by reforms proposed by Patriarch Nikon, in 1653. The reforms included, for instance, crossing oneself with three fingers instead of two, singing "Hallelujah" three times instead of two, processions walking in the direction opposite to the movement of the sun, spelling Jesus "Iisus" instead of "Isus". Also, Nikon asserted the need to revise Russian religious books, according to old Church Slavonic and Greek materials. In general, concerning formal rather than doctrinal matters, the Nikonian reforms were supposed to restore the original Byzantine liturgy, as well as to establish uniformity between Greek and Russian practices (Zenkovskiy 1970).

At first, Tsar Aleksey Mikhailovich supported the reforms proposed by Nikon. Only after some time, due to the growing conflict between the Tsar and the Patriarch, Nikon was soon deprived of his Patriarchal status. Notwithstanding, his reforms remained canonical, much to the chagrin of some Orthodox clerics. Among the fiercest opponents to Nikon was Archpriest Avvakum Petrov. He regarded the reforms as an attempt to destroy the Russian Orthodox Church, which, as he argued, was the only true Church of God after the fall of Constantinople. For his views, Avvakum was repeatedly imprisoned and finally sent to Siberia, where, in 1672, he wrote the first Russian autobiography, *The Life of the Archpriest Avvakum, by Himself*. In 1682, together with his fellow believers, he was burnt at the stake. The Old Believers to this day consider him a martyr.

The Nikonian reforms triggered a resistance, not only from the clergy, but also from the people. They perceived the ruling rituals and symbols as a source of identification with the theological traditions and ecclesiastic rules of Eastern Orthodoxy. Thus, opponents of the reforms, who considered themselves the only followers and saviours of the old faith and piety, called themselves *starovery*, which means the Old Believers. Despite being persecuted and excluded, over the centuries, the Old Believers managed to develop a distinct and unique culture, which, although counter to mainstream Orthodoxy, strongly influenced Russian religious and philosophical thought. In their literature, the Old Believers not only interpreted the ongoing events in light of the Bible, but also referred to the writings of the Church Fathers, Apocrypha, and traditional cosmological Christian writings.

What is more, the Old Believers' historiosophy was deeply rooted in Russian folklore. It merged popular demonology, old Russian myths, and common eschatological fantasies (Panchenko 2001). However, it is important to emphasise that the Old Believers movement was never a homogenous community. The two basic factions within the Old Believers movement were: *popovtsy*, who recognised priests and sacraments; and *bespopovtsy*, a more radical faction that rejected priests, sacraments, and all manifestations of the mundane world as permeated with an anti-Christian spirit. In time, a variety of groups and sects, which developed diverse interpretations of Church traditions, diverged primarily from the *bezpopovtsy* faction, such as *filippovtsy*, *beguny*, and *dyrniki* (Przybyl 1999). *Filippovtsy* were a community founded by the monk Philip from the Vyg desert, who considered the Tsar to be the incarnation of the Antichrist and refused to mention him in prayers. *Beguny* believed that one could not fight the Antichrist and, thus, the only possibility to escape evil powers is to remain in constant motion. Also, they rejected all manifestations of the state apparatus, including identity cards. *Dyrniki*, in turn, rejected the institutionalised Church and icons. They prayed facing east, through holes in the walls. For this reason, they were called "hole worshippers" (Crummey 1970).

For all factions of the Old Believers, the Nikonian reforms seemed a betrayal of true Orthodox faith and responsible for the rupture within Russian history, which allowed the country to fall into the Antichrist's grasp. The Old Believers were convinced that Russia was no longer the Third Rome, nor the Kingdom of God on Earth, but it was turned into the Kingdom of the Antichrist. The fact that Moscow was regarded as the Third Rome – understood not as a topographical concept, but an image of the Russian state – and that it had fallen into sin, ultimately destroyed the possibility of the salvation of humanity. In essence, the Old Believers believed that the world was turned upside down and what had once been considered sacral space was turned into a domain of evil forces, and there was no turning back (Wodziński 2005).

The fact that the Church Council, which approved the Nikonian reforms, started in 1666, which, understandably, was considered the year when the Antichrist would enter the world, was not without significance. Even though many believed Nikon's actions were a literal fulfilment of the biblical prophecies about the Endtime, the Old Believers did not develop a unified Antichrist ideomyth, nor a generally applicable vision of his arrival. Whereas some Old Believers held the opinion that the tangible Antichrist incarnated in Patriarch Nikon, others insisted that the Antichrist was Tsar Aleksey. In their view, by accepting the Nikonian reforms, he lost his "divine charisma" and, hence, legitimacy of his power. Consequently, he was seen as a charlatan and a usurper, to whom all negative values were attributed. Such thinking was based on a kind of reversal of sacralisation of power, and it assumed that if the real Tsar is the icon of Christ on Earth, the usurper automatically becomes the Antichrist.

According to renowned Russian semioticians, Boris Uspensky and Viktor Zhivov (2018: 205-337), sacralisation of power is the result of a predominance of mythical and traditional thinking, in which there is no difference between sign and meaning; *sacrum* and *profanum*. Considered to be the icon of Christ, the Tsar becomes Christ himself. He is believed to be the acting tool in the hands of God that ensures Orthodoxy and purity of faith in Russia. The Russian autocracy (*samodzerzhavye*) becomes a "dogma of faith." Interestingly, such an approach to power is inscribed in the Byzantine idea of the "symphony of powers," in which secular power symbolised by the Tsar and spiritual power embodied by the Church are equal and complement each other. However, the phenomenon of the sacralisation of power has been characteristic not only for Orthodox Russia. In his study *The King's Two Bodies* (1957), Ernst Kantorowicz argues that this phenomenon could be observed in numerous European countries, specifically the United Kingdom. In his view, in the Middle Ages and early modern period, the king was seen as a mortal individual, and, at the same time, the embodiment of the higher, divine order. The king was believed to have two bodies: the "body natural," which was mortal and imperfect, and the "body politic which was the embodiment of the transcendental political power, sanctified by God".

Another Tsar, who aroused much controversy among Old Believers and other Russians, was the son of Aleksey, Peter the Great (1672-1725). One of the most controversial figures in Russian history, Peter the Great became famous for introducing numerous reforms aimed at modernising Russia. The reforms included the creation of a regular army and first cadet schools, the introduction of a new administrative division, new taxes, and rank table, as well as changing the Byzantine calendar to the Julian one. Also, Peter the Great founded the new, modern capital of imperial Russia – the city of Saint Petersburg. The significant change, especially from the Orthodox believers' point of view, was establishing the Most Holy Synod and subordinating the Russian Orthodox Church to the state. As a result, beginning in 1721, Peter the Great bore both the titles of Patriarchal office and *imperator*.

For many Russians, Peter the Great's irreverent attitude towards religion was also problematic. In 1692, together with his friends, the Tsar founded a club called The All-Joking All-Drunken Synod of Fools and Jesters, which became famous for drunken celebrations, masquerades, and mockery of the Church. The Old Believers and most faithful Orthodox followers perceived such behaviour, as well as his westernising reforms, as demonic, and argued that Peter the Great was, in fact, the Antichrist. Not only did they insist that he was of Jewish origin and disguised himself under the false Christian name of Peter, but they also saw his two titles as usurped. In their view, these titles – similarly entangled in the compromised religious and secular powers embodied in Nikon and Tsar Aleksey – symbolised the two horns of the Beast from the Book of Revelation. Many Old Believers saw the two horns of the Beast in one of the fundamental symbols of the Russian state, the two-headed eagle which, during Peter's reign, went from gold to black (Cherniavsky 1966, Riasanovsky 1985).

Despite speculations that the Antichrist would be an individual, either the Tsar or the Patriarch, the Old Believers' historiosophy did not only focus on the tangible nature of this apocalyptic figure. In many communities, there was a belief that the Antichrist's rules, manifested by general apostasy and corruption of the Orthodox Church, were inherently spiritual. The conviction that the Antichrist would be spiritual rather than tangible was expressed, for instance, by the Archpriest Avvakum. According to him, even though the "spirit of the Antichrist" was present in the decisions of the Patriarch and the Tsar, the Antichrist himself had not yet arrived. Avvakum argued that the Patriarch and the Tsar, who symbolised religious and secular power, were the embodiment of the two horns of the Beast from the Revelation, rather than the Antichrist, who was alleged to come from imperial and Jewish lineage (Przybył 1999, Crummey 1970). Interestingly, within the Old Believers' movement, there developed also a third way of understanding the Antichrist figure, which was a fusion of tangible and spiritual approaches: the belief that the Antichrist was incorporated in the Russian imperial dynasty. From this perspective, each successor to the throne was viewed as a long-ruling embodiment of the Antichrist (Cherniavsky 1966).

In their apocalyptic vision of reality, the Old Believers perceived a temporary world as a battleground of the ultimate struggle between forces of good (Christ) and forces of evil (the Antichrist). They believed that since the Nikonian reforms became canonical, the Antichrist prevailed. In such a situation, three possibilities to oppose the Antichrist and his rules were considered: a revolt, establishing fortress communities where the true faith would be preserved, and hidden refuge. All these strategies aimed at a departure from the world under evil rule (Crummey 1970: 219-223). Even though socio-political issues were of a secondary nature, what was initially a religious movement turned into an anti-monarchist and anti-feudal revolt (Przybył 1999). To avoid oppressions, the Old Believers fled abroad or to distant territories of Imperial Russia, where they established colonies. The more severe persecutions were, the more extreme the behaviour of the Old Believers became. The most radical Old Believers, who were sure that the Antichrist was now ruling the world, not only abandoned their traditional way of life, but also decided to commit mass suicide by self-immolation. These eschatologically rationalised suicides were considered "baptism by fire" – an act of final purification before entering the Divine Kingdom (Robbins 1999).

Over the years, the Russian state ceased to persecute the Old Believers, yet, the schism within the Orthodox Church carried on to the present. The activity of the Old Believers was not limited to the *Raskol* and the years that followed. Their apocalyptic historiosophic conceptions flourished especially in the time of chaos and uncertainty. Fast-forward to the 20th and 21st centuries, with the tragic events of the two world wars, the Bolshevik Revolution, and the Cold War, coupled with the dynamic development of new technologies, and, finally the dissolution of the Soviet Union, all this only added new dimensions to the Old Believers' polemics about the Antichrist (Ageyeva 1997, Panchenko 2016).

The apocalyptic historiosophy the Old Believers developed is not the only source of what can be named the "Russian Antichrist". A crucial moment in the development of this figure in Russia was at the close of the 19th and the start of the 20th centuries. As the 1800s ended, eschatological and apocalyptic moods escalated again in the Russian Empire. It was commonly believed that history was coming to an end and that civilisation was in decline. A French expression for this period, *fin de siècle*, was often associated not only with its literal meaning – "the end of the century" – but also with the symbolic end of the world, or at least the world as it was known. This collision of the passing of the old and the promise of the new was expressed in art, which fluctuated between life and vitality, and eschatological melancholy. The dominant trends within literary and cultural movements of that time were decadence and symbolism (Bowers and Kokobobo 2015).

In most European countries, the notion of *fin de siècle* continued from 1880 to 1900. In Russia, it started in the 1890s and did not finish with the end of the 19th century – it lasted for two more decades, until the beginning of World War I (Matich 2005). During this period, Russian culture was strongly influenced by European trends, such as apocalypticism, interest in occultism and spirituality, the Nietzschean critique of Christianity, and Freudian psychoanalysis. Along with these Western influences, Russian art, literature, and philosophy were impacted by rapid social, economic, and political transformations. The explosions of industrialisation and urbanisation, together with a mounting crisis in the Russian autocracy and the gradual decline of the Russian Empire, led to the Bolshevik Revolution, which is viewed as the end of an era and which, together with the events of World War I and the Russian Civil War, triggered a storm of premonitions about the "last days".

The events that shook Russia in the decades leading up to the Revolution were seen not only as a fulfilment of St. John's prophecies encapsulated in the Book of Revelation, but also as a repetition of the Time of Troubles.[10] The deep sense of helplessness and despair it caused resulted in a shift towards mysticism, apocalyptic foreboding, and utopian nostalgia for the future (Pyman 2011). In this atmosphere of the imminent "end of history", various apocalyptic themes, including the Antichrist ideomyth, emerged in literary, historical, religious, and philosophical writings of the period. They were especially prominent in the oeuvre of thinkers representing the Religious Renaissance, which was one of the most significant and original formations of the Russian *fin de siècle* (Mazurek 2008). What united this intellectual movement, comprising various philosophical trends, was the recognition of a dominant culture-forming role of Russian Orthodoxy. Writers such as Nikolai Berdyaev, Dmitry Merezhkovsky, Vasily Rozanov, and Viacheslav Ivanov often referred both to early Christian patristic literature and mystical prophecies from the Book of Revelation. For them, Russian history seemed to be a struggle between two antithetic principles: Christ and the Antichrist. In this duo, the Antichrist was not only a symbol of evil forces, godlessness, and atheism, but also a metaphor for "dark spirituality" embedded in different socio-political orders, such as Russian autocracy, Communism, or liberal democracy (Isupov 1995).

Alongside ecclesiastical writings, Russian Religious Renaissance thinkers were influenced by the ideas of Fyodor Dostoyevsky and Vladimir Solovyov. Both the Grand Inquisitor figure in Dostoyevsky's novel *The Brothers Karamazov* and the

---

[10] The Times of Trouble (*Smutnoe vremya, Smuta*) was a particularly chaotic and tumultuous period in Russian history. It lasted from the heirless death of Fyodor I in 1598 until 1613, when Mikhail I Romanov was chosen by the Zemsky Sobor as the Tsar of Russia. During the interregnum, Russia struggled with invasions from the Polish-Lithuanian Commonwealth as well as numerous internal problems, including famine and plagues (Billington 1966). Up to this day, the term *Smuta* is often used while referring to especially turbulent periods of Russian history.

ecumenical ruler Apollon in Solovyov's philosophical treatise *The Short Tale about the Antichrist* exacted a lasting toll on the Russian image of the Antichrist. Even though the word "antichrist" is never used in the parable told by Ivan Karamazov to his younger brother Alyosha, it is evident that the Grand Inquisitor's power is of devilish origin. Likewise, Solovyov's Apollon is a deceitful individual who offers people ostensible peace, prosperity, and entertainment in exchange for their freedom. Here, the apocalyptic Antichrist figure has been presented not so much as Christ's archenemy, but as a "master of masquerade". He is a false Messiah, who performs fake miracles and deludes people with silver-tongue blasphemies in order to gain unlimited authoritarian power.

After Russia's Soviet experience, many considered Dostoyevsky's literary image of Communism as analogous to religion being prophetic. Being a castigation of social reality based only on positivist and scientific ideas of progressive humanism, the parable about the Grand Inquisitor was seen as a prognosis of negative consequences stemming from a totalitarian utopia. In the parable, Dostoyevsky conveyed a dystopian vision of a totalitarian state-Leviathan, in which true Christian values are replaced with anti-Christian equivalents. He harshly criticised Roman Catholicism as a source of atheism and Socialism. In his view, the recognition of absolute supremacy of the Pope is a distortion of Christian values, which, in effect, might lead to the fall of Christian civilisation (Walicki 1979).

Vladimir Solovyov's *The Short Tale about the Antichrist*, due to its prophetic acuity, is in many ways consistent with Dostoevsky's parable. It tells the story of Apollon, a thirty-three-year-old pacifist, philanthropist, and humanist, who becomes the leader of a universal state. Presenting himself as a God-like individual, he introduces numerous reforms to prevent poverty and to establish eternal peace. His purpose, however, is not to make humanity happy, but to gain total power based on false ecumenism and reversing Christian values. Fortunately, faithful Christians recognise him as a false Messiah, and, actually, the Antichrist. To escape his power, they flee to the desert to await the Parousia – the Second Coming of Christ. When Christ finally arrives, the Antichrist and his followers are defeated, and the millennial Kingdom of God arises on Earth.

The Grand Inquisitor, arguably, was not the only inspiration for Solovyov's Apollon-Antichrist. A figure of a thirty-three-year-old individual who rises to power by preaching principles of equality, freedom, and liberal democracy detached from Christian faith also appears in the writings of Konstantin Leontiev, often deemed the Russian Nietzsche for his views. Ten years before publishing Solovyov's work, in his *Letters to Vladimir Solovyov* (1879), Leontiev argued that Russia is destined to give rise to the Antichrist. As he saw it, the Antichrist is supposed to come from the Tribe of Dan and, thus, be born in the Jewish community in the Russian Empire. After the Antichrist's birth, Russia will have to choose its final path – it will either recognise the Pope's supremacy and fight the Antichrist of democracy, together with the Roman Catholic Church, or accept anti-Christian ideas of democracy which will lead to atheism and "murderous equality".

The apocalyptic scenario Leontiev suggests, alludes to a prophecy put forth by Seraphim of Sarov (1754-1833), a Russian saint canonised by the Russian Orthodox Church, in 2015. In St. Seraphim's revelation, the Antichrist was supposed to be a Jew born in Russia, in a huge city between Saint Petersburg and Moscow. This city, named Moscow-Petrograd, would be established during the "last days" to unite all Slavs against the powers of evil. Before the Antichrist is born, Russia would experience a protracted war accompanied by a terrible revolution, which would deprive the Orthodoxy of its purity. As St. Seraphim preached, bloody rivers would flood Russia and "the great disasters would prevail on Earth". St. Seraphim's powerful prophecy influenced many writers and thinkers anticipating an imminent Apocalypse. Since it emphasised accusations that the Antichrist would come from the Tribe of Dan, such a narrative was invoked especially eagerly by authors manifesting antisemitic views.

Seraphim of Sarov was not the only Orthodox saint who preached antisemitic views and identified all the evils of the world with the Jews. Echoing a similar sentiment is John of Kronstadt (1829-1909), the influential Orthodox priest canonised by the Russian Orthodox Church Abroad, in 1965, who was actively involved in the ultra-nationalist and antisemitic Black Hundred movement, also known as the Union of the Russian People, and responsible for numerous anti-

Jewish pogroms in the Russian Empire, in the years 1905-1907.[11] Due to his charismatic personality and adamant preaching of conservative values, John gained not only a significant following, but also became central to the Ioannides cult. They believed that with the end of the world looming and the imminent arrival of the Antichrist approaching, the only possibility for redemption is to follow Father John. Some of the Ioannides even believed that John was the next incarnation of Christ. Even though he renounced non-canonical manifestations of his cult, the apocalyptic ideas expressed by the Ioannides were not foreign to him. His sermons and writings often referred to political and social transformations taking place in Russia as signs of the doomsday. In his view, the most important sign of Antichrist rule was the emergence of Communist and Socialist ideas he believed were put forth by the Jews whom he considered the main enemies of Orthodoxy. As he argued, Russia could resist the impending catastrophe only by remaining the absolute monarchy.

The antisemitic views prominent at the beginning of the 20th century resonated strongly in what appeared to be an unprecedented widespread anti-Jewish discourse in Russia and beyond – *The Protocols of Elders of Zion*. This publication presented a warped world history filled with lies and accusations, claiming there is a Jewish conspiracy aimed at achieving global domination. Translated into around fifty languages, including Arabic and Japanese, *The Protocols* is claimed to be as famous as the Bible. Since its original publication, the work justified hostility towards Jews, and, thus, contributed to the notorious escalation of worldwide antisemitism at various stages of history. Not only did this text inspire pogroms, including those pushed by the Black Hundreds in the Russian Empire, in the years 1905-1907, but also was exported to the West; this cruel publication set the foundation of anti-Jewish Nazi ideology. For many years, the book was also used as a political weapon against Bolsheviks and Communists (Bronnen 2000, Cohn 2006, Landes and Katz 2012).

At the time of publication, *The Protocols of the Elders of Zion* was first considered to be a real document. Only later the pamphlet was disclosed as a forgery. Although it has not been proven, among academic circles there is a consensus that

---

[11] In 1992, in post-Soviet Russia, an extreme-right organisation was established using the same name, led by Alexander Shtilmark (Laqueur 1993).

this text was put together as "a document" at the beginning of the 20th century on the orders of the Okhrana, the Russian secret police. The authorship of *The Protocols* is usually attributed to the head of the Okhrana in Paris, Pyotr Rachkovsky, and two spies, Ivan Manasevich-Manuilov and Matvey Golovinsky. It is argued that the book is a combination of texts published in the latter part of the 19th century. They include Maurice Joly's *Dialogues in Hell*, a political pamphlet written as a dialogue between Machiavelli and Montesquieu, directed at Napoleon III, originally published in 1864; Herman Goedzsche's novel *Biarritz*, which came out in 1868; and Wilhelm Marr's leaflet, describing Jewish victory over the German people, published in 1879. Written in the style of minutes taken during what the text calls twenty-four secret meetings of the Jewish Sanhedrin[12], *The Protocols* resemble one of the chapters of the latter book, entitled "The Jewish Cemetery in Prague and the Council of Representatives of the Twelve Tribes of Israel". In short, it was a compilation of gothic 19th-century novels, anti-modern discourses, and anti-Jewish prejudices, portraying Jews as minions of the Antichrist (Aptekman 2006, Boym 1999, Hagemeister 2006, 2008).

While in Western Europe, *The Protocols of the Elders of Zion* owed its popularity to the White anti-Bolshevik immigrants who fled Russia after 1917, in Russia, the text's appeal took root earlier due to a controversial religious thinker, Sergey Nilus. Although *The Protocols* was first published in Russia, in 1903, in Pavel Krushevyan's newspaper *Znamya*, it only gained significant attention as an appendix to Nilus' book *The Great within the Small and the Antichrist as an Imminent Political Possibility* (1905).[13] In this collection of essays, Nilus expressed his views on the disastrous future of Russia and the world, plunging into anti-Christian chaos. He perceived processes such as industrialisation, urbanisation, and secularisation in Russia as clear evidence that the complicated plan of the Elders of Zion was being fulfilled. Referring to the prophecies of Seraphim of Sarov and

---

[12] In the ancient Jewish court system, after the destruction of the Second Temple in Jerusalem, the Sanhedrin was the supreme religious body consisting of 71 (Great Sanhedrin) and 23 (Lesser Sanhedrin) members.

[13] Another Nilus book containing *The Protocols of the Elders of Zion* is *Near is the Coming Antichrist and the Kingdom of the Devil on Earth*, published in 1911 by the Holy Trinity Monastery at Sergeyev Posad, which to this day remains a cult site among Russian nationalists.

John of Kronstadt, he argued that the world was leaning towards an eschatological catastrophe, and the only force capable of restraining the imminent arrival of the Antichrist was Orthodox Russia ruled by the Tsar (Hagemeister 2010).

Sergey Nilus was obsessed with the Antichrist. Born in 1862, Nilus was a "free-thinking and fun-loving young man in Paris, and a vivid reader of Nietzsche and Schopenhauer"; he later had a prophetic revelation about the Endtime and turned into a bigoted Orthodox Christian (Boym 1999: 104). Rumour had it that he even owned a trunk called the Museum of the Antichrist in which "he kept collars, boots, badges, and even some kitchen utensils, on which he believed he saw the sign of the Antichrist" (Aptekman 2006: 13). Not only did he see the malicious influence of the Antichrist in all manifestations of reality that surrounded him, but also connected the Antichrist's activity with the Jews, whom he perceived as an apocalyptic nation conspiring against the Holy Rus'. For Nilus, the Antichrist was not so much an abstract eschatological figure as an imminent political possibility threatening Russia he perceived as the last genuinely Orthodox Empire.

Nilus' antisemitic views coincided with a rise of radical and antisemitic attitudes among the most impoverished and religious strata of Russian society. However, as Michael Hagemeister suggests (2008), despite his belief in the eschatological Jewish plot, Nilus was no racist or antisemite in a political sense. Rather, since he perceived Jews as the Endtime nation playing an important role in the "cosmic drama of Passion and Salvation", his views were an expression of a "traditional Christian anti-Judaism". No matter how he might be classified, the antisemitic theology Nilus put forth through the use of *The Protocols of the Elders of Zion* played a pivotal role in creating a specific discourse among the Russian right, before the Bolshevik Revolution and after the dissolution of the USSR. Indeed, Nilus' oeuvre was not only popular in the late Russian Empire, but also became the ideological foundation of the so-called "new Russian right", which emerged in the late 1980s. According to historian Walter Laqueur, after Perestroika, Russian public discourse came from all different political perspectives, from democrats and liberals, as well as from conservatives and nationalists. The fall of the Soviet Union resulted in a revival of nationalist discourses, which led to a rediscovery of Nilus and his work. Republished by various publishing houses in the thousands of copies, Nilus' writings quickly achieved the bestseller status. Nilus, subsequently, became a cult figure in ecclesiastical circles and far-right milieus, associated mainly with the radical Pamyat movement.

Nilus was not alone in accusing Jews of a conspiracy orchestrated to cause a decline of the Russian monarchy and the 1917 Revolution. At that time, most of traditional Russian society perceived modernisation, urbanisation, industrialisation, and the Revolution that followed, as an attempt to destroy Orthodox Russia. The ideas of Communism and Socialism were believed to be foreign to Russia and pushed from outside its borders. The anti-religious activities of the Bolsheviks, including the destruction of churches, persecutions of hierarchs of the Russian Orthodox Church, as well as imposing atheism on the masses, led many people to see all this as a result of the Antichrist's activity. Such views were shared not only by peasants and clergymen, but also by prominent writers and thinkers, including Nikolai Berdyayev, Dmitry Merezhkovsky, and Vasily Rozanov. According to them, Bolsheviks turned the Holy Orthodox Rus' into the Kingdom of the Antichrist, where, in the name of progress and modernisation, faithful Christians were being persecuted. For them, what was supposed to be a Communist utopia turned out to be a deceitful anti-Christian dystopia, the primary aim of which was to destroy the true Russianness inevitably connected with Orthodox Christianity. Lenin, as a result, was viewed as some kind of a topsy-turvy Antichrist figure, who, disguised as a genius and a philanthropist, turned out to be a merciless tyrant. These interpretations alluded to the powerful images of Dostoyevsky's Grand Inquisitor and Solovyov's Apollon.

For many Russians, the Bolshevik Revolution was not only a result of a Jewish conspiracy, but also the fulfilment of eschatological prophecies contained in the Book of Revelation. The unprecedented horrors of World War I, the Bolshevik Revolution, and the Russian Civil War triggered an avalanche of premonitions about the "last days". Witnessing the end of the world as they knew it, many peasants and religious people expected the worst. They perceived the new regime as the start of the Kingdom of the Antichrist where all previously known values were turned upside down. It resembled the eschatological panic accompanying the persecutions of the Old Believers, who did not recognise the reforms introduced by Patriarch Nikon in the 17th century. According to scholar Lynne Viola (1990), such a way of describing reality had its roots in traditional folk Orthodoxy. As she argues, in times of turmoil and chaos, apocalyptic rumours about Armageddon, Parousia, and the coming of the four horsemen of the Apocalypse seemed to be the most effective discursive strategy used to describe the rapidly changing reality among religious people. The discourses about the end of the world not only imposed meaning on what was happening, but also gave hope that after the decay of the existing world, a new, better reality will come. After all, in the Christian tradition, it is believed that the Kingdom of God on Earth will be established only after the Apocalypse.

In time, the apocalyptic panic in Russia, intricately tied to events of the Revolution and the two world wars, calmed down. Russian historian Aleksey Beglov (2014: 123) suggests that since the late 1940s there has been a slow decline of radical eschatological expectations, which eventually lost its momentum in the 1960s. That does not mean, however, that the visions of the "last days", coupled with the Antichrist ideomyth, disappeared from Russian discourses. Instead, the centre of gravity of the Endtime Orthodox discourses moved from Russia along with the Russian Orthodox Church Outside of Russia, also known as the Russian Orthodox Church Abroad. The ROCOR was established in the early 1920s by Church clerics and hierarchs who had to flee Russia as a result of repressions perpetrated by the Bolshevik regime. In 2007, the canonical ties between the Orthodox Church Outside of Russia and the Moscow Patriarchate were re-established after more than eighty years of separation. To date, the ROCOR remains the most important cultural and spiritual centre of Russian communities abroad (Pospielovsky 1984). The relationship between the Russian Orthodox Church and the Russian Orthodox Church Outside of Russia has never been an easy one. The ROCOR, closely connected to so-called "white emigration" circles, was an ecclesiastical jurisdiction independent of the Moscow Patriarchate. Moreover, the Russian Orthodox Church Outside Russia, ardently anti-Communist, nationalist, and pro-monarchist, fiercely accused hierarchs of the Moscow Patriarchate of cooperating with the Communist and atheist regime, and collaborating with the secret services. The ROCOR, nevertheless, also was a target of accusations, as it praised Hitler's rise to power in the 1930s.

Apocalyptic thinking was relatively widespread among followers of the Russian Orthodox Church Outside of Russia. Also, it was an important component of the writings of influential representatives of the ROCOR, such as Boris Molchanov and Seraphim Rose, whose views affected not only the Russian community abroad but also the ideology of the "new Russian right". Molchanov, an Orthodox priest who emigrated in 1920, insisted heresy, materialism, and the collapse of Christian values all stemmed from an epoch of apostasy that the Bolshevik Revolution had ushered in. In his view, the only way to save the world from Antichrist rule was to restore Russian Orthodox monarchy. Seraphim Rose, an Orthodox priest who originally came from a Protestant family, echoed similar views, agreeing that the Bolshevik state was little more than the habitat of evil, yet saw the West as not being much better. For him, due to overpopulation, environmental catastrophes, the emergence of non-Christian rites such as New Age and Satanism, as well as technological advances that allowed authorities to spy on its citizens, the Western world was permeated with "multiplied lawlessness". In such circumstances, he suggested, the only thing left was to await the Antichrist, who would arrive in the 1980s. Both Molchanov and Rose saw an absolute moral decay of the modern world and the imminent arrival of the Antichrist (Shnirelman 2017). The apocalyptic prophecies preached by priests of the Russian Orthodox Church Outside of Russia were often accompanied by the belief that a Judeo-Masonic plot had orchestrated all misfortunes on Russia. In many discourses developed within Orthodox communities abroad, the Apocalypse was read as the universal prophecy which can be applied to any historical epoch. Therefore, the Communist state's attack on the Orthodox Church in Russia was believed to exemplify the apocalyptic struggle between good and evil. The Jews, in turn, were often portrayed as Satan's disciples, aiming at destroying Christianity and gaining unlimited power over humanity. Such narratives became especially visible after the State of Israel was established in 1948. According to right-leaning Orthodox priests, it was clear that the reconstruction of the Third Temple in Jerusalem was just a matter of time, suggesting the end of the world was imminent. At the same time, in Soviet Russia, anti-Zionist propaganda claimed the United States, with the newly established State of Israel, was striving for unlimited world power. His-

torian Viktor Shnirelman (2017) points out that the Orthodox narratives and Soviet propaganda had one thing in common: their antisemitism and Judeophobia were inspired by *The Protocols of the Elders of Zion*.
Although apocalyptic beliefs in Russia were beginning to fade, Perestroika and the subsequent dismantling of the Soviet Union revived such views. The fall of Communism, growing inter-ethnic conflicts, a general downturn of quality of life, as well as a gradual liberalisation of religious life, led to what Russian historian Aleksey Beglov (2014: 123) calls the "third wave of eschatological expectations". Even though the Soviet regime attempted to erase religion and metaphysics from the public discourse, it did not succeed in suppressing it. When the Soviet Union collapsed, various religious and mystical discourses blossomed in the public sphere. It resulted not only in the emergence of new religious movements, including The Church of the Last Testament, The White Brotherhood, and the Vissarion community, but also in numerous occult movements. According to historian Bernice Glatzer Rosenthal (2012: 402), occultism was revived in Russia as part of a search for spiritual dimensions in life and comfort in uncertain times. Disillusion with state-promoted atheism and ideologies of something called Marxist utopia led to a spiritual vacuum, and the new religious and occult movements were an attempt to fill the growing void with meaning. Both new religious movements and alternative spiritualism were a manifestation of a lack of trust in the official institution of the Church, and a weakening of established or conventional ways of religious expression (Panchenko 2004, Menzel 2012, Akhmetova 2010).
The collapse of the Soviet Union was a time of liberalisation of religious life and a time when the public debate was "liberated". There appeared hitherto prohibited discourses. They included both liberal and democratic narratives and radical-conservative ones. According to Viktor Shnirelman (2017: 132), conservative ideas did not appear in post-Soviet Russian discourse out of the blue. In fact, in the 1970s and 1980s, there was the growing popularity of nationalist ideas, and the resulting chaos and ideological void that came with the Soviet collapse gave nationalistic narratives the possibility to flourish. A proliferation of conservative, religious, and nationalist views was rooted in an increase of eschatological anxiety: it was not so much the actual state of the socio-political situation as a feeling of destabilisation, uncertainty, and lack of vision for the future.

Adding to all this, there were rising fears of some evil forces engineering a "conspiracy against Russia" and seizing power to destabilise the country. As a result, people searched for answers in religious prophecies and ecclesiastical writings, especially in conservative circles. People were particularly influenced by the works of Sergey Nilus, prophecies of Seraphim of Sarov, writings that originated among "white" emigrants, and *The Protocols of the Elders of Zion* which were widely published after the fall of the Soviet Union (Laqueur 1993, Shnirelman 2017). In 2010, *The Protocols* were officially prohibited and placed in the Russian Federal List of Extremist Materials (Minjust.ru), yet they were still disseminated through underground channels. Consequently, many Russians started to believe that this so-called Judeo-Masonic conspiracy was the real reason behind all the misfortunes happening to Russia. Ironically, the Judeo-Masonic conspiracy has been seen both in the establishment and the dissolution of the Soviet Union. There are profound contradictions going on with this logic. Despite the USSR was deemed the Kingdom of the Antichrist, the people would go on to see the dissolution of it as being caused by the Antichrist and his allies.

In the next chapter, leaning on the concept of conspiracy theory, I discuss the most popular post-Soviet discourses, in which the Antichrist and his minions are portrayed as the ultimate enemies of Russia and the cause of all the calamities the Russian state has encountered since the collapse of the Soviet Union, including the political turmoil, financial crisis, poverty, depopulation, among other things. While looking at this unusual mix of conspiracy and eschatology, I show how, in post-Soviet discourses, the Antichrist ideomyth embodies nearly every possible evil force in modernity: globalisation, ecumenism, sexual liberation, unlimited cash flows, and new technology.

III. The Antichrist and His Plot Against Russia

Just because you're paranoid doesn't mean they aren't after you.[14]

In post-Soviet Russia, there is a relatively widespread conviction that events such as the Bolshevik Revolution and the collapse of the Soviet Union were not the results of historical contingency, but of a complex vicious plot exercised by some evil forces aiming at destroying Russia. Depending on political needs, the enemy plotting against Russia has the face of a Jew, Muslim, Freemason, oligarch or liberal, operating both from outside and inside of the country. What unites these conspiratorial discourses is the conviction that Russia is a besieged fortress, as well as a belief that behind important historical and current affairs there is a group of malicious, yet influential, people who seek power over the world at the expense of the ordinary Russians.

Richard Hofstadter (1966), one of the first theoreticians who analysed conspiracy theories[15], insisted that they are an expression of political paranoia driven by fear. In a similar vein, Mark Fenster (2007) and Ilya Yablokov (2018) argue that, by using social anxieties, conspiratorial narratives are a tool of political manipulation. However, narrowing down conspiracy theories to clinical paranoid tenden-

---

[14] A humorous statement attributed to Joseph Heller, author of the novel *Catch-22*, first published in 1961.

[15] Apart from the works quoted, there exists a vast literature on conspiracy theories and how they are appropriated in the realm of politics and beyond. See for instance: Popper K. (1967). *The Open Society and Its Enemies*. London: Routledge & Kegan Paul; Pipes D. (1997). *How the Paranoid Style Flourishes and Where It Comes From*. New York: Free Press; Fenster M. (2008). *Conspiracy Theories: Secrecy and Power in American Culture*. Minneapolis: University of Minnesota Press; Coady D. (2006). *Conspiracy Theories: The Philosophical Debate*, Aldershot: Ashgate; Brotherton R. (2015). *Suspicious Minds: Why We Believe Conspiracy Theories*. New York: Bloomsbury Sigma; Byford J. (2011). *Conspiracy Theories: A Critical Introduction*. Houndmills, Basingstoke, Hampshire: Palgrave Macmillan; Bratich, J. (2008). *Conspiracy Panics: Political Rationality and Popular Culture*. New York: State University of New York Press; Barkun M. (2003). *A Culture of Conspiracy: Apocalyptic Visions in Contemporary America*. Berkeley: University of California Press; Bale, J. (2007). Political Paranoia vs. Political Realism: on Distinguishing Between Bogus Conspiracy, *Patterns of Prejudice*, 41 (1): 45-60.

cies, or a mere populist political tool, appears to be too reductionist. Such an approach not only marks conspiracy theories as an example of political extremism, but also fails to see them as specific explanatory models. Clare Birchall (2006) points out that Hofstadter and his followers failed to recognise that "conspiracy theories arise out of radical doubt about how knowledge is produced". From this standpoint, they are an example of "popular knowledge" available to all strata of the society which helps people to make sense of reality. Moreover, conspiracy theories can be approached as "stigmatised knowledge", defined by Michael Barkun (2003: 8) as claims marginalised due to their incompatibility with what is conventionally considered the truth. After all, as the epigraph to this chapter suggests, conspiracy theories do not necessarily have to be untrue, and the Watergate affair had proven that.

In this chapter, I approach conspiracy theories as specific modes of reasoning that convey a particular ideological message and aim to reveal what that message is. Since my primary focus is the apocalyptic Antichrist figure, I analyse the most popular post-Soviet conspiracy theories spread mostly by right-leaning and religious milieus that employ apocalyptic and eschatological notions. In them, individuals and collectives behind the alleged evil plot aimed at destroying Russia are portrayed as servants of the Antichrist, hindering the historical mission of Orthodox Russia to redeem humanity. In the first part of this chapter, I discuss what, according to the selected authors, is the core of the Antichrist's mission against Russia and why the Antichrist strives to destroy it. In the second part, I focus on convictions about the existence of the anti-Christian and anti-Russian Judeo-Mason plot aimed at seizing power over the world.

III.1. (D)evils of Postmodernism: Gradual Apostasy and the Mystery of Lawlessness

In many Russian circles, it is believed that there was no contingency in the catastrophes and disasters occurring in Russia throughout the centuries. Hence, the events such as the schism within the Russian Orthodox Church, known as the *Raskol*; Napoleon's invasion; the demise of the Russian monarchy; the Bolshevik Revolution; the collapse of the Soviet Union, and the chaos and turmoil that followed were the result of a multilevelled plot put forth by enemies of the country.

In this context, Russia has always been portrayed as the besieged fortress. Depending on a historical moment and political needs, they were the Mongols, the Poles, the Napoleonic troops, Freemasons, the Bolsheviks, the West, the United States, Yeltsin's administration, the oligarchs, and many others. Though the enemies have continuously changed, they always had one thing in common: unlimited means and abilities to use in their struggle against Russia.

Although conspiratorial narratives were widespread among the Soviet urban population beginning in the 1970s, their full bloom happened in the early 1990s. It coincided with a high interest in astrology, UFOs, and other paranormal phenomena (Panchenko 2018). After the collapse of the Soviet Union, like many other marginalised ideas, conspiracy theories have moved from fringes of public discourse to the mainstream.[16] This process was accelerated by popular culture and the development of the internet, as well as circulation of writings by influential journalists, political scientists, academics, media personalities, and religious figures, including Metropolitan Ioann Snychev, Alexander Dugin, Mikhail Nazarov, Oleg Platonov, Tatyana Gracheva, and Olga Chetverikova. The popularity of conspiracy theories in post-Soviet Russia was the result of a society turning to all-embracing "master narratives" capable of imposing order and meaning on the incomprehensible and chaotic reality as people struggled with anxieties rooted in globalisation, emergence of the free market, rapid social and political changes.

In any case, post-Soviet Russia is not isolated in its fascination with conspiracy theories. In the last three decades, they have gained significant popularity all over the world, and, above all, in the United States, where the belief in conspiracy the-

---

[16] To read more about the growth in popularity of conspiracy theories in post-Soviet Russia see: Oushakine S. (2009a). "Stop the Invasion!": Money, Patriotism, and Conspiracy in Russia, *Social Research*, 76 (1): 71-116; Khlebnikov, M.V. (2012). *Teoriya Zagovora. Opyt Sotsyokul'turnogo Issledovaniya*. Moskva: Kuchkovo Pole; Bagdasaryan V. E. (1999) *Teoriya Zagavora v Otchestvennoy Istoriografii Vtoroy Poloviny 19-20 vv.* Moskva: Signal; Ortmann S., and Heathershaw J. (2012) Conspiracy Theories in Post-Soviet Space *The Russian Review*, 71 (4): 551-564; Laruelle M. (2012) Conspiracy and Alternate History in Russia: A Nationalist Equation for Success?, *The Russian Review*, 71(4): 565-580; Yablokov I. (2018) *Fortress Russia: Conspiracy Theories in the Post-Soviet World*. Cambridge: Polity Press; Borenstein E. (2019) *Plots Against Russia: Conspiracy and Fantasy After Socialism*. Ithaca and London: Cornell University Press.

ories steadily increases (Hellinger 2019, van Prooijen 2018). What is more, conspiracy theories are not limited to one cultural milieu. Rather, they are continually being imported and exported across time and space. As Elliot Borenstein argues in his book *Plots Against Russia: Conspiracy and Fantasy After Socialism* (2019: 49), the most famous example of how "memes of conspiracy migrate" is the case of *The Protocols of the Elders of Zion* and how that publication influenced anti-semitism worldwide. More recent examples of conspiracy theories travelling back and forth include the concept of the New World Order, the Dulles' Plan, as well as the belief in the Computer-Beast controlling humanity from its headquarters in Brussels.

Interestingly, conspiracy theories not only travel around the world, but also tend to spread in the same manner as apocalyptic fears. Referring to eschatological and apocalyptic motifs of the ultimate catastrophe, they impose the Manichean view on politics and history and help to unite a given community against the evil Other (Murawska 2017). As well, conspiracy theories tend to suggest that there is an absolute truth concealed behind a misleading veil of current affairs, which only the chosen ones – "seers, prophets and apocalyptic thinkers" – can see (Hagemeister 2006: 252). In view of the Apocalypse, understood as a discourse which "unveils" what is concealed (Collins 1979, Shnirelman 2016: 195), conspiracy theories may be used as tools to look beyond the "political myths" behind which a specific ideology exists (Barthes 1957).

In contemporary Russia, conspiracy theories appear mostly on the internet, which is a breeding ground for such discourses. They can also be found in numerous newspaper articles, TV broadcasts, as well as utterances of prominent public figures, such as journalists, politicians, scientists, and writers. Moreover, they drive entertainment and popular culture – there are countless post-Soviet Russian TV series, movies, books, and video games utilising conspiratorial ideas. Why are these motifs so appealing? Karl Popper (1967), who introduced the notion of conspiracy theories to the academic discourse, saw in their popularity an answer to the processes of secularisation, which led to the removal of religion from the public space. In his view, since the place of deities was taken over by omnipotent individuals and groups governing politics and economics, and "miracles" became replaced by "secrets", people started to believe that the truth is hidden from the "ordinary man in the street" behind a "superficial and misleading veil".

However, interpreting conspiracy theories as a mere reaction to secularisation does not seem to be a fully satisfying explanation of their popularity. According to Elliot Borenstein (2019), who specialises in Russian studies, people tend to look for patterns even when they are not there, especially when chaos and anxiety prevail. Conspiracy theories act as mediating and "healing" narratives that order the chaotic structure of the reality. Their apparent complexity, which often comes down to explaining everything in Manichean categories of good and evil, is also not without significance in this context. Borenstein insists that another aspect that contributes to the popularity of conspiracy theories in Russia is the binarism embedded in traditional Russian culture as theorised by Yuri Lotman and Boris Uspensky in their study *Binary Models in the Dynamics of Russian Culture (to the End of the Eighteenth Century* (1985). As the Tartu-Moscow Semiotic School duo suggests, Russian culture is deeply immersed in Orthodox Christianity, and, thus, there is no neutrality – the world is viewed in the paradigm either/or: either holy or diabolical, either good or bad, either Christian or anti-Christian. Borenstein emphasises that although this model does not explain the whole Russian culture, it undoubtedly points out one of its most essential aspects.

The conviction that the West is Russia's greatest enemy that aims at destroying it at any cost fits perfectly into this binarism. In this Manichean vision, the West represents evil, while Russia is perceived as an embodiment of positive values. These views are especially popular among post-Soviet Russian right-wing and religious milieus, whose intellectual lives revolve around media, such as Alexander Prokhanov's reactionary newspaper *Zavtra*, Oleg Platonov's journal *Russkiy Vestnik*, and the Orthodox TV channel Spas. In the program "Conservative Club", broadcasted on this channel in 2017, Igor Panarin, a conservative Russian historian and political scientist, gave an interview to Boris Kostenko. He insisted that everything that had happened in Russia since 1816 was the result of an elaborate plot orchestrated by Masons together with Western special forces. In his view, events such as Napoleon's invasion, the two world wars, and the fall of the Soviet Union were organised according to carefully prepared plans aimed at depriving Russia of solid spiritual foundations and weakening its geopolitical position.

Panarin is not alone in his conviction that Western actions aimed at destroying Russia have increased, especially in the last two centuries. This view is shared by numerous post-Soviet authors representing a conservative and religious worldview, such as Oleg Platonov, Mikhail Nazarov, and Alexander Dugin. Platonov and Nazarov are well known not only for their "profound" analyses of Russian history in light of a Western anti-Russian conspiracy, but also for their antisemitic views and the belief that *The Protocols of Elders of Zion* is an authentic historical document (see 3.2.). Sharing some of these views, specifically the conviction that there exists an elaborate conspiracy directed against Orthodox Russia, Alexander Dugin is supposedly one of the best known and most controversial public figures in post-Soviet Russia. Well-known and often evoked also in Western scholarship[17], Dugin is something of a one-person operation. He is a philosopher, a writer, a political activist, a scholar, the leader of the neo-Eurasian movement, and the host of numerous radio and television broadcasts, including the television program *Landmarks* on the Orthodox channel Spas. Known best for his extensive publishing activity, in the years 2009-2014, Dugin was the acting head of the Department of Sociology of International Relations at the Faculty of Sociology at the M.V. Lomonosov University in Moscow.

Even though Dugin is frequently described as a neo-imperialist and neo-fascist, his political views are difficult, if not impossible, to be unambiguously classified.

---

[17] Much has been written about Alexander Dugin, his ideas, and his influence on post-Soviet politics and society, both in Russia and the West. Often (exaggeratedly) named "Putin's adviser", the "most dangerous contemporary politician", and even "Putin's Rasputin", Dugin has been the subject of numerous academic and non-academic books and articles. See for example: Umland A. (2009). *The Nature of Russian "Neo-Eurasianism": Approaches to Aleksandr Dugin's Post-Soviet Movement of Radical Anti-Americanism*. New York: Sharpe; Shekhovtsov A. and Umland A. (2009). Is Aleksandr Dugin a Traditionalist? "Neo-Eurasianism" and Perennial Philosophy. *The Russian Review*, 68(4): 662-678; Lichtmesz M. (2014). Alexander Dugin – Der Postmoderne Antimoderne . *Sezession*. Available at: https://sezession.de/45827/alexander-dugin-der-postmoderne-antimoderne-2 [Accessed 31 August 2020]; Shnirelman V. (2016). Aleksandr Dugin: Vozvedenye Mosta Mezhdu Eskhatologey i Konspirologey. *Gosudarstvo, Religiya, Tserkov' v Rossii za Rubezhom*, № 4: 194-221; Tolstoy A. and McCaffray E. (2015). Mind Games: Alexander Dugin and Russia's War of Ideas, *World Affairs* 177(6): 25-30; Lynch C. (2018). Did Philosopher Alexander Dugin, aka "Putin's brain", Shape the 2016 Election? *Salon.com*. Available at: https://www.salon.com/2018/05/05/did-philosopher-alexander-dugin-aka-putins-brain-shape-the-2016-election/ [Accessed 31 August 2020].

As Orthodox Church historian Vladimir Moss (2014) argues, over the years, Dugin "has been linked with the extreme right and with the extreme left, with fascism and with Communism, with Orthodoxy and with paganism". Not only was Dugin a part of an occult dissident culture existing in late-Soviet Saint Petersburg, but he also was a co-founder of Eduard Limonov's National Bolshevik Party, which existed from 1993 to 2007. Although Dugin sharply criticises postmodernism, one can argue that his ideas are a specific postmodernist blend of various ideologies, political views, and religious concepts. His conception of neo-Eurasianism, for instance, can be classified as "postmodern fascism". According to political science scholar Lee Trepanier (2015), Dugin's geopolitical vision indeed presupposes creating "an authoritarian regime that is, on the one hand, nationalist, expansionist, and autarkic, while, on the other hand, spurns any metaphysical values or objective epistemological claims".

Describing himself as an Old Believer, Dugin is particularly interested in "understanding the role of the Orthodox Church and Russia in the last times" (Moss 2014). For this reason, the end of the world and the Antichrist figure occupy a prominent place in his considerations. In his 1993 book *Conspirology*, Dugin not only interprets historical and political events occurring in Russia in the light of underlying international conspiracy, but also addresses geopolitical concepts with Christian eschatology. For him, the end of the world and the arrival of the Antichrist are not metaphors, but real political possibilities. In this regard, Dugin echoes many of the authors analysed in this study. Practically all of them see mundane phenomena and events such as political conflicts, economic crises, and social transformations in an eschatological context.

What is more, they tend to describe them as the result of an apocalyptic plot. Polish ethnologist Santana Murawska (2017) suggests that such a discursive strategy owes its popularity to the fact that conspiracy theories tend to spread in a similar manner as apocalyptic fears. According to her, the proliferation of eschatological conspiracy theories is associated primarily with an intensifying fear of the end of the world and the Apocalypse, which often caused rapid changes affecting a given social group. The development of new technologies is also significant. In a globalised world dominated by new social media and the internet, where it is increasingly difficult to assess the credibility of news, people, events, and institutions, conspiracy theories serve as a "safe" interpretative scheme.

Apart from inscribing geopolitics into eschatology, Dugin insists in his book that conspirology is a secular derivative of the profoundly religious worldview. He sees conspiracy theories in a similar vein as Karl Popper. However, whereas Popper was a zealous defender of liberal democracy, Dugin preaches anti-progressist, anti-modernist, and anti-liberal values. Dugin's theories of neo-Eurasianism, Traditionalism, mondialism, and conservative revolution are genuinely inspired by European traditionalists and occultists such as René Guénon, Miguel Serrano, Julius Evola, and Alexandre Saint-Yves d'Alveydre. His interpretation of their writings remains, however, quite subjective. Yet Dugin, as Shnirelman (2016) points out, not only fails to acknowledge the antisemitic and fascist elements of their intellectual output, but he does not practice proper scientific distance and tends to approach their works literally.

Shnirelman, furthermore, asserts that Dugin employs "metaphysical dogmas" in analysis rather than a coherent theoretical apparatus. Consequently, his study severely lacks professional empirical credentials. It turns out to be a mere blend of esoterism, Christian eschatology, and antisemitism, in which Dugin tries to prove that Russia is in a permanent "metaphysical war", not so much with the West as with Judaism, which is its ideological fundament, Shnirelman (2016) argues. In many of his works, Dugin suggests that only by putting all available information together, one can see a broader picture and understand the dangerous situation in which Russia found itself in after the demise of the Soviet Union. In his view, the Russian Federation is surrounded by enemies and conspirators who are attempting to destroy it both from outside and within. Dugin insists that the West and its supporters not only are waging a "hybrid war"[18] against Russia, aimed at gaining an unquestioned world hegemony, but are also infiltrating Russia with immoral and anti-Christian ideas of democracy, liberalism, human rights, and tolerance.

---

[18] Unlike its use in political science, the notion of a "hybrid war" is used here in a slightly different sense. It indicates the combination of different "measures" used against Russia and aimed at weakening its political potential, rather than a war strategy combining conventional and unconventional methods.

This view is shared by other post-Soviet conservative authors, including Tatyana Shishova and Irina Medvedeva, who are a writing team of psychologists, defenders of conceived life, and firm believers of corporal punishment of children. In their book *The Special Mission of the Antichrist* (2009), Shishova and Medvedeva insist that Russian elites, infected with what they call a "Western virus" of radical liberalism, became an instrument of rejecting core Russian national values. As they see it, Russian elites are, in fact, the "fifth column" working for the West. Consequently, as they argue, the Russian government not only promotes Satanism, and preaches impudence and inequity by prohibiting an open expression of Orthodox faith, but also introduces laws that, under the guise of the "protection of reproductive health", enable contraception, sterilisation, and abortion. These efforts, they insist, lead to a propagation of sodomy and homosexuality, and seriously damage the Russian society.

The belief that the West infiltrates Russia is relatively widespread in post-Soviet Russia, specifically among right-wing circles. Conspiracy theories pushed on religious and conservative websites and forums, such as Protivkart.ru and Evangelic.ru, along with YouTube videos, espouse that plans to destroy Russia date back to 1871. It was when Pike's Plan, a mysterious document created by Albert Pike, an American writer, poet, and a prominent Freemason, was released. In the text, Pike is claimed to describe a plan to destroy Roman Catholicism in order to create a world Church of Lucifer. In a contemporary twist, many post-Soviet authors argue that after dealing with Catholicism, Pike and his supporters were planning to destroy Orthodoxy and Russian civilisation. It was believed that it could be achieved only by creating a "fifth column", consisting of nihilists, atheists, and godless people that could infiltrate Orthodox Russia from the within. Thus, the Bolshevik Revolution, which irretrievably destroyed the Russian Empire in an effort to create a so-called godless utopia, resulting in the death of the Tsar and his family, is seen as the start of Albert Pike's plan. In post-Soviet Russia, the Pike's Plan conspiracy theory conveniently points fingers at the alleged guilty parties that introduced Communism to Russia and blame modern Catholicism and ecumenical ideas developed since the Second Vatican Council. Such an approach remains relatively persistent in post-Soviet conservative narratives, including the works of Oleg Platonov, Mikhail Nazarov, Vladimir Osipov, and Olga Chetverikova.

Another popular conspiracy theory, claiming that the West will destroy Russia from the within, is the narrative about a Dulles' Plan. As the allegations go, during the early years of the Cold War, then CIA director Allan Dulles described how the United States would destroy the Soviet Union by "installing false values" in Soviet people's consciousness. The USSR was expected to collapse as a result of a gradual corruption of the Soviet culture and moral values dear to the Soviet people. Interestingly, after the collapse of the Soviet Union, the belief in the existence of a Dulles' Plan gained considerable popularity in Russia, especially among radical Communist and national-patriotic milieus. Such theories of malicious trickery against Russia not only have been republished in various Russian journals, newspapers, and pamphlets, but have also been perpetuated by leading politicians and public figures, including the leader of the Communist Party of the Russian Federation, Gennady Zyuganov, and the last Soviet KGB head, Vladimir Kriuchkov (Golunov and Smirnova 2016).

Russian folklorist and literary scholar, Alexander Panchenko (2016), argues that the popularity of this conspiracy theory "can be explained by what in psychoanalytic anthropology is called projective inversion". According to him, the Dulles' Plan serves as an easy justification for all failures and ills overwhelming the post-Soviet Russian society. As Panchenko suggests, contemporary Russians seem to be unison in saying: we are not the ones who are guilty of how bad it is now in Russia; it is Allan Dulles and the American intelligence to blame. Interestingly, despite its extensive popularity, in 2015, the text *The Dulles' Plan for Destruction of the USSR (Russia)* was placed on the Russian Federal List of Extremist Materials by a municipal court, in the city of Asbiest (Minjust.ru).

As with *The Protocols of the Elders of Zion*, *The Dulles' Plan for Destruction of the USSR (Russia)* turned out to be a forgery. In his article, "The Dulles' Plan: Soviet Literature, Conspiracy Theories, and Moral Panics in Russia on the Verge of the Twentieth and Twenty-First Centuries" (2018), Panchenko tracks its emergence and developments, insisting that the narrative has its roots in the duology *The Eternal Call*, published in 1970 and 1979. In the novels, one of the most recognised writers during the Brezhnev era and editor of the journal *Molodaya Gvardya*[19], Ivanov created the dark character Arnold Lakhnovkiy as a dedicated Trotskyist, and a collaborator of Nazi Germany, who developed a secret plan aimed at destroying Russia. The plan assumed, alongside a military conflict, the slow destruction of the core Soviet/Russian values by corrupting the Soviet youth with a "cult of sex, violence, sadism, and treachery" (Borenstein 2019: 90-91). Interestingly, the publication of Ivanov's novel coincided with the airing of the 1970s cult Soviet TV series *The Seventeen Moments of Spring*, in which the Soviet spy Isaev-Stierlitz attempts to break the secret peace negotiations between the Nazis and the Allies, led by Dulles. According to Panchenko, both Ivanov's novel and the cult series established the Dulles figure as an anti-Russian conspirator in the Soviet, and later Russian, popular imagination.

The association of Trotskyists with Jews, relatively new in Russian society, was orchestrated through Soviet propaganda. Panchenko (2016: 126) argues that by implicitly tying being a Trotskyist and an enemy of the Soviet state, Ivanov's novels take on antisemitic overtones. It is no surprise that in the second half of the 1970s and the 1980s, among the nationalist-patriot milieus, *The Eternal Call* became what Pachenko calls a "manifesto of legal antisemitism" and a kind of "Soviet adaptation of *The Protocols of the Elders of Zion*". Elliot Borenstein (2019: 89) also points to a certain convergence between the Dulles' Plan and *The Protocols*. For him, they are examples of what he deems antisemitic rubbish that not only "take a primitive view of human psychology", but also "assume a downright slipshod approach to secrecy" that evil conspirers find pleasure in revealing their immoral plans.

Numerous post-Soviet authors embrace this cognitive pattern outlined by conspiracy theories such as the Pike's Plan and the Dulles' Plan. One of them is Valeriy Filimonov, a conservative Orthodox writer and one of the leaders of the "anti-INN movement". In his article, "When the Antichrist Will Come" (2016), Filimonov insists that the West continuously infiltrates and destabilises Russia by

---

[19] The monthly literary journal, established in Moscow in 1922, was an organ of the Komsomol, a Communist youth organisation. Nowadays the journal represents the Orthodox and national-patriotic milieus.

using the false rhetoric like "peace and security", "war against international terrorism and extremism", "electronic democracy", and "tolerance". Like many other post-Soviet Russian right-wing authors, Filimonov believes that the West aims to change Russian people's consciousness and program them to follow the Antichrist. The West is considered to be preparing the world for the Antichrist arrival and the Apocalypse by corrupting and manipulating Russia with anti-Christian values.

However, as many authors propose – among them Valeriy Filimonov, Alexander Dugin, Tatyana Shishova and Irina Medvedeva – when looking at the apocalyptic hierarchy of Russia's enemies, the West is not the final challenge. Rather, it is just a tool of the Antichrist, believed to be not only the archenemy of Christ, but also the archenemy of Russia, often described as the last vessel of genuine Christian values. In their writings, these authors suggest that the Antichrist seeks to destroy Orthodox Russia by using the support of his faithful servants: the so-called "bearers of apostasy". They include not only the West as a political entity, but also Catholics, Communists, Jews, and Masons. In short, the list consists of all groups and individuals that have ever conspired against Russia. This view is expressed with particular conviction by Ioann Snychev, who, from 1990 to 1995, was the Metropolitan of the Eparchy of Saint Petersburg and Ladoga, and, thus, one of the most influential figures in the Russian Orthodox Church of that time. In his article "Creators of Disasters" (1994), he insists that, as a result of hostile forces and conspirators, Russia lost its metaphysical purity and entered the path of apostasy. In his view, the chaos after the dissolution of the Soviet Union led to yet another "Great Russian Time of Troubles", also known as *Smuta*, which broke the symphony between sacral and secular powers he deemed the constitutive feature of the Russianness, deeply immersed in the Orthodox tradition. This claim by Snychev directly invokes the concept of "sacralisation of power" developed by Boris Uspensky and Viktor Zhivov in their book *Tsar and God* (see 2.2.).

Echoing such sentiment, the majority of post-Soviet authors explored in this study believe that the destruction of Russia by the Antichrist and his minions will be achieved through "metaphysical infiltration". As they argue, this infiltration is manifested primarily in spreading the "mystery of lawlessness", which is supposed to lead to "gradual apostasy" – turning away from God and true Christian

(Orthodox) values. The "mystery of lawlessness" is interpreted as a spiritual presence of the Antichrist in what is viewed as the temporary world. Equally important, this concept has its roots in the second letter of St. Paul to the Thessalonians, in which he writes:

> 7 For the mystery of lawlessness is already at work. Only he who now restrains it will do so until he is out of the way. 8 And then the lawless one will be revealed, whom the Lord Jesus will kill with the breath of his mouth and bring to nothing by the appearance of his coming. 9 The coming of the lawless one is by the activity of Satan with all power and false signs and wonders, 10 and with all wicked deception for those who are perishing, because they refused to love the truth and so be saved. 11 Therefore God sends them a strong delusion, so that they may believe what is false, 12 order that all may be condemned who did not believe the truth but had pleasure in unrighteousness (2 Thess 2:7-12).

According to St. Paul, the "mystery of lawlessness" is, indeed, the proliferation of godlessness and evil that heralds the arrival of the Lawless One, the Antichrist. In other words, the "mystery of lawlessness" can be interpreted as a spiritual presence of the Antichrist that only after reaching its apogee will lead to the arrival of the Antichrist in the flesh.

Whereas the spiritual presence of the Antichrist is traditionally equated with the gradual departure from Christian values, many post-Soviet authors believe that the corporeal arrival of the Antichrist in the world will be the "omega point" of human history. This view is shared, for instance, by Yuriy Vorobevskiy, whom Viktor Shnirelman (2017: 378-379) calls a "self-proclaimed direct follower of Sergei Nilus". In his book *The Path to the Apocalypse: The Omega Point* (1999), Vorobevskiy argues that the Antichrist figure is tightly associated with the Christian paradigm of history unfolding from Paradise to the Apocalypse. Thus, as he insists, when the time arrives, the world will come to its ultimate end, and people will be forced to live in the eternal nightmare characterised by no boundaries between what is true and what is false. At this point, intentionally or not, Vorobevskiy invokes the views of other post-Soviet authors, including Alexander Dugin and Patriarch Kirill of Moscow and all the Rus', who link the arrival of the Antichrist with postmodernism.

Whereas Vorobevskiy perceives the "apogee of apostasy" in a very negative vein as the last moment of history, other authors, such as Mikhail Nazarov and Oleg

Platonov, offer a slightly more optimistic perspective. According to them, the Antichrist is not only the embodiment of disasters connected to the Apocalypse, but also an omen of the Parousia. From this perspective, the Antichrist's rule is seen as the announcement of the Second Coming of Christ and the inauguration of the new era. This view is deeply rooted in Christian eschatological tradition, in which Christ is believed to renounce his power and redeem people from the influence of the Antichrist through suffering, death, and, finally, the resurrection. Since Christ's victory over the Antichrist is supposed to be the beginning of that new era, there exists a belief that human history can reveal its hidden meaning only from the perspective of its end. Subsequently, all earthly circumstances acquire a new dimension – there are no ordinary events, but God's particular plan (Bethea 1989, Fomin 1999).

Such a reading of history evokes the concept of *historia sacra* put forth by St. Augustine in his treaty *City of God* (426). In the Augustinian heuristic interpretation of history, the end is inscribed in all temporary events and phenomena. As German historian Rudolf Bultmann (1975) sums it up, "history is swallowed up in eschatology", and the end of the world is imminent. Thus, in many post-Soviet Russian discourses, the temporary world is viewed as not reliable and moving towards its inevitable end. It is also considered as permeated with the spirit of the Antichrist; therefore, the crises, social experiments, national catastrophes, and utopian reforms are described in apocalyptic terms. Modernisation and progress, in turn, are perceived as the continuous destruction of the world and gradual isolation from all foundations of history, which may be revealed only through the Apocalypse.

As many of these authors see it, the "mystery of lawlessness", which will culminate in the arrival of the Antichrist, is not a recent appearance. They point out that it is enough to look closely at how European history has unfolded to understand that the invisible evil has been operating for a while now, and the effects of these activities are becoming more pronounced. For authors such as Nazarov, Platonov, and Dugin, the beginning of the "mystery of lawlessness" working and the decline of genuine religiosity and spirituality was triggered by the East-West Schism, in 1054. In their view, the disjunction of the ecclesiastical communion between Eastern and Western Christianity launched a process of apostasy that led to the increasing approval of atheism, progressivism, rationalism, and individualism in the West. These anti-Christian values, they argue, injected to the temporary world after the East-West Schism has left a significant mark on great historical epochs, including the Renaissance, the Reformation, and the Enlightenment (Dugin 1996, Nazarov 1999).

Oleg Platonov (2010a, 2011), a Russian ultranationalist writer and the head of a Moscow-based think tank, the Institute for the History of Russian Civilisation, insists that all epochs of human history have been permeated with false humanism, which has reinforced the spirit of the Antichrist. According to him, the ideas of humanism and progression turned out to be particularly problematic, as they deny the divine nature of humanity, contradict Christian ethics, as well as promote consumerism, and a technocratic attitude to life. Overall, Platonov and his fellow authors believe that Western Catholicism not only turned out to be "a damaged limb" that fell from a healthy body of Christianity, but also that it was a source of distortion and degeneration of Christian moral values, which, in the course of history, has led to the development of contemporary anti-Christian democracy. These post-Soviet authors allude to Dostoyevsky's claim that Western Christianity was the main source of Socialism and atheism (Walicki 1979).

What particularly worries post-Soviet conservative and religious authors is the fact that Orthodox Russia has not escaped the process of apostasy. Alexander Dugin argues in his book *The Metaphysics of the Good News* (1996) that the apostasy within Orthodoxy started in the 15th century when the Turks conquered Istanbul. For Dugin, the fall of Byzantium, accompanied by a loss of political independence, led to the annihilation of a fundamental tenet of the Orthodox Church. Like in the West, secular aspects of life have gradually separated from the spiritual, and the "symphony of powers" lost its importance; what Dugin calls the critical steps on the "Russian road to apostasy" were the Time of Troubles in the 16th century and the schism within the Russian Orthodox Church in the 17th century. Dugin argues that the latter was particularly destructive since it resulted in dividing the Russian nation into two parts: the one that has maintained the true Orthodox faith and remained loyal to the Holy Rus', or the Old Believers, and the other that adopted the Nikonian reforms and became the acolytes of Antichrist. In short, Dugin considers the *Raskol* to be the most tragic moment in Russian history, which was not only a result of moral decline within the Russian society, but also the beginning of the end of history, and the moment when the spirit of the Antichrist was unlocked in the temporary world (Dugin 2011).

The image of the spiritual Antichrist present in many of these discourses is practically identical to St. Paulician's "mystery of lawlessness", understood as a gradual apostasy and a breakup from the Christian tradition. However, out of these authors, only Dugin explicitly refers to a concept of spiritual Antichrist. This is how Dugin describes the spiritual Antichrist in an essay, "The Return of Beguny", published in the book *The Russian Thing: Essays on National Philosophy*:

> The spiritual Antichrist is everywhere – this is all that we have inherited. He is outside, he is inside, he has eaten us, as previously he has eaten, through and through, to the blood, and arteries, stupid bodies of our progenitors. We are born from dead parents, into the deadly world. Our passports are the pranks of the counterfeiters. Our names are bad jokes. Our country is a mirror of misapprehension. And outside, it is even worse, nastier, scarier, emptier, lousier, more rotten. There he established his throne of interest a long time ago, about three centuries... (Dugin 2001).

As Dugin explains it, the spiritual Antichrist symbolises the ubiquitous forces of evil that cannot be seen, but can easily be recognised. Also, he sees it as a mass spiritual decline, which will lead to the replacement of Christian purity with anti-Christian false values. In Dugin's eyes, even Orthodox Russia did not remain innocent – it also succumbed to the Antichrist's influences. Thus, the spiritual Antichrist, who has been ruling in the West for at least three centuries now, has managed to infiltrate Russia and "engulf its blood and arteries", Dugin insists.

In his description of the spiritual Antichrist, Dugin alludes to one of the many questions that divided the Old Believers in the years following the schism in the 17th century. Breaking ties with religious and secular authorities, the Old Believers insisted that, beginning in 1653, the Russian Orthodox Church began falling away from Christ and worshipping the Antichrist, a false Messiah. Consequently, the Old Believers were convinced that the spirit of eternal destruction was unlocked, and the spiritual Antichrist not only infused people's lives, but also permeated the Russian reality on all levels. It is important to note, however, that the conception of the spiritual Antichrist developed among the Old Believers gradually. At first, along with a traditional exegesis of the Scriptures, specifically the Book of Revelation, in which two Beasts appear, they believed that Tsar Aleksey and Patriarch Nikon are the personifications of the Antichrist. Only later, the more complex interpretations of the Antichrist's nature flourished, especially among *bezpopovtsy*, who understood the arrival of the Antichrist in metaphysical terms. For them, the Antichrist was a wicked spirit of heresy rather than a particular individual; phenomena such as secularisation, globalisation, and modernisation were not only the signs of the imminent arrival of the Antichrist, but also the proof that the Antichrist had already begun building his Kingdom on Earth.

Dugin's line of thought is followed by authors Tatyana Shishova and Irina Medvedeva. They insist that the spiritual Antichrist has recently become particularly active, especially after the dissolution of the Soviet Union and the end of the bipolar world order. In the fight for hegemony, they see the United States and other Western countries agreed to serve the Antichrist, and, for his benefit, wage spiritual war with the Russian Federation aimed at the final destruction of genuine Orthodox values it represents. Part of this spiritual war with Russia is a so-called "information war" carried out through the media to discredit the country internationally. Anna Irbulatova (2017), an investigative journalist who echoes this view, insists that the Western media not only produce countless lies about the world and put the blame on Russia, but also bribe some Russian journalists to promote these lies. Ironically, it is the Russian Federation that is often accused of conducting an extensive information war with the rest of the world, which has become particularly intense after the aggression against Ukraine and the incorporation of Crimea, in 2014.[20]

---

[20] See for instance: Darczewska J. (2014). The Anatomy of Russian Information Warfare: The Crimean Operation, a Case Study. *Punkt Widzenia*, (42). Available at: http://aei.pitt.edu/57173/1/42.pdf [Accessed 31 August 2020]; Jaitner M. (2015). Russian Information Warfare: Lessons From Ukraine. In: Geers K. (Ed.). *Cyber War in Perspective: Russian Aggression Against Ukraine*. Tallin: NATO CCD COE Publications. Available at: https://ccdcoe.org/uploads/2018/10/Ch10_CyberWarinPerspective_Jaitner.pdf [Accessed 31 August 2020]; Sengovaya M. (2015). Putin's Information Warfare in Ukraine: Soviet Origins of Russia's Hybrid Warfare. *Institute for the Study of War*. Available at: http://www.understandingwar.org/sites/default/files/Russian%20Report%201%20Putin%27s%20Information%20Warfare%20in%20Ukraine-%20Soviet%20Origins%20of%20Russ

These post-Soviet authors argue that the information war is only one of the numerous means employed by the anti-Christian West to destabilise and conquer Russia. According to them, the greatest threat to Russian spiritual purity is the promotion of "rotten values", such as democracy, liberalism, and the free market. Known for anti-Western and antisemitic views, who argues in his book *The Mystery of Russia: Historiosophy of the 20th Century* (1999) that by spreading notions of human rights and democratic values the West imposes a philosophy of materialism and individualism on Russia. As Nazarov suggests, the main purpose behind this strategy is creating a homogenised world in which it would be easy to control and manipulate people, as well as eliminating the "absolute spiritual values" of Orthodoxy and replacing them by anti-Christian falsehood.

Vladimir Osipov (2012), head of an extreme-right nationalist party, the Union of the Russian People, also perceives democracy as little more than a corrupt system. Democracy, as he sees it, is the embodiment of evil: it allows special services to track citizens; its "sick" tax system robs the most unfortunate people of money, and it enables the destruction of the family thanks to the concept of gender. By negating traditional values and the Christian idea of the family, he charges, Western democratic systems legalise, and, hence, impose homosexuality on other people. This homophobia is not surprising given Osipov's work is characterised by anti-liberalism, and an obsession with the protection of a traditional family model understood as a sanctified relationship between a woman and a man and additionally legitimised by having children.

This obsession with moral purity, as well as a negative attitude towards democracy, can be found in the works of practically all the authors examined here. According to political scientist Konstantin Kostiuk (2002), the distrust of liberalism and democracy is, indeed, relatively widespread in post-Soviet Russia. It is present not only among the religious and conservative circles, but also other groups in the Russian society that associate democracy with the "Yeltsin decade". For

---

ias%20Hybrid%20Warfare.pdf [Accessed 31 August 2020]; Ajir M. and Vailliant B. (2018). Russian Information Warfare: Implications for Deterrence Theory. *Strategic Studies Quarterly*, 12 (3): 70-89. Available at: https://www.airuniversity.af.edu/Portals/10/SSQ/documents/Volume-12_Issue-3/Ajir.pdf [Accessed 31 August 2020].

them, 1990s Russia was an era of chaos and disintegration, intensified by the financial crisis of 1998. Consequently, many Russians believe that the failure of the Russian transformation was a result of poor decisions of Yeltsin's administration inspired and financed by the West. It ended up in establishing a reign of oligarchs who "created their own parallel infrastructure which substituted for a state", as journalist Arkady Ostrovsky puts it, quoted in work by researcher Naphtali Rivkin (2017). As a result, in post-Soviet Russia, the word "democracy" has acquired a pejorative meaning. The biggest sceptics began to ironically name the political system that emerged in Russia after 1991 as "dermocracy", combining the word "democracy" with the Russian word *dermo* meaning "shit".

A distrust towards democracy in the post-Soviet Russian society has been accompanied by a negative attitude towards the international system of economic relations. It is reflected in the works by discussed authors, many of whom believe that the free market and global trade are only an excuse used by the West to introduce anti-Christian orders in the Russian Federation. The right-wing authors, such as Mikhail Nazarov and Vladimir Osipov, believe that the main goal behind adopting a liberal economy worldwide is to enable better-developed countries to drain the Russian Federation and deprive it of its resources. They also insist that the global economy is supposed to accelerate processes of globalisation that lead to establishing a world government ruled by the United States.

These views are shared in *The Project Russia* book series, published from 2005 to 2010, which discusses "spiritual, social, political, and economic issues" concerning Russia and the rest of the world. The book series not only achieved a bestseller status (the first edition had a press run of one million copies), but also was widely discussed in Russian political circles. Thus, one can assume that the views expressed by its authors have, indeed, resonated in the post-Soviet Russian society. The project's authors and financial backers were for some time a subject of speculation. Many believed that it was created and supported by Putin and his followers; however, in 2010, after the publication of the fourth part of the series, *The Project Russia: The Great Idea*, one of the authors was revealed. It turned out to be Yuriy Shalaganov, the director of The Institute of Strategic Security Foundation and chairman of the Moscow regional branch of the Union of Russian Gardeners. As Shalaganov argues throughout the series, the global stock market established in the 1920s in the United States and exported to other countries cannot be controlled anymore. Moreover, he believes that since the stock exchange in recent years was overtaken by the virtual reality and artificial intelligence, thanks to the internet it will spread even wider, eventually resulting in one currency for everyone, and, finally, leading to the establishment of the Kingdom of the Antichrist.

According to Panchenko (2016), many post-Soviet Russian conservative authors typically connect everything involving a cash flow with the "mark of the Beast". For them, the Antichrist has a hand in the stock market, credit cards, as well as everything marked with a bar code. This interpretation derives from the traditional exegesis of the Book of Revelation, in which St. John anticipates "[the Beast] causes all [...] to be given marks on their right hands, or on their foreheads; and that no one would be able to buy or to sell unless he has that mark, the name of the beast or the number of his name" (Rev: 13-16). What is more, the aversion towards modern financial systems often has antisemitic undertones. Since the Jews have historically been associated with money and finance, conspiracy theories abound in post-Soviet Russia in which Jewish figures are Antichrist servants and control world cash flows and financial systems, and, in so doing, support the establishment of his evil kingdom. Ironically, it was antisemitism that closed many doors to Jewish people, forcing them to earn a living by being merchants and working in finance.

The early 2000s, panic erupted in the Russian Federation with the implementation of the individual value-added tax (VAT) identification number (INN). This is perhaps the most striking example of eschatological hysteria that resulted from the belief the Antichrist and his servants are controlling world cash flows. The panic was triggered by an article in which the Athonite Elder, Hieromonk Rafail (Berestov), warned people against accepting the INN number. He insisted that by accepting the number, a person automatically gave their soul away to the Antichrist (Akhmetova 2010: 182-188). Whereas conservative priests of the Russian Orthodox Church supported Hieromonk Rafail's theories, the more liberal, including those within the ROC hierarchy, sharply criticised such incitements. In 2001, to appease such rapidly growing apocalyptic fears, the Synod of the Russian

Orthodox Church officially proclaimed that new technologies do not influence the salvation of the soul. Meanwhile, the Patriarchate of Moscow asked the secular authorities to respect those who prefer not to have an INN and suggested that such people should be provided with an alternate solution.

In many ways, the attempts of the liberal circles of the Russian Orthodox Church to ease the moral panic set off by Hieromonk Rafail have failed. The most radical INN opponents continued their protest, some of them fighting it to this very day. In some cases, the resistance towards the INN has turned quite extreme. Underground groups even emerged, persuading people to abandon everything they own and to "flee to the forest". Their fanatic conduct resembled the Old Believers, who fled persecutions and believed the Antichrist ruled the world, as well as the behaviour of "catacomb churches", whose members refused to accept Soviet passports in the 1960s. Kathy Rousselet (2015), who has completed extensive research on the Russian Orthodox Church, sees the INN opposition not only as the symptom of the apocalyptic fears deriving from the Book of Revelation, but also as an implicit critique of the post-Soviet state and a dire fear of globalisation. As she suggests, by presenting itself as a mediator between the most radical INN opponents and the representatives of the state, the Russian Orthodox Church used the situation to strengthen its political position.

When it comes to the modern world of business – biometric cards, electronic payments, bar codes, and individual VAT identification numbers – coupled with technological development in general – post-Soviet conservative writers are divided in their views. Whereas some of them consider all these modern-day manifestations to be signs of the imminent arrival of the Antichrist, others criticise this eschatological obsession and argue that the power of the Antichrist is, indeed, out there, but it should be looked for elsewhere. It is important to emphasise that the attitudes of the ROC clergy and their followers towards the new media development are not only highly ambiguous, but also overloaded with affectivity, prejudices, and conjectures. On the one hand, they perceive the internet as a useful channel of social and cultural communication; on the other hand, they view it as an immoral, anti-Christian tool (Dolińska-Rydzek 2016).

Oleg Platonov is an excellent example of such post-Soviet Russian views. As he argues in his book *The Russian Resistance: The War with the Antichrist* (2010), the most anti-Christian of all new technologies is the internet, which is based on the zero-one system that can be reduced to the number of the Beast from the Book of Revelation – 666. In 1997, as he explains it, the U.S. government decided to invest $500 million in creating a universal computer network, which would control every household, first in the United States, and, later, all over the world. Platonov insists that in order to establish such a network, about forty international companies started to work on introducing biometric cards, the primary task of which was to install this global computer network. The final result of these activities was to create the supercomputer that will track every action of every person in the world.

The legend about the "computer named Beast" tracking every action of every person in the world is widespread in post-Soviet Russian conservative discourses. As this conspiracy theory goes, a supercomputer exists in an EU administration building in Brussels. Its existence aims to connect banks all over the world and to progressively enforce a new money system together with some Socialist economic push. It is believed that after gaining control of everyone around the world, the Computer Beast will assign an individual number to each person, which will be tattooed on the right hand and replace credit cards. The number reportedly would consist of three groups of six numbers, which means that it will be the apocalyptic mark of the Antichrist as foretold in the Book of Revelation (Barkun 2003: 44, Fuller 1995:181). Panchenko looked into the origins of this rumour, and not only identified sources of the story, but also traced the changes it underwent over the years. Based on his research, it appeared the narrative originates in the 1970s among extreme evangelical circles in the US, and entered post-Soviet discourses through different channels as a result of "travelling through time and space".

According to Viktor Shnirelman (2017: 127-130), there are a few texts that significantly influenced the perception of new technologies as well as processes associated with globalisation in post-Soviet Russia, and, thus, contributed to the development of a narrative about an omnipresent and omnipotent Computer Beast. As he argues, one of them is an anonymous 1981 article, "The Attack of the Beast", which appeared in the Russian journal *Niva*, published in Richmond, Virginia, by Pavel Vaulin, a Soviet émigré professor at the University of South Alabama. It is believed the article was actually a translation of an excerpt from a book by Mary Stewart Relfe, a radical evangelical preacher; in her book, *When Your Money Fails*, published in that very same year, she insists that the international banking system is based on the "number of the Beast" – 666. There is mention of the existence of the Computer Beast, situated somewhere in Luxembourg and controlling all banking operations. Shnirelman notes that another important channel through which the Computer Beast narrative was exported to post-Soviet Russia were the works of the Greek elders from the Mountain of Athos, who also repeatedly referred to Relfe's book.

In the post-Soviet context, the development of new media and new technologies is often associated with postmodernism and globalisation. Dugin, for instance, suggests in many of his works that, aside from the moral decline and turning away from God, a characteristic feature of postmodernism is the "transhumanisation by using modern technologies". In his view, modern technologies lead to a breaking up with sacrum and transcendence, and, in consequence, narrow the human cognition and negate the divine nature of humanity. What is more, as he insists, the digitisation of the reality accelerates the coming of a postmodern era, in which all true values are either displaced to the ideological peripheries or turned inside out. As a result, what is good is represented as evil, and it is the shortest way to enable the Antichrist to come to the world and control humankind under the guise of introducing universal happiness and peace. By arguing that postmodernism confuses good with evil, Dugin not only alludes to how Ilya Glazunov represented Christ and the Antichrist in his painting as indistinguishable twins, but also suggests that the emergence of this philosophy is an introduction to the Apocalypse. The negative attitude towards postmodernism, considered to be a wicked and valueless philosophy, is, indeed, widespread in religious and conservative circles in post-Soviet Russia. The disagreement with the chaos of postmodernism and devaluation of religion in the public sphere was primarily a result of the uncertainty and the longing for grand narratives, the end of which Jean-François Lyotard announced in 1979 in his book *The Postmodern Condition: A Report on Knowledge*. It all contributed to the emergence of a so-called "conservative turn", and, with it, the increasing popularity of the entire spectrum of right-wing ideas in various post-Soviet Russian discourses. The term "conservative turn", used interchangeably with "conservative revolution", refers originally to the ideological turn that took place in Germany in the 1920s, and significantly influenced the formation of the Nazi ideology.

The "godfathers" of the post-Soviet Russian turn are well-known intellectuals and media personalities. Not only do they often refer to conservative traditions in Russian philosophy and historiosophy, but also tend to evoke theories developed in interwar Germany, including "political theology" put forth by German lawyer and political scientist Carl Schmitt. What is more, being an eclectic, and, ironically, kind of postmodern amalgam of the often contradictory traditionalist and radical ideas, the Russian "new conservatism" has gained popularity both among the intelligentsia and the masses. As Maria Engström insists (2012: 181), contemporary Russia "is not very different from the rest of the world, where diverse religious, nationalist or paranormal ideologies of salvation have been characterised as the principal ideological commodity of the twenty-first century".

Even though the Russian neo-conservatism emerged in the late-Soviet era within the circles of a non-conformist underground in Moscow and Saint Petersburg, it is mostly associated with Vladimir Putin's rise to power. For many, the "conservative turn" not only marks a shift in post-Soviet discourses, but also for several years now it has been noticed in Russian politics, both on internal and external levels. According to Marlene Laruelle (2016), a French sociologist, historian, and political scientist specialising in Russia, one of the symbols of the "conservative turn" is funding the Izborsky Club, started in 2012. It is a community of well-known conservative experts, closely related to the Kremlin and acting as its "advisory body", headed by a conservative writer, Alexander Prokhanov.

Vladimir Ilyin (2016), whose name brings to mind another Ilyin and one of the most famous representatives of Russian interwar conservatism[21], argues that the

---

[21] Ivan Ilyin (1883-1954) was a Russian religious and political philosopher, and a part of the so-called "white emigration". Influenced by the Slavophile tradition, Ilyin was a radical nationalist, monarchist, and a harsh critic of democracy. His views on politics were rather controversial, especially due to his support of fascism, as well as his explicit antisemitism. Many post-Soviet artists and thinkers, including Oleg Platonov, an ultranationalist writer

post-Soviet "conservative turn" was a response to the failure of liberal-democratic reforms that marked the decade after the breakup of the Soviet Union. Sergei Oushakine, who sees something similar that occurred in the Russian Federation in the early 2000s, introduced the term "patriotism of despair". This is, as he explains, "an emotionally charged set of symbolic practices called upon to mediate relations among individuals, nation, and state and thus to provide communities of loss with socially meaningful subject positions" (2009: 5). The acceptance of patriotic and conservative values serves as a kind of the "symbolic practice", aimed at dealing with the trauma of 1990s Russia with its savage transformation and corrupt privatisation, as well as a break with historical continuity and disintegration of identities, both individual and collective. At the time, as oil prices increased and the society enjoyed relative prosperity, the situation only strengthened a positive attitude toward a revived conservatism.

Whereas the modern Russian conservatism is shaped on the moral level by values promoted by the Russian Orthodox Church and patriotic education, on the political level it is characterised by the glorification of the Russian imperial past, the strong division between "us" and "them", and extreme anti-Westernism (Shevtsova 2007, Engström 2014, Akopov 2016). One of the most important premises of the post-Soviet neo-conservatism is challenging the Western hegemony and the attempts to establish a homogenous globalised world ruled by the United States. In the late 1980s and early 1990s in Russia, globalisation and ecumenism were associated mainly with the increase of poverty, financial destabilisation, mounting environmental problems, and deteriorating quality of life. Consequently, Russian eschatology of that time was linked to an anti-globalisation movement (Shnirelman 2017: 416).

It is reflected in numerous post-Soviet right-wing, and especially religious, discourses. According to authors such as Oleg Platonov, Mikhail Nazarov, and Olga Chetverikova, globalisation, which is tightly bonded with ecumenism, is used by the Antichrist and his minions to gain hegemony in the world on both the political and spiritual levels. For this reason, globalisation and ecumenism are considered

---

and Holocaust denier, and Nikita Mikhailov, a renowned film director, admit to being inspired by Ilyin's ideas. As argued by Andrzej de Lazari (2014), references to his works are also present in Putin's rhetoric.

a serious threat to the Russian national culture. It is important to emphasise, however, that the Russian right-wing and religious milieus are not the only ones believing that globalisation and ecumenism are the Antichrist's doing. The anti-ecumenical sentiments are equally widespread within the most radical circles of the American religious right, the representatives of which also believe that the unification of various religions will result in establishing the Kingdom of the Antichrist (Barkun 2003). Such views are also embraced by the Polish radical right, which has noticeably flourished in the last few years.

It is important to note that the post-Soviet sentiments towards globalisation and ecumenism go deeper than the early 1990s and the collapse of the USSR. According to Shnirelman (2017), the negative attitude towards these processes was transplanted to post-Soviet discourses from the writings of radical authors related to the Russian Orthodox Church Outside of Russia. The most prominent opponents of globalisation and ecumenism, he argues, are Boris Molchanov and Seraphim Rose. According to them, ecumenism is the betrayal of genuine Christianity; not only is it aimed at unifying all religions and nations, but it also leads to establishing the universal state ruled by the Antichrist. Similar anxieties were caused by globalisation, which they perceived as a reason for the collapse of nation-states and ethnic cultures. In their view, globalisation was aimed at establishing a totalitarian "new political order" in which authorities, inspired by the Antichrist, will control each individual and make them live what they call a spiritless, Godless life as it already exists in the West. The post-Soviet authors, in fact, do not add much to these conceptions – by equating ecumenism and globalisation with mondialism, they insist that it is all aimed at weakening Russia and establishing the Kingdom of the Antichrist (Snychev 1995, Ilyashenko 2004, Nazarov 1999). So, why would the Antichrist and his servants want to harm Russia so severely? According to the right-wing observers, the answer is quite simple: it is due to Russophobia. Eliot Borenstein (2019: 99-101) argues that, though the beliefs underlining the hysteria over Russia's alleged enemies may seem bizarre since Vladimir Putin came to power, it has moved from the fringes to the mainstream of the Russian public debate. In August 2016, he notes, the Russian Ministry of Culture allocated 1.75 million roubles for a study of "technology of cultural Russophobia and state-administrational responses to this challenge". For many people, it is pretty strong evidence the Russian Federation is taking all this Russophobia very seriously. Also, as Borenstein points out, invoking Russophobia works well as a discursive strategy aimed at rallying "the population against an implacable enemy while reminding that same population of its collective identity". What is more, by explaining Russophobia as a deep fear of how powerful Russia is, authors such as Metropolitan Ioann, Nazarov, Platonov, and Dugin, allude to ideas of the Russian messianism and the conviction that Russia has a pivotal role to play in the Endtime.

But what exactly is Russophobia and where does this notion come from? According to the most conventional definitions, the notion of "russophobia" is defined as a negative, and even hostile, attitude towards everything related to Russia. It is considered to be an integral part of the propaganda spread by anti-Russian forces. Since Russophobia covers a broad spectrum of emotions – from fear to hatred – it is believed that enemies of Russia use it to mobilise their social base and to establish regional or global domination by imposing their values on the Russian society or Russian-speaking communities abroad (Kuleshov 2017). Nevertheless, the term "Russophobia", as well as the phenomenon itself, are highly ambivalent and acquire different meanings in different times and contexts. One of the most outlandish definitions of "Russophobia" can be found on the Russian psychological portal Psyportal.net (2012), where – with surprising seriousness – anonymous authors suggest that Russophobia is like any other phobia, and, thus, it can be treated by cross-cultural communication, accompanied by traditional psychotherapeutic methods, such as hypnotherapy and pharmacological treatment.

Interestingly, the notion of Russophobia goes back to 1869, when Fyodor Tyutchev first used it in a letter to his daughter. It was not until the late 1980s when the term made its mark with the publication of an essay by Igor Shafarievich, a well-recognised Soviet mathematician and algebraist. Published first outside of the samizdat in 1989, Shafarievich's essay, "Russophobia", condemns liberal Russian émigré authors and Western scholars, such as Grigoriy Pomerants, Richard Pipes, Alexander Yanov, and Andrei Siniavsky, for distorting the Russian history and spreading damaging stereotypes about Russia in the West.

According to Shafarievich, all those authors mistakenly claim that the fundamental feature of the Russian nation is a "slavery soul" and, therefore, Russians strive for strong rulers and leaders such as Ivan the Terrible, Peter the Great, and Joseph Stalin. Also, Shafarievich criticises the fact that they often identify the idea of Moscow the Third Rome as the manifestation of Russian nationalism (Berglund 2014).

Another assertion about Russia popular in Western scholarship, which irritates Shafarievich, is the claim that there are only two alternatives of how post-Soviet Russia can develop: either into a "democracy of the Western-type" or "totalitarianism" based on the xenophobic nationalism and chauvinism. In other words, Shafarievich argues that slandering Russia and insisting that it should follow the path of the development analogous to other Western countries are, indeed, the symptoms of Russophobia. Interestingly, after a negative reception of his essay, especially in the West, Shafarevich published an article, "Russophobia Ten Years Later" (1991), in which he reasserted all of his arguments. He again objected to the supposition that Russia should follow the same democratic path of the Western countries and insisted that it should not be detached from its Orthodox core.

What is more, Shafarievich (1991) insisted in his essay that "Russophobia is the ideology of a specific social class, which is a minority and put itself in opposition to the rest of the people". He calls this social class a "little nation" and suggests that it not only opposes the "big nation", but that it also intends to take control over it. The "little nation" is for him a reform-oriented elite that tries to change the worldview and way of living of the majority of "ordinary Russians", which such high-society types considered to be backward and inept. The notion of "little nation" that Shafarievich evokes in his essay was used first by Augustin Cochin, a French historian, to describe a group of intellectuals responsible for the French Revolution. Following this line of thought, Shafarevich saw the "little nation" also in other groups responsible for important historical events, such as the French Huguenots, English Puritans, and Prussian intellectuals. As he insisted, in Russian history, the role of the "little nation" was played by the intelligentsia, dominated by people of Jewish descent, who despised the traditional Russian way of life and attempted to spread Russophobia all over the world (Shafarevich 1989, 1991).

Due to such assertions, the author of "Russophobia" was soon labelled a leading antisemite of post-Soviet Russia. He was also considered to be the leading ideologue of the Russian chauvinistic nationalism represented by Pamyat, the Russian organisation established in the 1980s and known for its right-wing monarchist views and harsh antisemitism. Even though there are opinions that Shafarievich was not an antisemite, and the primary motivation behind his essay was to break the taboo of the overrepresentation of Jews in the Russian intelligentsia (Berglund 2014), his "little nation" could easily be interpreted as the Jewish community in Russia. For this reason, as Kevin O'Connor argues (2006: 149), "Russophobia" was quickly taken up by Russian nationalists, especially those connected to *Nash Sovremennik*, a Russian monthly conservative journal, founded in 1954.

Moreover, the notion of Russophobia inspired numerous authors related to the post-Soviet Russian right, including Alexander Prokhanov, Sergey Kara-Murza, and Oleg Nemenskiy. Whereas Prokhanov (2007) argued that the phenomenon of Russophobia was the result of a fundamental misunderstanding between Russia and the West, both Kara-Murza (2015) and Nemenskiy (2014) insisted that Russophobia has always been much more than just a phobia. In their view, it has been an ideology used by political opponents of Russia, specifically the United States. In the same vein, Dmitry Peskov, Putin's press secretary, argues that an example of the American Russophobia is the fact that the US politicians are continuously demonising Russia, for instance, by accusing the Russian Federation of manipulating recent elections in the United States (King 2017).[22] Peskov's claim demonstrates that the discursive strategy of employing Russophobia as a catch-all term

---

[22] The question of Russia's involvement in the 2016 US presidential election received wide coverage in the international media. Even though it has not been officially proved, many believe that Donald Trump owes his win to some alleged form of Russian interference. See more in: Shane S. and Mazzetti M. (2018). Inside a 3-Year Russian Campaign to Influence U.S. Voters, *The New York Times*, Available at: https://www.nytimes.com/2018/02/16/us/politics/russia-mueller-election.html [Accessed 31 August 2020]; Ackerman S. and Thielman S. (2016). US Officially Accuses Russia of Hacking DNC and Interfering With Election, *The Guardian*. Available at: https://www.theguardian.com/technology/2016/oct/07/us-russia-dnc-hack-interfering-presidential-election [Accessed 31 August 2020]; Moscow Denies Russian Involvement in U.S. DNC Hacking (2016), *Reuters*. Available at: https://www.reuters.com/article/us-usa-election-hack-russia/moscow-denies-russian-involvement-in-u-s-dnc-hacking-idUSKCN0Z02EK [Accessed 31 August 2020].

is present also in the official political discourse of the Russian Federation. It is predominantly used to emphasise the uniqueness of Russia and to accuse political opponents of evil intentions hidden behind their actions and utterances, which are labelled as anti-Russian.

Andrzej de Lazari (1996: 81) argues that Igor Shafarevich, a contemporary Russophile, has a significant impact on post-Soviet Russian discourses. According to de Lazari, Shafarevich has taken on a position similar to that of Nikolay Danilevsky and his book, *Russia and Europe*, in the second half of the 19th century. Shafarievich, as with Danilevsky and other Russophiles, maintains that Russian culture is unique and has nothing in common with the West, and is something of a symbol of the post-Soviet Russian anti-Westernism.

For more than two decades, Shafarevich's idea of the "little nation", whether he intended it or not, has fuelled the post-Soviet Russian antisemitism. Consequently, in numerous post-Soviet Russian discourses, Jews have been portrayed as minions of the Antichrist, and the greatest enemies of Russia, striving for its destruction. Moreover, the Jews seem to be perceived as a corporeal incarnation of the "mystery of lawlessness" We can see more of this in Tatyana Gracheva's book, *Invisible Khazaria*. In the next chapter, I will explore how the book touches on speculations about establishing the New World Order, ruled by the Antichrist, and the accompanying antisemitic convictions and their manifestations in post-Soviet eschatological conspiracy theories.

III.2. Antisemitism and Eschatology: The New World Order and Invisible Khazaria

> (...) And from among the prophets God assigned only three – Moses, who was the creator of God's Law, Isaiah who predicted the Messiah – Christ from the Tribe of Judah, and Jeremiah, who predicted the anti-Messiah – the Antichrist from the Tribe of Dan
>
> (Gorenstein 1975: 6)

The Tribe of Dan, invoked by Fredrich Gorenstein in his 1975 novel, *The Psalm*, which was first published in the samizdat, is the biblical tribe from which the Antichrist is believed to originate. In his book, Gorenstein turns against the traditional exegesis of the Antichrist figure, and, along with a Jungian concept of the

Self, he portrays the Antichrist not only as the enemy of Christ, but as a representative of the dark forces, whose presence is necessary to fulfil the will of God. Here, the arrival of the Antichrist does not indicate the end of history. Instead, as Harriett Murav suggests (1993), by witnessing critical events of Soviet history, such as the famine in Ukraine, the German occupation, Stalinism, and the Brezhnev era, Dan guarantees the continuity of the novel. Since the Soviet history is presented in the novel in the context of the Apocalypse, the utopian myth of building a bright Soviet future is replaced by a dystopian story of starvation, displacement, rape, and murder. Hence, Dan is not only an abstract literary image, representing the Russian eternal Other, but also a carnal being, which reverses traditional understanding of the Antichrist figure. He takes over functions traditionally ascribed to Christ; he becomes both the judge and the Saviour. Nevertheless, we should keep in mind that this kind of literary vision is an exception. The dominant Antichrist image we can find in Soviet and post-Soviet discourses is the Antichrist being a Jew, who conspires against Russia.

According to the exegetical tradition, the Tribe of Dan is the only tribe that does not appear among 144 redeemed tribes of ancient Israel mentioned in the Book of Revelation. Named the "lost tribe", it is believed to have fallen into blasphemy, which was the reason why it could no longer be counted among the People of God. Numerous exegetes of the Scriptures insisted that it is the tribe in which the Antimessiah-Antichrist will be born. This view was expressed, for instance, by Irenaeus of Lyon (ca. 130-200).

Irenaeus insisted that the Antichrist will not only be a Jew from the Tribe of Dan, but he will also be the embodiment of the Beast from the Book of Revelation, as well as the Man of Sin evoked in St. Paul's Epistle to the Thessalonians. In subsequent centuries, the myth of the Antichrist as a false Messiah, from the so-called lost tribe, was reproduced by numerous thinkers, philosophers, and artists, both within the Western and Eastern Christian traditions. One of the most persistent antisemitic narratives that perpetuated the image of Jews as Christianity's greatest enemies were created: the belief that they not only rejected Christ as the true Messiah, but also gave the Antichrist to the world (di Nola 2000, Shnirelman 2017).

As noted earlier, the antisemitic belief that Jews are a malicious collective plotting against Christianity resonated particularly strong in *The Protocols of Elders of*

Zion, and fits in well with this study. In his article, *"The Protocols of the Elders of Zion*: Between History and Fiction" (2008), Michael Hagemeister argues that the pamphlet, a prime example of a conspiracy theory, in many ways resembles apocalyptic narratives. As with the Book of Revelation and other discourses of this kind, it attempts to "unveil" what is hidden and expose the true nature of things. By uncovering what Jews discuss during their secret meetings, *The Protocols* claim to display what is hidden from everyday people and unmask the evil Jewish plot behind all historical events and phenomena. This line of thought is followed by Svetlana Boym (1999) and Marina Aptekman (2006), who suggest that *The Protocols* can be approached as an example of "contemporary mythology". In their view, the pamphlet not only is a response to emotional needs generated by political and economic crises, but also conveys ideological and political messages by turning them into ostensibly authentic narratives. This works exactly like other mythological discourses evoked and analysed by Roland Barthes in his collection of essays *Mythologies* (1957).

Sergey Nilus was the big promoter of antisemitic ideas articulated in *The Protocols of the Elders of Zion*. Born in 1862, he was a flamboyant playboy, who later became a religious thinker obsessed with the idea of the Antichrist. In 1905, he included *The Protocols* as an appendix to his book *The Great within the Small and the Antichrist as an Imminent Political Possibility*. After the Revolution of 1917, Nilus' writings were recognised as anti-Soviet and forbidden in the USSR. It was during Perestroika when Nilus' work was rediscovered and embraced by the Russian public discourses, mostly by conservatives and nationalists. His works, including those containing parts of *The Protocols of the Elders of Zion*, were republished by various publishing houses and reached bestseller status. Nilus became something of a cult figure in ecclesiastical and far-right circles, mainly revolving around the radical right-wing national-patriotic Orthodox Christian movement Pamyat.

Both Nilus' writings and *The Protocols of the Elders of Zion* have become essential texts for the far-right ideology in post-Soviet Russia. Before its new surge in popularity on the Runet[23], *The Protocols* was easily available and reached a broad audience, sold in the thousands in general bookstores, Orthodox speciality bookshops, and street stalls (Shnirelman 2017: 145, Laqueur 1993). Even though it was officially banned in 2010 and placed on the Russian Federal List of Extremist Materials (Minjust.ru), the pamphlet is still distributed through unofficial channels. Many observers fear there are still many readers of *The Protocols of the Elders of Zion*, especially in conservative and right-wing circles. As a result, unfortunately, the dangerous rhetoric in this text continues to appeal to many post-Soviet public figures, along with a large number of influential writers and artists, with potentially explosive consequences.

Antisemitism, eschatology, and conspiracy theories abound throughout the analysed works, and it is pretty clear what the source is. Consequently, the Jews and political opponents claimed to be of Jewish origin are portrayed the embodiment of evil and ultimate enemies of Russia, which, in turn, is believed to be the Katechon – the only Christian (Orthodox) empire capable of withholding the arrival of the Antichrist (Shnirelman 2016, 2017). Some claim that since the start of Russia's existence, a Judeo-Masonic plot has been hounding its efforts. Such believers, as the argument goes, are not necessarily antisemites, but it is all still very instrumental in escalating hostilities towards Jewish people.

Although a discussion on the phenomenon of Russian antisemitism can fall into all kinds of oversimplifications, the land's history cannot deny centuries of antisemitism in one form or another.[24]

---

[23] It is a Russian-language section of the Internet. Due to its specific socio-cultural context as well as political implications, the Runet has been researched both within and outside of Russia. See more in: Etling B. et al (2010). *Public Discourse in the Russian Blogosphere: Mapping RuNet Politics and Mobilization*. Available at: https://cyber.harvard.edu/publications/2010/Public_Discourse_Russian_Blogosphere [Accessed 31 August 2020]; Fossato F. (2009). Discussion: Is Runet the Last Adaptation Tool. *Digital Icons*, Available at: http://www.digitalicons.org/issue01/pdf/issue1/Web-as-an-Adaptation-Tool_N-Fossato.pdf [Accessed 31 August 2020]; Konradova B. and Schmidt H. (2014). From the Utopia of Autonomy to a Political Battlefield of the Russian Internet. In: Gorham M. et al. (Ed.). *Digital Russia: the Language, Culture and Politics of New Media Communication*. London, New York: Routledge.

[24] Antisemitism, and its consequences worldwide, has been thoroughly studied in the twentieth century. There are countless academic and non-academic works tackling the history of Jewry in Central and Eastern Europe, as well as manifestations of antisemitism in Russia

According to American political scientist and philosopher Stephen Eric Bronnen (2000: 2), "antisemitism [in Russia] was never simply an independent impulse", but, rather, a "part of a broader project directed against the civilising impulse of reason and the dominant forces of modernity". The Jews seemed like a perfect "target" to blame. Considered strangers "unfaithful" to the national culture, they were defined by features such as "cosmopolitanism, rootlessness, modern law, and finance", often perceived as negative. In the most extreme cases, the Jews were equated with "evils of modernity" and considered the inherent enemies of the traditional Russian national community (Boym 1999: 102). Marina Aptekman (2006: 667) suggests that a consequence of portraying the Jews as "demonic enemies of Russia", in post-Soviet Russian conservative discourses they have become "mythological" figures. As a result, the Jews are no longer perceived as tangible, real people targeted by the Black Hundreds as was the case at the beginning of the 20th century. Instead, the word "Jew" has become a label used to identify an adversary. From this standpoint, it underwent a change of the meaning, similar to that of the word "antichrist".

Nowadays, antisemitic themes in Russia are not as common as in pre-revolutionary or Soviet times. Nevertheless, they still strongly shape right-wing and conservative worldviews. Even though post-Soviet conspiracy theories see the enemies of Russia also in many other presumably evil collectives, such as the Islamists, the sectarians, the American secret police, the US-controlled internal forces, the Reptilians, and the Freemasonry, the belief in the existence of an apocalyptic

---

and beyond, for instance: Cohn-Sherbok D. (2002). *Antisemitism: A History*. Stroud, Gloucestershire: Sutton Publications; Slezkine Y. (2011). *The Jewish Century*. Princeton: Princeton University Press; Goldstein P. et al. (2012). *A Convenient Hatred: The History of Antisemitism*. Brookline: Facing History and Ourselves; Petersen H. and Salzborn S. (2010). *Antisemitism in Eastern Europe: History and Present in Comparison*. Frankfurt am Main: Peter Lang; Gibson J. and Howard M. (2007). Russian Antisemitism and Scapegoating of Jews. *British Journal of Political Science*, 37 (2): 193-223; Lazare B. (1995). *Antisemitism: Its History and Causes*. Lincoln: University of Nebraska Press; Greenberg L. (1944-1951). *The Jews in Russia*. New Haven: Yale University Press; Löwe H.D. (1993). *The Tsars and the Jews: Reform, Reaction and Antisemitism in Imperial Russia 1772-1917*. New York: Harwood Academic Publishers; Rossman V.J. (2013). *Russian Intellectual Antisemitism in the Post-Communist Era*. Lincoln: University of Nebraska Press; Paperni V. (Ed.) (2004). *Antisemitism and Philosemitism in the Slavic World and Western Europe*. Haifa: University of Haifa Press; and many others.

Jewish plot remains the most widespread. It can be found not only in numerous pamphlets, brochures, and texts published officially or distributed through unofficial channels, but also on the Runet. When put the entry "Jewish plot" (*evreiskiy zagavor*) on the Russian segment of the internet, one will find a never-ending discussion across websites and forums about how the Jews are reportedly responsible for all of the world's problems through history.

Of particular interest, on Orthodox websites, or those regularly read by Church followers, one can find numerous discussions about the links between Jews and the Antichrist. Among the recurring motifs, there are: the belief that the Antichrist will be a false Jewish Messiah coming from the Tribe of Dan; the conviction that the tax identification numbers (the INN), the postal codes, and the magnetic credit cards are the "seal of the Antichrist"; and, finally, the view that the processes of globalisation and ecumenism are veiled attempts to build the Zionist Kingdom of the Antichrist, or, as many authors argue, to establish the New World Order, in which Christianity will be abolished.

The conviction that there exists a multi-levelled, complicated plot aimed at establishing the New World Order, in which a world government will replace sovereign national governments, is one of the most popular conspiracy theories in Russia and beyond. According to Michael Barkun, author of *Culture of Conspiracy: Apocalyptic Visions in Contemporary America* (2003), the belief in the New World Order often has an apocalyptic component. As he argues, many adherents of this theory insist the New World Order equals "an impending world dictatorship in which the Antichrist would seize control through a combination of co-opted international organisations and marvels of electronic surveillance" (2003: 55). In the end, processes and phenomena such as democratisation, globalisation, and technological progress are believed to result in establishing the Kingdom of the Antichrist on Earth. In his book, Barkun (2003: 40) identifies two main sources of such convictions: the Christian millenarianism with its speculations about the Endtime and "a body of historical and political pseudoscholarship that purported to explain major events in terms of the machinations of secret societies".

It should be noted that the term "New World Order" does not belong exclusively to conspiracy theories. In politics, it is a neutral term commonly employed to address important changes taking place in international political and economic affairs. As such, it has been used in various situations by politicians, including statesmen Woodrow Wilson, Winston Churchill, and Mikhail Gorbachev. In their speeches, they used this term as a reference to a new period of history after changes in the balance on the international arena. On September 11, 1990, US President George H.W. Bush gave a speech entitled "Toward a New World Order" in which he talked of a "New World Order" leading to the establishment of a supra-government. In his talk, Bush discussed objectives of the post-Cold War global politics and prospects of international cooperation between the greatest political powers. This was the moment that triggered the proliferation of conspiracy theories addressing the issue.

The term "New World Order" was immediately picked up by American religious fundamentalists, obsessed with the imminent arrival of the Antichrist. They believed that since the US president spoke about the NWO so openly, it meant that the forces of evil were becoming more powerful and the Endtime was near. For them, the promise of the New World Order was, in fact, the threat that the Kingdom of the Antichrist would soon materialise as a result of actions undertaken by the Illuminati, the Freemasons, the New Age movement, and the US political institutions (Barkun 2003). This fear was a leading theme of a bestselling book, *The New World Order* (1991) written by Pat Robertson, an American televangelist and religious, political commentator. In his book, Robertson not only insists that hidden, powerful forces control US politics, but also refers to a whole range of popular conspiratorial themes, including the Illuminati, Freemasons, and evil Jewish bankers. Also, he argues that Satan is the mastermind behind the plot aimed at establishing the one-world-government, and that the end of the world, foreseen in the Book of Revelation, is near.

As Barkun argues (2003: 45), American Christian fundamentalists and anti-government populists are the two American countercultures that gave rise to the majority of conspiracy theories in contemporary mass culture. Meanwhile, the popularity of multiple conspiracy theories preached by these circles was not limited to the United States. They have evolved, mutated, and travelled across different cultures. As a result, the New World Order narrative, coupled with other conspiracy theories, ended up in Russia. What is particularly interesting, even though imported from the US, the Russian variant of the NWO theory is permeated with anti-Western attitudes. It tends to portray the political reality as divided between the powers of good, represented by the Russian Federation, and the devilish New World Order supported by the United States (Yablokov 2015). An example of this contemporary political picture is Mikhail Nazarov's book, *The Mystery of Russia: Historiosophy of the 20th Century* (1999), in which he argues that establishing the New World Order brings about a gradual global incorporation of the Jewish-American cosmopolitanism and aims at destroying Orthodox Russia.

In *The Mystery of Russia*, apart from discussing Russian history in the light of a conspiracy theory, Nazarov offers a "multileveled deconstruction" of the political situation in the 20th and 21st centuries:

> We see that this "New World Order" becomes overgrown with political and military instruments under the auspices of the UN ("nowadays the UN, as well as UNESCO, are almost entirely composed of masons from different countries" – proudly reported a Masonic source in the 1960s). What is striking is such an explicit manifestation of the material power of Jewry in the "preventive war" led via America against Iraq (...) – and the whole world is paying for this war... And most importantly – we see that the current government of Russia unconditionally supports all these measures and participates in this process, having before its eyes the same ideal of the "ultimate" consumer society, permeated with apostasy... (Nazarov 1999: 62).

An obsession with a Judeo-Masonic plot aimed at corrupting Russia permeates Nazarov's writings. *The Mystery of Russia*, claiming to reveal the truth about the United States, argues that the US is, in fact, a puppet state in the hands of wealthy Jews who, thanks to their money, manipulate the course of history. The way he sees it, Bush's 1991 announcement of the National Security Strategy revealed the dark plans to control the world. As Nazarov insists, the US president not only declared establishing the New World Order, but also emphasised that America will play a dominant role in this process by promoting false values of peace, security, and freedom. Nazarov's work appears to explain much of today's Russian religious conservatism. Not only does he combine an American conspiracy theory about the New World Order with anti-American ideas employed by the Russian far-right, but he also twists it with antisemitic visions, stating that America is controlled by Jews and Masons, who are servants of the Antichrist.

As many Russian conservative and religious authors argue, the Judeo-Masonic-controlled United States uses international organisations such as the UN, NATO, and the European Union to seize power everywhere. As well, they resort to military means such as attacking Iraq, bombing Serbia or intervening in Syria to build greater profits (Osipov 2012, Snychev 1993). Nazarov (2005) and Platonov (2010a), Holocaust deniers who believe *The Protocols of Elders of Zion* is an authentic historical document, insist that Jewish money has enabled what they call the "world's backstage" to gain considerable political influences and to weaken Russia throughout the centuries. According to them, Jews and Masons have sponsored the adversaries of Orthodox Russia – both internal and external – in all historical conflicts, ranging from the Crimean War and World War I to the Bolshevik Revolution and the Cold War. They believe Jews with their money, or, more specifically, Jewish bankers, throughout history have worked feverishly to destroy Russia and have prepared the world for the arrival of the Antichrist.

In his book, *The Battle for Russia* (2010), Platonov insists that world Jewry not only organised the Bolshevik Revolution, but also is responsible for the disintegration of the USSR. As he explains it, there was the original aim to destroy the Holy Rus', and the "symphony of powers" between the Tsar and the Patriarch, followed by the dismantling of the Soviet Union to get the New World Order established under the leadership of the United States. Platonov's ideas mirror ideological disarray that can be found in other post-Soviet Russian conservative and religious authors. According to political scientist Andreas Umland (2007), Platonov's views are a mixture of "pathological anti-Americanism, delusional conspirology, apocalyptic images of the future and fantastic statements about the upcoming new birth of the Russian nation". Platonov, a self-proclaimed heir and continuator of Metropolitan Ioann Snychev, an antisemite and ardent Stalinist, represents a whole conglomerate of what are often mutually exclusive ideas (Shnirelman 2017: 393). From this standpoint, he is not very different from Mikhail Nazarov and Aleksander Dugin.

In addition to all this, there is a theory of the Invisible Khazaria put forth by Tatyana Gracheva. Since 2009, Gracheva, a head of the Department of Russian and Foreign Languages at the Military Academy of the General Staff of the Armed Forces of Russia, published a series of books about the Invisible Khazaria and its dark plans to destroy Russia and prepare the world for the Antichrist. As Gracheva suggests, the Invisible Khazaria is a secret community, consisting of people working for the most important international organisations such as the United Nations, NATO, and the European Union. Gracheva's books include *The Invisible Khazaria: Algorithms of Geopolitics and Strategies of Secret Wars of the World's Backstage* (2009), *The Memory of the Russian Soul* (2011), and *The Last Temptation of Russia: To Which War Russia Should Prepare Itself* (2013). These books were bestsellers and translated into several languages, including English and Polish.

The Khazars, the main villains in Gracheva's work, were, in fact, a semi-nomadic Turkic nation that established a great empire in the 7th century, the khaganate. In the 9th century, to centralise a heterogenous state, Judaism was introduced as an official religion of the Khazar empire. This decision led to objections among some of the groups, and, subsequently, led to internal tensions that significantly weakened the empire. It coincided with a dynamic development of the Orthodox Kievan Rus', ruled by the Count Svetoslav, who ravaged the khaganate in 965. After this defeat, the Khazar state was never rebuilt, and the Khazars scattered around the world. As Gracheva insists, it was when the defeated and humiliated Khazars decided to take revenge on the Russian state. In her view, to achieve this purpose, they not only provoked events such as the two world wars and the Bolshevik Revolution, but also established supranational institutions such as the European Union and NATO. Gracheva believes that all these actions have three primary goals: introducing a new anti-Christian religion, consolidating the political and economic power, and establishing the unified state of what she calls the Global Khazaria.

According to Gracheva's geopolitical views, the only obstacle to the Invisible Khazaria's sinister goal is Orthodox Russia. In *The Memory of the Russian Soul*, she writes:

> "The global consolidation of power" means building the global state (the Global Khazaria) led by the Antichrist, after starting the world war. It is the ultimate goal of the Khazar bankers. Russia, as a stronghold of Orthodoxy and a national statehood in the world, has become the main obstacle to the implementation of these sinister plans (Gracheva 2011: 15-16).

The Global Khazaria, as envisioned by Gracheva, in many respects, resembles the New World Order. Not only is it depicted as a universal, unified state where sin prevails, but, also, as Gracheva suggests, it will be ruled by the Antichrist. As the story goes, by taking control of all capital and information, the Khazars will gradually exterminate the Western states and manipulate the masses into believing that Russia is humanity's enemy. In the face of impending Apocalypse, Gracheva warns the Russian people against the final clash between forces of good and forces of evil and suggests that in order to survive, people have to return to the Church and establish small communities, resembling those created by the Old Believers in the face of the *Raskol*.

Curiously, Gracheva's conception of the Invisible Khazaria is not a complete figment of the imagination. Reliable sources are scarce, but it refers to numerous myths that stem from the Khazars and resonates with other notions and theories explored in this study. Echoing Nazarov and Platonov, this Global Khazaria employs anti-globalist and anti-Western approaches in its goal to destroy Orthodox Russia and Christianity it represents. The only difference in Gracheva's work is that the main plotters against Russia are not Jews and Masons, but the Khazars who, by the way, happen to be followers of Judaism. In many ways, the image of the Invisible Khazaria culminates with the most popular conspiracy theories, bringing it all together, as pushed by analysed Russian conservative authors. It, indeed, refers to a whole conspiratorial repertoire, including motifs such as Russophobia, evil Judeo-Masonry, establishing the New World Order, and the existence of backstage planners in controlling the world.

Shnirelman (2012) provides an interesting perspective on Gracheva's Invisible Khazaria. As he puts it, Gracheva's books have not only little in common with reliable historical analysis, but also are full of antisemitic prejudices. Hence, the Invisible Khazaria should be perceived as a contemporary version of *The Protocols of the Elders of Zion*, in which the seemingly neutral word "Khazaria" replaces the antisemite myth about the Judeo-Masonic conspiracy against Christianity. As Shnirelman argues, this strategy dates back to the Soviet era, when the Khazar myth was employed as a euphemism for the ideologically marked word "Jew". Overall, in post-Soviet Russian discourses, the Khazars play the same role as Jews – they serve as an image of a collective enemy of Christianity, with Orthodox Russia its prime target. Also, they are portrayed as minions of the Antichrist, or his collective emanation in history and politics, just like the Judeo-Masons.

The belief that the Antichrist can be represented by a collective goes back to early Christianity. In the First Epistle of John, the author warns the believers that there exists a collective of "antichrists", who stand against the Christian doctrine, and are a threat to the stability of the community. Subsequently, this discursive strategy was employed not only to denote heretics, religious dissenters, and non-believers, but also as a plea for hostility towards certain ethnic and religious groups viewed as a threat. As this study shows, in post-Soviet Russian far-right and conservative religious narratives, labels "antichrists" and "servants of the Antichrist" are often used to designate a vicious collective, in most cases consisting of people of Jewish origin, planning to seize world power and destroy Orthodox Russia, which is deemed the only genuinely Christian state.

What unites all these texts is a particular hermeneutic style of explaining the reality in terms of a conspiracy, as well as abundant references to apocalyptic and eschatological themes. Other features characteristic for post-Soviet nationalist writings are the ambiguity, confusion of facts, and recurrence of motifs such as the greatness of Russia hindered by hidden enemies, the imminent arrival of the Antichrist, and a devilish character of the West. Moreover, these narratives very often appear to be serious academic research and render the conventional scholarship as irrelevant by winning a significant following. According to Shnirelman (2017: 438), these authors who describe Russian history in the light of a Judeo-Masonic plot, or any other clandestine operative, create the "alternative history", in which the existence of sinister external forces justifies all misfortunes and mistakes. Interestingly, the "alternative history", written often by amateur historians and famous writers, may be defined as "a therapy in which problems of today are re-mediated with images of the past glory" (Sheiko and Brown 2014, Laruelle 2012). In such works, Russia is portrayed as always persecuted by ominous forces, conspiring and aiming at establishing the New World Order – or the Global Khazaria – ruled by the Antichrist.

By imposing an overarching narrative to explain the surrounding reality, an alternative history in many respects resembles conspiracy theories: it also explains the reality in a mythological way, by creating an alternate cognitive apparatus, and creating a kind of "reality in itself". Even though it is difficult to say how prevalent conspiracy theories and "alternative history" truly are in post-Soviet Russia, one can observe their growing popularity. It is rendered by the same processes as those that have contributed to the increase of conspiracy theories in the United States: the decreasing trust in media combined with the widespread availability of conspiratorial narratives (Barkun 2003, Khlebnikov 2012: 3-16).

While looking at conspiracy theories and other examples of the so-called "stigmatised knowledge" (Barkun 2003), it is essential to keep in mind that what once was considered marginal can very quickly enter the mainstream. The radical, xenophobic, and antisemitic discourses, which have recently been normalised in various European countries, including France, Germany, and Poland, can serve as an example. Expanding from all this, the post-Soviet discourses are an exemplification of views shared by the majority of Russian contemporary nationalists and fundamentalists, and belong to the same semantic realm. By combining conspiratorial and eschatological motifs, they situate the current political situation with the final struggle between good and evil. Subsequently, upheavals over the last century – the Bolshevik Revolution, World War II, the collapse of the Soviet Union, and post-Communist era that followed – are seen as efforts to annihilate Russia. Meanwhile, in the next chapter, we will see similar strategies employed by post-Soviet Russian authors, but without that conspiratorial component.

IV. "Without Doubt, the Antichrist is a Real Political Possibility of Our Times": Russia, the Antichrist, and Political Theology

The quote used in the title of this chapter comes from the article, "The Mystery of Lawlessness", written by Metropolitan Ioann Snychev, the second most important person in the Russian Orthodox Church in the first half of the 1990s. The article, the title of which was taken from St. Paul's Second Letter to the Thessalonians, was first published in 1992 in the newspaper *Sovetskaya Rossiya*, which, beginning in 1974, was the official press organ of the Supreme Soviet and Council of Ministers of the Russian Soviet Federative Socialist Republic. Interestingly, after the dissolution of the USSR, the newspaper kept its name and was still on friendly terms with the Communist Party, headed by Gennady Zyuganov.

Written in a prophetic style, the article depicts the reality of the early 1990s as the Endtime, characterised by the collapse of moral values, insecurity, turmoil, and anarchy. For Snychev, the contemporary world, marked by a proceeding apostasy and departure from Christian values, is ruled by the Forerunners of the Apocalypse. Among them, Metropolitan Ioann mentions founders of the ecumenical movement, whose aim is to build a universal community led by a charismatic leader, who preaches democracy's false values of liberalism and freedom – the Antichrist. According to Snychev, the only way of stopping this destroyer's march and establishing his Kingdom on Earth is to revive the Holy Rus' by restoring the symphony of secular and Church powers.

Snychev's article concludes with a stern warning: the arrival of the Antichrist is a "real political possibility of our times". This claim is a direct reference to Sergey Nilus' book *The Great Within the Small and the Antichrist as an Imminent Political Possibility* (1903), in the second edition of which Nilus included *The Protocols of Elders of Zion*. Portraying the Antichrist as a political force is not mere poetic hyperbole. Instead, such a discursive strategy transforms the Antichrist ideomyth from the realm of metaphysics to the psychical world. Thus, the Antichrist is perceived as a political enemy, and the apocalyptic horrors believed to accompany his arrival are moved to the realm of politics.

The discursive strategy, in which the Antichrist is perceived as a political enemy, be it a religious dissenter, ideological opponent, or alien socio-political system, fits in with Carl Schmitt's notion of the political enemy. Once seduced by the Nazi ideology, Schmitt was a German jurist and political theorist who developed a vision of politics based on the friend/enemy dichotomy. In his book, *Concept of the Political* (1963: 27), he argued that even though a political enemy "need not be morally evil or aesthetically ugly", such a person has to represent values utterly foreign to a given collective. Politics is seen as the result of a community's struggle with the Other, based on an inevitable conflict between "us" and "them". What is more, according to Schmitt (2005), this struggle is inscribed into a broader context of a particular political theology set on the assumption that "all significant concepts of the modern theory of the state are secularised theological concepts". We can see an extension of Schmitt's theory in Snychev's strategy of portraying the Antichrist as the ultimate political enemy of Orthodox Russia, deemed the only genuine Christian state.

Snychev is not the only post-Soviet Russia author who portrays the Antichrist as the ultimate political enemy of Russia. Such a discursive strategy is employed by many contemporary Russian scholars, thinkers, politicians, activists, and religious figures, whom Alexander Verkhovsky (2004: 129) labels "Russian Orthodox nationalists". In considering the Schmittean theory of politics, as well as the concepts of sacral geography, it is interesting to explore how and why authors such as Snychev, Duschenov, Chetverikova, and Dugin describe the contemporary world as the stage of the apocalyptic drama and situate geopolitical phenomena in religious and eschatological contexts. By analysing their books, articles, and utterances, I aim at demonstrating how religious ideas, specifically the Antichrist ideomyth, are used instrumentally in politics today. It is also useful to look at discursive strategies they employ while constructing a collective identity based on imagined geographical boundaries.

IV.1. The Antichrist: Image of a Political Enemy

From 1990 to 1995, Ioann Snychev was the Metropolitan of the Eparchy of St. Petersburg and Ladoga and, thus, one of the most influential figures in the Russian Orthodox Church of that time. In his writings, he insisted that Russians are the

"God-bearing nation" and their destiny is to save humankind. As he saw it, the true Russianness not only is the culmination of autocracy, religiosity, and collectivism, but it is also the only force that can oppose the Antichrist and his Kingdom. Moreover, Snychev was an apologist of Ivan the Terrible and argued that the Tsar should have been canonised, as he came to represent the real union of secular and divine powers (Snychev 1997). To this day, his works enjoy relatively widespread popularity. Not only can they be found in the Church *lavkas*, but also they are often republished on various websites and forums on the Runet.

Known for his nationalism, antisemitism, and anti-Westernism, Metropolitan Ioann to this day remains one of the most controversial figures associated with the Russian Orthodoxy. Whereas some criticise him for inciting conflicts, the others consider him a spiritual guide and the most significant authority of the Russian Orthodox Church. As well, many questions have arisen over his writings. It is commonly believed that the actual author of books and articles published under his name was actually Konstantin Dushenov, the nationalistic publicist and the head of the Rus' Pravoslavnaya analytical agency, which, in 2004, was sharply condemned by Patriarch Aleksey for preaching an extremist outlook and discrediting the Russian Orthodox Church. In 2007, Dushenov was found guilty for "inciting hatred and enmity, as well as humiliating the dignity of a group of persons on the grounds of nationality, origin, attitude to religion", and sentenced to three years in prison.

These writings and utterances, regardless of the author – whether it was Metropolitan Ioann Snychev or Dushenov – are negative about everything that is not Orthodox, and often refer to eschatological motives, including the Antichrist ideomyth. In the article, "The Mystery of Lawlessness", it is argued that:

> Our homeland, our nation, is now experiencing rough, hard times of turmoil and anarchy. Shrines are being violated and spat upon; the state has been betrayed and abandoned for plunder of unscrupulous and greedy money-grubbers, priests preach the new official religion – the cult of spiritual and physical depravity; the cult of unrestrained profit – at any price (...). The process of apostasy, of the decay of a vivid and solid Christian worldview, foretold by the Lord Jesus Christ almost two thousand years ago, is close to completion. Apparently, God destined us to be the contemporaries of the "last times". Without doubt, the Antichrist is a real political possibility of our times (Snychev 1992).

This article pushes the Antichrist ideomyth from religion to political discourse, but also portrays the Antichrist as the embodiment of everything that was going wrong in post-Soviet Russia. Unlike in conspiracy theories, here the Antichrist is not responsible for a complex plot against Russia, but serves as a metaphor for political changes taking place in the world after the Cold War.

This is not the only post-Soviet text imposing a political feature on the Antichrist ideomyth. Other right-wing writers, thinkers, and public figures, including an associate professor at the Moscow State Institute of International Relations Olga Chetverikova and an Orthodox author Valeriy Filimonov also portray the Antichrist as an inherent enemy of the Russian Federation. For instance, Filimonov (2016) insists that the Antichrist will appear as a global political leader, who tempts people with false idols of "peace and security", "war against international terrorism and extremism", "electronic democracy", and "tolerance". As a charismatic deceiver, the Antichrist will offer the most successful solutions to resolve all contemporary crises. However, as the argument goes, his solutions will be a great spiritual deception. Consequently, humanity will be blinded and fall into the Antichrist's devious trap, and people will be turned into slaves of his dark forces. Only at this point, the Antichrist will reveal his true, devilish nature. According to Filimonov, the Antichrist will blind people with the promise of the Kingdom of God on Earth, and only later disclose himself as the Endtime tyrant, who replaces spiritual values with material goods and preaches Christian values detached from God.

Filimonov's vision explains why humanity will trust the Antichrist, even though he is described in the Scriptures as the Man of Sin, the Son of Destruction, and the Lawless One. In the same vein, the majority of post-Soviet Russian discourses describe the Antichrist as a deceitful and cunning, yet clever, individual, who deludes people with false miracles and silver-tongued blasphemies. In this portrayal, the Antichrist is "the wolf in sheep's clothing" as revealed in the Gospel of Matthew, the evil hypocrite that will present himself as good and trustworthy, and evokes the two figures that have shaped the Antichrist ideomyth: Dostoevsky's Grand Inquisitor and Solovyov's Apollon. Furthermore, it alludes to the prophecy of Boris Molchanov, one of the most influential figures of the Russian Orthodox

Church Outside of Russia, who insisted that solving humanity's problems through false miracles, the Antichrist will lead the world to the ultimate catastrophe Another problematic aspect of the Antichrist's nature is that he resembles Christ. In different post-Soviet Russian discourses, including Ilya Glazunov's art, Christ and the Antichrist are portrayed as almost identical, indistinguishable twins. Depicting the Antichrist as the mirror reflection of Christ not only points out to the difficulty in distinguishing good from evil in the modern world, but also alludes to the exegesis of the Antichrist figure put forth by Church Fathers. According to their forewarnings, as the ultimate enemy of Christianity, the Antichrist represents spiritual antipodes of Christ and the values he preaches. Moreover, all signs heralding the arrival of the Antichrist are seemingly identical with those related to the Second Coming of Christ, but with the opposite spiritual intent. The metaphysical pluses turn out to be only apparent and are swapped by the minuses. What is considered good, turns out to be evil, and it becomes impossible to distinguish between the two.

The confusion triggered by attempts to guess who is who in the Christ/Antichrist entanglement is perfectly reflected in the words of Mikhail Nazarov. In *The Mystery of Russia*, he writes:

> (…) if Christ is born of the Virgin and the Holy Spirit, the Antichrist – in a particularly perverse way – will be borne by a harlot and due to devil's influence; he will also begin his deceitful preaching at the age of thirty-three years and will continue to deceive people for three and a half years. Thanks to the power of the devil, he will perform miracles, make prophecies, he will come as a "Messiah", and the Temple in Jerusalem will be restored for him, etc. He will impress most of the people – those spiritually blind – by solving earthly problems using the method of "bread and circuses" (Nazarov 1999).

Nazarov combines both ways of portraying the Antichrist typical for post-Soviet Russian discourses. Not only does he argue that the Antichrist will be a perverse reflection of Christ, who will start his activities at the age of thirty-three, as was the case with Christ, but, also, that the Antichrist will first present himself as a Messiah, and only later reveal his true evil nature. As Nazarov suggests, the Antichrist will turn out to be a deceptive leader, who offers people what they demand – "the bread and circuses", just like anti-Christian emperors of ancient Rome.

The complex nature of this entanglement is also tackled by Alexander Dugin, one of the most controversial public figures in post-Soviet Russia. Dugin was a part of the occult dissident culture that flourished in late 1980s Saint Petersburg, and significantly inspired his conception of "integral Traditionalism". Even though he sharply criticises postmodernism, one can argue that his conceptions are a specific postmodernist blend of various ideologies, political views, and religious concepts. Moss also suggests that since Dugin is particularly interested in "understanding the role of the Orthodox Church and Russia in the last times", one of the essential parts of his philosophy is a specific "eschatological ecclesiology". For this reason, the Endtime and the Antichrist's arrival occupy a vital place in Dugin's arguments.

In his book, *Ways of the Absolute* (1990), Dugin not only develops a concept of a "total Traditionalism" – an esoteric revolt against the modern world – but also offers an original vision of the complex Christ/Antichrist entanglement. As he puts it, the relationship between Christ and the Antichrist resembles an ancient symbol of the amphisbaena – a dragon-snake with two heads, one of which belongs to Christ and the second to the Antichrist. In other words, Christ and the Antichrist represent two interdependent metaphysical poles of the reality, in which Christ is the Tsar, and the Antichrist is an evil usurper.

In this duo, Christ combines human and divine nature in himself and is an image of God on Earth. The Antichrist, in turn, as with the ancient Roman deity Janus, is a two-faced devilish traitor and rascal, who spreads existential nihilism and mingles conflicting values. Interestingly, while portraying the Antichrist as a false Messiah seeking to replace the redeemer, Dugin invokes both Christian and Islamic eschatological traditions. In traditional Islamic writings, there exists an Antichrist-like figure of Dajjal, the arrival of whom will coincide with phenomena such as gradual apostasy, spreading of evil in the world, and increasing the number of people worshipping worship Satan.

Dugin continues his explorations of the Antichrist and his wicked nature in another book, *The Radical Subject and Its Double* (2009). In it, he alludes to the eschatological tradition of Islam. Also, he argues that the Antichrist is not only a Christian equivalent of Dajjal, but also he invokes the historiosophy developed by *beguny*. This Old Believers faction rejected all manifestation to the state authority and believed that only by remaining in motion could they avoid the power of evil. Seeing himself as an Old Believer, Dugin insists that "if Christ is the lion, the Antichrist is a lion too". Further, he refers to a New Age idea of "metaphysical vampirism". He suggests that the Antichrist is a vampire embodying the modern culture, in which "the dark forces are sucking out people's money, strength, intelligence, talent, time, thoughts, attention, astonishment, desire, psyche". Along *beguny*, Dugin portrays the Antichrist as "a lion [who] drinks the blood of another lion" and argues that he is a metaphysical vampire, who not only feeds on Christ's blood, his antithesis, but also drains people from everything positive, and plunges them into misery and chaos (Dugin 2009a).

However, as Dugin suggests, there is no symmetry between the two lions, since Christ and the Antichrist are not, and can never be, symmetrical. The only figure, with whom the Antichrist can be compared to, is the so-called Radical Subject. In his original and complex concept of the new metaphysics, which is the foundation of the *Fourth Political Theory* (2009), Dugin describes the Radical Subject as an eschatological and traumatic figure, participating in processes that are beyond the conventional metaphysics. Somewhat like the Nietzschean *Übermensch*, the Radical Subject stands above humankind, yet, in the metaphysical hierarchy, he is still much lower than Christ. According to Dugin, the Radical Subject and the Antichrist represent "extreme forms of eschatological, apocalyptic reality in which we are immersed", and, thus, the metaphysical tension between them is an ontological symptom of the present world. In this perspective, the contemporary political reality, characterised by globalisation, liberalism and the development of post-industrial society, "can be easily recognised as the era of the Antichrist – the Endtime" (Dugin 2009b, 2011).

The 1990s in post-Soviet Russia, marked by rapid social, political, and economical changes, dynamic globalisation, and the development of new technologies, are often portrayed as the Endtime. Such a discursive strategy can be found not only in conspiracy theories (see 3.1. and 3.2.), but also in political views put forth by authors associated with religious and conservative milieus. In both types of discourses, the eschatological motifs blend with antisemitic prejudices. In the writings of analysed authors, the alleged Jewish ancestry of the Antichrist is evoked both in the context of disclosing a grand conspiracy against Russia inspired by this ultimate evil force and in numerous notions of contemporary geopolitics. Russian authors, such as Vladimir Osipov, Yuriy Vorobievskiy, and Konstantin Kedrov, motivated by interpretations of the Scriptures by Irenaeus of Lyon and Hippolytus of Rome, insist the Antichrist, originally from the Tribe of Dan, would be of Jewish origin. Ironically, Church Fathers and the post-Soviet Russian authors rather conveniently forget that Christ was Jewish.

Konstantin Kedrov, a Russian writer, philosopher, and a member of the PEN Club, argues that the Jewish ancestry of the Antichrist is indicated by the number 666 ascribed to one of the beasts from the Book of Revelation. In his book, *The Parallel Worlds* (2001), which is his authorial answer to the "global challenges" that include the question of life after death, Kedrov suggests that 666 is, in fact, an encrypted name, which can be figured out by using gematria. Drawing upon the Sumerian language, he decodes the "number of the Beast" as "Geshygeshisheas", which, as he insists, is a distorted anagram of the name of Jesus in a Hebrew transcription – "Yehoshuhand". According to Kedrov, a distortion of Christ's name works precisely like the prefix $ἀντί$ in the Greek word "antichrist" – it indicates that "Geshygeshisheas" is a false Messiah and a "dialectical counterpart of Jesus", who will attempt to replace him. For Kedrov, Christ and the Antichrist are two equal metaphysical aspects of reality. Unlike Dugin, he sees the Antichrist as symmetrical to Christ.

Portraying the Antichrist as symmetrical to Christ is, indeed, the most widespread way of imagining the Christ/Antichrist entanglement in post-Soviet Russian discourses. Yuriy Vorobieskiy, a Russian writer and journalist, whom Shnirelman (2017: 378-379) calls the "self-proclaimed direct follower of Sergei Nilus", ardently associates the Antichrist with the Jewry. His book *Path to the Apocalypse: Omega Point* (1999), stylised as a mystical prophecy, Vorobievskiy illustrates one of the most popular scenarios of how the Antichrist will come to the world. As he argues, the Endtime has already been inaugurated, because the Antichrist was born, yet not revealed.

As Vorobievskiy sees it, the Antichrist's life will be a masquerade and mockery of the life of Christ. Not only will his mother be a fallen woman from the Tribe of Dan, who will be the antithesis of the Blessed Virgin Mary, but he will also reveal himself only at the age of thirty, when Jesus began teaching and gathering the faithful around him. Due to his fraudulent activities, Vorobievskiy argues, the Antichrist will seize power over humankind and rule the world for three and a half years. After this time, his reign will end, and Christ will defeat him in the ultimate fight. In short, Vorobievskiy imagines the Antichrist as a political leader with a Jewish background, who will present himself as the Saviour and only later will he reveal his true nature of a cunning, greedy, and ruthless tyrant.

Another persistent discursive strategy that emphasises a relationship between the Antichrist and Jewishness is that the Antichrist will be a false Jewish Messiah. This view is based on the conviction that since Jews rejected Jesus as the Christ and the Anointed One, the Messiah they are awaiting is, in fact, Christ's enemy – he is the Antichrist. Following this line of thought, Metropolitan Ioann Snychev argues that Jews could not have accepted Jesus as their Messiah. As he insists in his book, *Overcoming the Time of Troubles: A Word to the Russian Nation* (1995), since Jews wished for their Messiah to be a ruthless, charismatic, and powerful political and military leader, it was impossible for them to accept Jesus, who preached love and peace. According to Snychev, a peaceful Messiah such as Christ could never enable Jews to achieve their main goal of becoming masters of the world. Moreover, in his writings, Snychev not only expresses an antisemitic opinion that Jews cannot be trusted, because their primary aim is to gain the dominant position over other nations, but also argues that Orthodox Russians are the only nation capable of opposing the Jews.

Pitting the Russians and Jews against each other as the most critical conflict in the final drama of the Endtime is not a particularly new strategy in Russian discourses. On the contrary, it originates from the writings of Seraphim of Sarov (1754-1833), a Russian saint, known for his passion for eschatology. As he saw it, Jews and Slavs are the nations of God's Providence, and, thus, only they have a particular role to play during the Last Days. Because Jews did not recognise Jesus as the Messiah, since the fall of Constantinople, the Russians are the only nation preserving the true Christian faith (Orthodoxy), and became God's favourite people. With the Endtime approaching, Seraphim of Sarov argues, Russians will seek leadership in the Orthodox Tsar, who will lead the united Slavs to defeat all forces hostile to Christianity. In his writings, St. Seraphim often referred the prophecies from the Book of Ezekiel and the Book of Revelation, and insisted that Russia would be the land of Magog, the so-called Supreme Prince ruling the peoples of Rosa, Mosha, and Tubal, where Rosa and Mosha were associated with Russia and Moscow.

The conviction that Russia will play a crucial role in the drama of the Apocalypse is relatively widespread in post-Soviet Russian discourses. Discussed authors, whose writings are deeply immersed in Russian messianism, tend to portray Russia either as the Katechon, and the only force capable of restraining the Antichrist (see 6.1.), or, along with the writings of Seraphim of Sarov and Konstantin Leontiev, as the place where the Antichrist will be born in a Jewish community. Although in the majority of conservative and religious writings, Russia is claimed to be the place of his origin, various prophetic visions point to other potential birthplaces of the Antichrist. For instance, a Russian woman named Pelageya Ryazanskaya, who died in 1966 and whose prophecies gained popularity after the collapse of the Soviet Union, prophesied that the Antichrist would be born in the United States. Even though Pelageya was criticised for the "occult distortion of Orthodox dogmas" by the representatives of the Russian Orthodox Church, including Patriarch Aleksey and Andrey Kuraev, and there was a suspicion that her writings were indeed a forgery procured in 1993 by her grandson, her prophecies, as well as the belief that the Antichrist will come from the West, remain relatively popular among "ordinary Orthodox Russians".

The origin of the Antichrist is not the only question that bothers conservative and religious authors. Another troubling issue is when the Antichrist will come to the world. Although the Scriptures do not explicitly say when the "last days" can be expected, over the years, many religious thinkers, including discussed post-Soviet Russian authors, had tried to forecast the exact time when the Antichrist was or will be born. Whereas some authors focus on solving the riddle of the precise date of the Antichrist's birth, the others approach this question more freely, situating the Antichrist's arrival in the indefinite future.

Interestingly, in their speculations, these authors do not necessarily refer exclusively to the Orthodox tradition. For example, Vladimir Osipov (2012), the head of the extreme-right nationalist Union of the Russian People party, who defines himself as a "Russophile" and calls for establishing a constitutional monarchy in

Russia, looks at the Jewish mystical tradition. As he insists, the Antichrist will be born on the ninth day of the Hebrew month of Av, Tisha b'Av. It is traditionally a day of fasting to commemorate the destruction of both Solomon's Temple by the Neo-Babylonian Empire and the Second Temple by the Roman Empire in Jerusalem, which falls in July or August. As he puts it, the birth of the Antichrist will be followed by the Jews recognising him as the true Messiah and building the Third Temple in Jerusalem. Osipov's interpretation not only alludes to antisemitic prejudices present in post-Soviet Russian discourses, but also evokes early Christian prophesies that the construction of the Third Temple, on the Temple Mount in the Old City, a holy site for both Jews and Muslims, will herald the Messianic Age, and, in his view, initiate the Antichrist's reign.

It is important to note that post-Soviet Russian discourses analysed in this study are not limited to abstract speculations who the Antichrist will be, nor where and when he will be born. On the contrary, discussed authors very often explicitly indicate which politicians should be recognised as the Antichrist and why. Their accusations not only stem from traditional Christian exegesis of the Scriptures, but are also deeply rooted in Russian historiosophy, which sees the Antichrist in strong historical political leaders, such as Lenin or Napoleon. Following this tradition, contemporary Russian and Western politicians are frequently considered the incarnation of the Antichrist, whose political career heralds the imminent Apocalypse. Such discourses can be most often found on the Runet, however, there exist also numerous articles and books in which today's politics is intertwined with religious eschatological narratives.

The Western politician most often portrayed as an embodiment of the Antichrist is Barack Obama. Being an Afro-American democrat with fairly liberal views, who supports same-sex marriages and female reproductive rights, Obama is like the worst nightmare of a right-wing and religious extremist in the United States, and beyond. Therefore, no one should be surprised that he is one of the most common candidates for being the Apocalyptic Beast. This is underlined in a survey conducted by the Public Policy Polling in 2013: one in eight Americans (13%) believed that Obama might be the Antichrist (Harris 2013). This conviction is shared by numerous post-Soviet Russian authors, specifically the ones active on various forums and websites on the Runet. What they see as Obama's fiendish character include the left-handedness, alleged Jewish or Muslim origin, participation in the Masonic lodges, as well as being born before his parents married (even though it is not necessarily true). In 2009, when Obama received the Nobel Peace Prize, the award simply hardened these views, which, for these people, was ample evidence of who he truly is. As it is argued on the website Okkultnye Novosti, the proof is that Antichrist will come to the world as a "man of peace", and only later reveal his true nature as the ruthless tyrant.

On the other hand, some of the Russian religious and conservative authors suggest that portraying Obama as the Antichrist is an exaggeration. According to the Archpriest Andrey Tkachev, who is at the same time a writer and a television personality, Obama is not charismatic enough to be the actual Antichrist. Rather, being "too small" for this status, he is only a forerunner of the Apocalyptic Beast (Tkachev 2013). Echoing such a sentiment, an Orthodox blogger under the nickname Akurochkin argues that there is a secret plan in which Obama is supposed to adapt the world for the arrival of the real Antichrist. In other words, he is not the Beast, but a demon and an architect of the New World Order (*A False Antichrist Barack Obama* 2012). This interpretation alludes to the passages from the Book of Revelation, indicating that when the Endtime begins, there will be the two beasts. The beast from the sea will precede the beast from the earth, and the latter will be the Antichrist. In this context, Obama is believed to be the beast from the sea, rather than the ultimate adversary of Christ.

Another popular Western candidate for the Antichrist is Prince William, the grandson of Queen Elisabeth. Since it is believed that the adversary of Christ will be charming, handsome, and skilful, this choice seems to be relatively apparent. A 2004 photograph put out by the Associated Press, an international news cooperative, showed a photo of a smiling Prince William in a slaughterhouse with a lamb in his arms. Even though for an average observer, it looks innocent enough, seekers of a hidden agenda disclose it as an apocalyptic symbol. They insist that William is posing as Christ, because he was chosen by the suspected backstage plotters to overtake the world. What is more, as many argue, since he holds a lamb's back hoof, it is clear that he sends a message to the Illuminati and hails them. For the preachers pushing such beliefs, this is the proof that Prince William has accepted his role as the World's Dictator and the Antichrist, and will be crowned when he turns thirty-three (*Is Prince William the Antichrist?* 2010). Ironically, Prince William is now thirty-eight and has yet to be crowned, even as the King of England.

Yet another individual who is often portrayed as the Antichrist is the Pope. Although this discursive strategy applies more to the dignity itself, rather than to a specific person, there exist numerous conspiracy theories, according to which Pope Francis is the Beast as he comes from the Jesuit order, considered a heretic sect. A Russian author with a particularly fierce hatred of the Pope and Western Christianity is Olga Chetverikova, MGIMO professor, whose lectures can easily be found on YouTube. As she is quick to argue, the Pope is a political leader, rather than a religious one, and uses his privileged position to influence both global politics and religious consciousness of people worldwide. In her view, the Catholic Church, under the Pope's leadership, disseminates a seemingly Christian content, which is riddled with what she calls "anti-Christian rhetoric". Chetverikova insists that the main goal behind it is to implement the Masonic formula of "introducing order through chaos" and make it easier for the Antichrist to seize power over the world. For her, ecumenism is particularly dangerous as it leads to blurring the boundaries between religions, and, consequently, enables the establishment of the Kingdom of the Antichrist (Chetverikova 2015, 2016, 2017). In her writings and speeches, Chetverikova alludes to the whole range of conspiratorial motives and presents the contemporary political reality as a result of machinations of secret societies such as the Masonry and Illuminati.

Chetverikova's ideas resonate among authors such as Mikhail Nazarov and Oleg Platonov, whose theories about the all-encompassing plot are explored in this study. For instance, Nazarov (1999) argues that reforms introduced during the Second Vatican Council, including the efforts toward ecumenical dialogue between all religions, led to the gradual devastation of Western Christianity, and turned it into a godless, anti-Christian religion. According to Platonov (1998), in turn, the Pope does not de-Christianise the Catholic Church to enable the Antichrist to seize power over humanity as much as he is the Antichrist himself. In other words, as Platonov argues, the Pope, who deceitfully presents himself as the "vicar of Christ", seeks to displace and replace Jesus Christ, and become the only head of Christianity. Thus, he resembles the ruthless Grand Inquisitor in Dostoyevsky's *The Brothers Karamazov* (see 2.1.).

Portraying the Pope as a figure resembling the Grand Inquisitor, and, hence, the Antichrist, is above all a result of anti-Catholic resentments widespread in Russian discourses. Such views are mainly present in the writings by conservative and religious authors. They tend to be motivated by unfavourable references to Catholicism expressed in the 19th century by numerous Slavophiles, as well as writers and thinkers such as Fyodor Dostoyevsky and Vasily Rozanov. In such discourses, the opinion prevails that the East-West Schism between Catholicism and Orthodoxy in the 11th century was, in fact, the beginning of apostasy and gradual atheisation in the West. The further corruption of the Catholic Church followed with the Union of Brest at the end of the 16th century, the Reformation, and culminating with the Second Vatican Council. The Papacy is viewed as a relic of the past, which perpetuates an erroneous belief that someone other than Christ may be the head of the Church. The Pope, according to such critics, also serves as a symbol of the moral demise of Western Christianity.

Seeing the Antichrist in the Pope has many sources and is not limited to Russian discourses. It also characterises the American New Christian Right, which has its roots in Protestantism. According to the representatives of the American New Christian Right, Catholicism is a heresy, which, having turned away from the actual teaching of Christ, fell into the realm of the Antichrist. The Pope is for them a false Messiah greedy for political power. In general, such discursive strategies date back to the 12th century, and biblical interpretations provided by Joachim di Fiore (ca. 1135-1202), who argued that the Antichrist will come to the world as a false pope, and will, indeed, be a heretic that will deceive both Christians and Jews. Interestingly, Martin Luther associated the papacy with the Antichrist, when, in the turbulent times of the Reformation, he insisted that the Pope was the embodiment of the devil, identical with the Antichrist.

Even though the Antichrist is mostly associated with the corruption and misappropriation of Christianity, this apocalyptic figure often appears in speculations tied to political doctrines. For many post-Soviet writers, the most anti-Christian state was, undoubtedly, the Soviet Union, where the Marxist-Leninist ideology replaced religion. Ironically, for many of these observers, it is the Antichrist who is also responsible for the collapse of the Soviet Union that triggered democratic reforms and enabled religion to flourish. This outburst of eschatological expectations erupted from rapid social, political, and economic changes. Consequently, Lenin and Trotsky, ardent opponents of Orthodoxy, along with Gorbachev and Yeltsin, linked to the restless 1990s, were all seen as the Forerunners of the Apocalypse.

Among contemporary Russian politicians deemed the Antichrist, Mikhail Gorbachev is the undisputed number one. Numerous authors believe that Glasnost and Perestroika were the results of devilish machinations, and Gorbachev is the main adversary of Christ. As is an aversion towards the papacy, these views are also shared by American conservative and religious milieus. Among many American books alleging that Gorbachev is the Antichrist, it is worth mentioning *Gorbachev! Has the Real Antichrist Come?* (1988), written by Robert Faid, a self-described "nuclear engineer", and *Mikhail Gorbachev is Gog and Magog: The Biblical Antichrist* (2010) by Randolph Wright, since they significantly inspired numerous post-Soviet Russian authors. Both books, written in a prophetic manner, are an attempt to prove that not only is Gorbachev the son of Satan, who aims to destroy the world, but also that dismantling the USSR was the first step on the path to the Apocalypse and Parousia. According to Faid and Wright, the truthfulness of these claims is confirmed by the birthmark on Gorbachev's forehead, which is apparently the mark of the Beast announced in the Book of Revelation. As noted, in the Post-Soviet Russian context, there exist numerous theories probing the connection between Gorbachev and the Antichrist. An interesting example is an article, "M.S. Gorbachev's Gematria and Christology" (2014) by Sergey Aleksandrovich Nekrasov, an associate professor at the Platov South-Russian State Polytechnic University and a member of the Russian Academy of Natural History. In his article, Nekrasov applies gematria and attempts to prove that English sentences such as "Michael Gorbachev is the Devil", "M Gorbachev the devil spawn", and "M S Gorbachev Number Six Six Six" adds up to 666, which is the number of the Beast foretold in the Book of Revelation. Also, Nekrasov insists that Nero was accused of being the Antichrist only due to a mistake in calculations. In his view, not only was the dissolution of the USSR a result of cosmic interconnections, but also Gorbachev *is* the Antichrist, who plunged Russia, the last genuinely Christian state, into chaos and destruction.

Boris Oleynik, the Ukrainian poet and publicist, agrees. Unlike Nekrasov and the American authors, however, he does not believe that the first (and only) president of the USSR is the Antichrist. For Oleynik, Gorbachev is much lower in the eschatological hierarchy – he is a mere servant and emissary of the ultimate enemy of Christ. In his book, *The Prince of Darkness* (2003), Oleynik suggests that events such as the Chernobyl disaster, the sinking of the ship Nakhimov, as well as political and military crises in all the post-Soviet states – from Nagorno-Karabakh to Vilnius – were the results of the "mystery of lawlessness". Another factor that Oleynik's said confirms a close relationship between Gorbachev and the Antichrist is that he worked closely with the Western leaders, including George Bush, with whom he was meeting secretly in strange circumstances.

Gorbachev is not the only Russian politician whose affinity with the West has been used to prove an anti-Christian character of his actions. According to numerous post-Soviet Russian authors, Yeltsin is also seen as an emissary of devilish powers because, as they argue, he is responsible for the chaos that emerged from the democratic reforms of the 1990s. For instance, Vladimir Osipov (2012: 233) points out that, from 1961 to 1990, Yeltsin was a member of the Communist Party, and, thus, his character is smeared with anti-Christian elements. As Osipov argues, Yeltsin's participation in religious celebrations is a malicious mockery of the Orthodox faith. Gennady Zyuganov also called Yeltsin the embodiment of the Antichrist. After losing in the presidential election in 1996, Zyuganov argued that Yeltsin is the Antichrist foretold by St. John in the Scriptures. The fact that Yeltsin was missing a finger on one of his hands was proof enough, he insisted (Ryan 1999: 316-320). In the end, as with other statements Zyuganov made, it was pure populist folly. Zyuganov also demonstrated a lack of knowledge of the Book of Revelation as the seal of the Antichrist was supposed to appear on the forehead, and the right hand (Rev 13: 16-17), and Yeltsin had a finger missing on his left hand.

Whereas some factions of the Old Believers insisted that being the Antichrist could have been inherited within the Romanov dynasty, several authors are convinced that subsequent presidents of the Russian Federation can embody the Antichrist. Vladimir Putin is in this regard no exception. Even though in the religious and conservative circles he is generally portrayed as the man of the moment and the Saviour, in recent years there have appeared voices critical of Putin, and situating his presidency in the context of the imminent Apocalypse. According to them, not only did Putin contribute to economic and political crises that have lately affected Russia, but also he is the reason for an increasing number of murders, suicides, and divorces in their society. Moreover, in such discourses, Putin is portrayed as a charismatic and influential political leader, who "owns the keys to life and death", meaning that he controls Russian nuclear weapons. Putin, often portrayed as an individual striving for absolute power, is also deemed responsible for the moral decline of contemporary Russia; therefore, he is believed in some circles to be a servant of devilish forces or even being the Antichrist (Larkin 2018).

There is a revealing letter written by Aleksey Potupin, a follower of the website Apocalypse.Orthodoxy.ru, to Andrey Mazurkevich, an administrator of the website. Potupin writes:

> And we know the Antichrist will masquerade as a true Orthodox individual, and Vladimir Putin is actually doing this. He presents himself as the real Man, the Saviour of the Universe. As the Messiah. Therefore, I say loudly, my dear Orthodox People, he had sneaked really close. On the Russian throne, on the throne of God himself, the Antichrist wished to rule – Vladimir Putin (Potupin and Mazurkevich 2001).

Potupin, leaning on traditional interpretations of the Scriptures, describes Putin as the sneaky Antichrist, who presents himself as the Messiah. For him, the fact that Putin was elected the president of the Russian Federation is a fulfilment of prophecies in the Book of Revelation, and the beginning of the Endtime. Interestingly, in his response, Mazurkevich argues that it is Gorbachev, who is the Antichrist, not Putin. To support this argument, he not only quotes the apocalyptic early-Christian writings, but also refers to Oleynik's book.

It is important to note that Potupin is not alone in his claims that Putin is the Antichrist. Such discourses can be found all over the Runet. Most often, they are published by Putin's adversaries, for instance, pro-Ukrainian activists, and extremely religious circles, the so-called Orthodox fundamentalists, who are strongly intertwined with the national-patriotic movement (Kostiuk 2000, Verkhovsky 2002). Although marginal, these discourses demonstrate that, depending on the political situation and needs of particular social groups, the political leaders are portrayed as either divine or devilish.

One of the most conspicuous examples of the latter is a short video, *The Devil*, which portrays Putin as the Antichrist. Circulating on the Internet, and changing its titles and domains over the last few years, the video was most likely first put out just before the parliamentary elections in 2007. It was on Mariya Gaydar's YouTube channel – the daughter of a former Russian prime minister, and a Putin opponent. To prove anti-Christian elements in Putin's character, the video producers not only attempt to disclose the demonic aspects of his presidency, but they also interpret his regime in the light of the Book of Revelation and Orthodox prophecies about the Endtime. Putin's takeover of the Federal Security Service of the Russian Federation in 1998, which was a threefold quotient of 666, and the official beginning of his presidency on December 31, 1999, when "the whole world awaited the arrival of the Antichrist", are read as the signs of the Apocalypse. As well, the video argues that the diminutive form of Putin's name, Volodya, is an anagram of the word *dyavol*, which means "the devil".

Post-Soviet Russian discourses that portray a political leader as the Antichrist not only refer to a traditional exegesis of the Scriptures, but also invoke a broad semantic field of the Russian Antichrist ideomyth. Describing a political leader as Christ or the Antichrist alludes to a centuries-old Russian tradition of sacralisation of power. As Uspensky and Zhivov suggest, this discursive strategy has its roots in the medieval Byzantine culture, in which it was believed that God sanctifies the power of Tsars and Kings. Consequently, the Tsar is regarded not only as the head of the state and the guardian of the Church, but also the God's anointed representative and the icon of Christ on Earth. However, if the Tsar turns out to be a usurper, he loses the "God's charisma" and the legitimacy of that power. The person becomes the anti-Tsar, to whom all negative values are attributed (Uspensky and Zhivov 2012).

Portraying a political leader as the Saviour and Messiah implies that he may also show his "dark side", and turn out to be a false Messiah, the Antichrist. According to Cezary Wodziński (2005), a Polish philosopher and expert on Russian culture, such a semantic rotation depends mainly on ideological, political, and religious needs of specific groups. As Wodziński suggests, the good Tsar equated with Christ turns out to be his antithesis, the Antichrist, during a crisis, which is often perceived as an end of a certain epoch. As rapid changes may lead to a deteriorating quality of life, and, in consequence, society may perceive the leader, who was previously providing goods and protection, as the source of erupting violence and chaos. For example, Wodziński notes the Time of Troubles and the *Raskol*, when all familiar values turned to dust and the reality as people knew it was unrecognisable. A similar process took place in Russia in the turbulent 1990s, when many people no longer understood the world around them and turned to eschatological narratives to impose some realm of meaning on the new reality that engulfed them. The discursive strategy of interpreting political phenomena in the context of the Apocalypse is, in many regards, an attempt to make sense of historical events and to capture increasingly complex political and social processes. This strategy shares similarities with the political theology put forth by Carl Schmitt, in which religious concepts are secularised and serve to describe secular phenomena. According to Schmitt (1963: 27), the essence of politics is grounded in the friend/enemy division, in which the political enemy is recognised as "existentially something different and alien". More importantly, in Schmitt's view, the enemy is "not merely any competitor or just any partner of conflict in general", but the public adversary antagonistic towards a given community.

In the subsequent years, the friend/enemy division Schmitt put forth inspired Ernesto Laclau and Chantal Mouffe, post-Marxist political theorists, who developed the concept of "political antagonism". As they argue in the book *Hegemony and Socialist Strategy: Towards a Radical Democratic Politics* (1985), the discord between morally superior "us" and the immoral "them" is a reaction to discursively constructed, yet often imagined, dangers and threats. Subsequently, the Antichrist not only symbolises the political Other, but also, being the epitome of apocalyptic fears, becomes an important reference point for a collective identity.

According to Erin Runions (2009), a religious studies scholar, political theology based on interpreting the Bible as being political rather than religious is an example of "masculinist political decisionism". However, even though she suggests the Antichrist figure "ironically disrupts the masculinist authority of decisions made in the name of Christ" and creates a possibility of an encounter with the political Other, post-Soviet Russian discourses prove just the opposite. In them, the Antichrist figure serves as the radicalised metaphor of evil and is employed to perpetuate political divisions and strengthen hostility towards the Other. This discursive strategy emphasises the demonic character of an adversary and justifies missionary efforts and extremism of various groups that refer to this ideomyth. It is based on the conviction that since our enemy is the Antichrist, any radicalism is legitimised. After all, as indicated in these works, no holds should be barred in the fight with the ultimate archenemy, who strives to destroy the beloved homeland, Orthodox Russia. Here, politics is perceived as a constant struggle between "us" and hostile "them", and a political conflict acquires the cosmic and ultimate meaning. Thus, political, social, and economic events are situated on two levels: phenomenological and metaphysical ones. They are believed to occur simultaneously in the world as we know it, and in some hidden reality that only the chosen ones can see (Shnirelman 2017).

IV.2. Sacral Geography and the Kingdom of the Antichrist

The practice of portraying a political enemy as the Antichrist in post-Soviet Russian discourses is closely linked to the belief that before seizing power over the world, he will seduce people with false values of democracy, liberalism, and human rights. Enjoying the support from people, the Antichrist will establish a nihilist kingdom, where everything is ambiguous and relative. As Russian religious and conservative authors envision it, the Kingdom of the Antichrist will be a political space – a state or a union of states – where Christian values will be abandoned, and forces of evil will prevail. Notably, many post-Soviet authors, including Dugin, Chetverikova, and Nazarov, argue that numerous signs are indicating that the Antichrist has already begun building his kingdom. As part of the evidence, they name social and political phenomena such as American hegemony, the growing dominance of democratic and liberal values, accelerating globalisation and technological progress, increasing drug and alcohol addiction, as well as an ever-increasing ecological catastrophe, caused by the rapid development of capitalism.

In his article "Autocracy of the Spirit" (1997), Metropolitan Ioann Snychev insists that nowadays we are witnessing the time of "decay of vivid and solid Christian worldview". As he argues, people abandoned Christ and succumbed to the charm of Paradise on Earth. According to Snychev, however, Paradise on Earth is, indeed, only a mirage, and, once built, it will turn out to be the Kingdom of the Antichrist, based on a postmodern confusion of good and evil. Orthodox Russia is for Snychev the last bastion of Christianity, and the only way of defeating the Antichrist is the revival of the Holy Rus', meaning the restitution of the symphony of secular and divine powers. Only then, as he believes, will Russia become the Katechon – the only force capable of restraining the arrival and final victory of the Antichrist (see 6.2.).

Similar views are shared by Kirill, the Patriarch of Moscow and all Rus'. Before becoming the Patriarch, he was considered a modernist and reformer. Still, after gaining his current position, he turned out to be an ardent opponent of reforms within the Russian Orthodox Church, as well as all manifestations of moral liberalism, including abortion, euthanasia, same-sex relationships, and even civil marriages. In addition, he openly advocates for the annexation of Crimea and supports separatists in Donbas. As with Snychev, who represented a rather radical wing of the ROC, the Patriarch Kirill argues that we are now witnessing the beginning of the era of the Antichrist. As he sees it, with today's distinctions between what is Christian and what is anti-Christian more of a blur, the likelihood that the Kingdom of the Antichrist will soon be established is increasing. In the Patriarch's view, the postmodern civilisation – in which good and evil, truth and falsehood, sainthood and sin are becoming more and more confusing – is close to being ultimately destroyed on its own wish (Strelchik and Kirill 2009, Patriarch Kirill 2010).

As indicated, both Metropolitan Ioann and Patriarch Kirill are not alone in their condemnation of postmodernism. Reflecting a lot of this, many authors see postmodernism as one of the manifestations of "mystery of lawlessness" resulting in this elaborate conspiracy against Orthodox Russia (see 3.1.). A slightly different perspective on postmodernism is offered by Dugin, who identifies the present day as an epoch of Postmoderna. As he argues in *The Fourth Political Theory* (2009), Postmoderna is the last significant historical era preceding the Apocalypse. For

Dugin, the contemporary world, marked by globalisation, liberalism, and the emergence of post-industrial societies, "can be easily recognised as the era of the Antichrist: the Endtime". The Fourth Political Theory Dugin put forth stems from a conviction that there is a need to set an ideology superseding liberal democracy, Marxism, and fascism that dominated the twentieth century. According to Dugin (2009a, 2011), it can be done only by "deciphering the paradigm of postmodernism" that led to the spread of liberalism and enabled the West's overwhelming domination over the world. Dugin perceives postmodernism as a process of establishing the global Kingdom of the Antichrist, where deceptive values promoted by the West, such as permissiveness, tolerance, and secularisation, will prevail. In many regards, this Fourth Political Theory is a continuation of Carl Schmitt's political theology, in which the political reality is described in religious terms.

Even though many of Dugin's works do not hesitate to refer to conspiracy theories (see 3.1. and 3.2.), his Fourth Political Theory aspires to be a profound, even scientific, geopolitical concept. He sees it as a significant alternative to the Western imperialism that dominated the geopolitics after the dissolution of the Soviet Union. Interestingly, many scholars dealing with post-Soviet Russia, including Andreas Umland (2007), insist that the Fourth Political Theory is an ideological foundation of Putin's rhetoric and an expression of the actual political aspirations of the Russian Federation. Despite some similarities, there are, however, numerous differences between Putin's real political actions and Dugin's relatively radical concept. Overall, Dugin calls for a break with the USSR's past and creating a new quality in global geopolitics. As the thinking goes, Russia is supposed to become a powerful anti-Western Orthodox empire destined to protect the world from the anti-Christian West, specifically the United States (Doroszczyk 2016).

Both the Fourth Political Theory and Dugin's conviction that a complex eschatological conflict exists between Russia and the West are rooted in his earlier geopolitical notion of neo-Eurasianism.[25] He elaborated on it in his 2000 book, *The*

---

[25] Much has been written about neo-Eurasianism and its impact on post-Soviet Russian discourses, see for example: Laruelle M. (2012). *Russian Eurasianism: Ideology of Empire*. London: Johns Hopkins University Press; Laruelle M. (2017). *Eurasianism and the European Far Right: Reshaping the Europe-Russia Relationship*. Lahnam: Lexington Books; Umland A. (2009). *The Nature of Russian "neo-Eurasianism": Approaches to Aleksandr*

Foundations of Geopolitics, which is used as a textbook in officer schools in the Russian Federation. According to Dugin, geopolitics is based on an inevitable confrontation between the two types of civilisations: traditional and collectivist tellurocracies that are land powers, and thalassocracies – liberal and individualistic maritime powers. Whereas the first type is represented by Eurasia headed by Orthodox Russia, the latter is embodied by the United States and its allies. As Dugin suggests, the US perceives Orthodox Russia as a leader of the Eurasian zone being a major obstacle on its way to "planetary globalism". In his view, the West is mainly concerned with the emergence of the "continent of Eurasia" due to Russia's growing political, military, and, above all, spiritual potential.

Since the end of the Cold War, Dugin argues, the primary goal of the West, under the command of the United States, is to seize world power and lead everyone towards the Apocalypse. In his book, *Mysteries of Eurasia* (1991), Dugin describes the anti-Christian political strategy of the West:

> Powers, groups, ideologies and state formations, which are collectively called "the West" and which, after the victory in the "Cold War", are the sole masters of the world. Behind the façade of "liberalism", they exercise a coherent eschatological theological doctrine in which the events of secular history, technological progress, international relations, social processes, etc., are interpreted from an apocalyptic perspective. The Western Antichrist tries to convince the world that, in fact, his planetary and spiritual enemy – the continent Russia and its secret pole, us – is the "Antichrist" (Dugin 1991).

As Dugin insists, the West not only tempts people with false values of wealth, freedom, and liberalism, but also attempts to convince the world that Russia is the Antichrist. In Dugin's view, such a way of portraying Russia is nothing new, and it did not come to existence only after the Cold War. For example, he notes, US President Ronald Reagan called the Soviet Union the "Evil Empire" in 1973. As Dugin sees it, Reagan did it in order to divert the world's attention from what he

---

Dugin's post-Soviet Movement of Radical Anti-Americanism. New York: Sharpe; Shlapentokh D. (2007). *Russia Between East and West: Scholarly Debates on Eurasianism*. Leiden: Brill; Bassin M. (2016). *The Gumilev Mystique: Biopolitics, Eurasianism, and the Construction of Community in Modern Russia*. Ithaka: Cornell University Press; Suslov M. and Bassin M. (2016). *Eurasia 2.0: Russian Geopolitics in the Age of New Media*. Lahnam: Lexington Books.

deems the devilish aspirations of the United States and to reduce Russia's credibility on the international stage. Even though Western countries have stuck to this discursive strategy, Dugin believes the 21st century is witnessing a significant weakening of the West, meaning there appears a chance Russia can challenge the political balance of power imposed by the US and create a new multipolar international order (Curanović 2012).

Dugin's political concept is based on a specific "sacral geography" deriving from a belief that modern geopolitics is deeply rooted in religion. According to political scientist Marlène Laruelle (2012), a premise that religion is the foundation of civilisations and the main force of historical development is an example of "cultural fundamentalism". As such, Russia's distinctiveness from the West is viewed as resulting from a clash between cultural and religious "essences of peoples", rather than social and economic struggles. In his political theory, Dugin not only divides the realm of politics into two essentially different opposing camps of the Homeland and the Atlantic powers, but also situates this conflict in two parallel dimensions: the dimension of contemporary politics and the "hidden convert mystical dimension", in which the Russian Federation is portrayed as the embodiment of the Holy Rus' (de Lazari 1996).

This double duality evokes the notion of two Cities put forth by St. Augustine in the early 5th century. In the treaty *On the City of God Against the Pagans*, he insisted that there exist "the City of God" (*civitas Dei*) and "the Earthly City" (*civitas terrena*). Whereas the first is the metaphorical Jerusalem and the quintessence of God's mercy, "the Earthly City" is tantamount to Babylon and symbolises human arrogance and contempt for divine creation. Hence, based on a false faith and attachment to earthly material goods, it is the Kingdom of the Antichrist and a treacherous utopia, where good is only apparent. Interestingly, St. Augustine's idea in many ways coincides with political theology developed by the Old Believers, who believed that, as a result of evil powers at work, the so-called Promised Land of peace, equality, and freedom, has turned into the Kingdom of the Antichrist where all values were distorted (see 2.2.).

Dugin's neo-Eurasianism not only is a continuation of the concept of Eurasia popular among the "white emigration" in the years after the Bolshevik Revolution, but it is also an expression of anti-globalism, anti-Westernism, and imperial sentiments present in post-Soviet Russian discourses. It is also deeply immersed in Russian messianism, one of the dominant features of which is emphasising the uniqueness of the historical development of Russia. Since the 19th century, there has been a heated debate over the direction Russia should take being pushed by Slavophiles and Westernisers. Over time, a "third way" emerged, based on the assumption that Russia is a unique space between East and West. The supporters of this concept argue that Russia, being positioned "between the (Roman) Western and the (Byzantine) Eastern civilisations, should choose its own, different and exclusive middle way" (Storchak 2003: 30, Bouveng 2010). For Russia, such a middle-road approach may be the best route to unify all of Eurasia and lead it against the Western Antichrist, Dugin (1997: 197) insists.

After the collapse of the USSR, Dugin's notions of neo-Eurasianism have been promoted by many circles as the new Russian idea (Trenin 2002). However, some conservative authors criticise it harshly. According to Metropolitan Ioann (1994), by focusing on geography and ethnology rather than spirituality and religion, one can end up overlooking the most important aspect of Russia's mission in the world. This view is shared by both Dushenov (2015) and Platonov (2010a). As they argue, focusing on the political conflict between the West and Eurasia draws attention away from what is really important in the Endtime. In their view, Orthodox Russians should focus on resurrecting the Holy Rus', which will serve as the Katechon, and enable the ultimate defeat of the Antichrist. Nevertheless, they concede that the popularity of neo-Eurasianism is much easier to comprehend than complex theological pursuits.

Despite this criticism, what unites Dugin's neo-Eurasianism and the writings of these authors is anti-Westernism. Many Russian authors insist that since Russia represents a system of values other than that pushed in the West, the conflict is inevitable. Interestingly, for the majority of these conservative and religious authors, the conflict between Russia and the West is not a mere political rivalry, but an earthly reflection of the spiritual battle between Christ and the Antichrist. Here, the tangible world becomes the scene of the eschatological struggle between forces of good and evil, represented respectively by Russia and the West. Subsequently, in many post-Soviet Russian right-wing discourses, the political antagonism between Russia and the West is described in apocalyptic terms.

As these narratives show, in the hierarchy of enemies Russia faces, the West undoubtedly occupies the top spot. Perceived through the apocalyptic lens, it is viewed as a nihilistic Kingdom of the Antichrist. For Platonov (2010a), the process of the West moving towards the Antichrist was initiated by the East-West Schism in 1054. By rejecting the true principles of the faith, that of the Orthodox, Catholicism has fallen like a "broken, rotten piece; like a damaged limb from a healthy body", he claims. Dugin follows this line of thought in his book *Logos and Myth* (2010), arguing that the detachment deprived Catholicism of the Christian vitality, and turned it into a purely political organisation, often used as a weapon in the power struggle. Furthermore, as he insists, the politicisation of Catholicism has turned the West into the postmodern kingdom of *logos*, where religion is substituted by philosophy.

Even though Western Europe, closely connected to Catholicism and Protestantism, is believed to be the traitor of true Christianity, it is the United States that many of discussed authors consider being the centre of the anti-Christian power. According to Nazarov (1999), the anti-Christian character of the US is highlighted by the way it was established. As he sees it, the multicultural nature of the country, worshipping capitalism and decorated with Masonic symbols, was built on the bloodshed of Ingenious peoples and African slave labour. Hence, in Nazarov's view, the US, with its aspirations to become the "universal Empire" is, indeed, the prototype of the Kingdom of the Antichrist. The US slogan of "defending democracy" is, for Nazarov, a mere guise for imperial ambitions and attempts to establish the anti-Christian hegemony in the world. Nazarov perceives US talk of "universal democratic values as fundamentally false and argues that it is confirmed by the fact the US did not hesitate to use the nuclear bomb on civilians. Moreover, as Nazarov insists, the American intentions to dominate the world are openly declared in the "National Strategy of the United States". Hence, the US is achieving its aims by promoting materialist ideology to other parts of the world with pop culture and capitalist notions.

Platonov (2010: 656) shares these views. He believes that America's cult of money, lack of what he calls a "national core", coupled with sinful pop culture promoting homosexuality and drug use are all detached from any Christian truth, and, ultimately, representing the Kingdom of the Antichrist. The arrival of the Antichrist is most certainly near, echoes Sergey Fokin (2015), an author on the portal Logoslovo.ru, arguing that economic and migration crises observed in the US and elsewhere, as well as terrorism in the Western Hemisphere, indicate the Endtime has started. However, in his views of contemporary politics, Fokin adds something new. He insists that the centre of the Apocalyptic drama will move to the United Kingdom because the US will soon go bankrupt due to the financial crisis triggered by the fast-growing debt initiated in 2008. According to Fokin, after the US bankrupts itself, international organisations, such as the United Nations and NATO, will move their centres to Western Europe, which will instantly sink into a crisis caused by terrorism and immigration.

In Fokin's view, only the UK will remain untouched, and, hence, it would become the "new Babylon of Europe", and the place where the Antichrist would arrive. Interestingly, this fits in with some views that Prince William is the Antichrist, as mentioned earlier, and was shared among Old Believers communities in Siberia, in the 1980s. Elena Ageyeva (1997), a historian that specialises in Old Believers' literature, argues that Fokin's view stems from anti-Western sentiments in the late-Soviet society and the accompanying Soviet propaganda, which led people to believe the war was inevitable with the UK. Meanwhile, anti-Western attitudes did not disappear with the dissolution of the Soviet Union. On the contrary, despite the initial fascination with everything Western in the early 1990s, Russian society quickly became disappointed with what was considered the "Western style of living". Consequently, the resentments towards the West and the United States began to grow (Duncan 2005: 277, Gudkov 1997, Ball 2003: 239).

Dmitri Trenin, a director of the Carnegie Moscow Centre, insists that since the late 1990s, Russian society became more and more convinced its post-Soviet problems were invented, or certainly encouraged, by the US. Many Russians started to believe that the US intelligence, together with their alleged allies within the Russian Federation, "plan to solve the world's geopolitical problems at the expense of Russia" (Trenin 2002: 101). This claim alludes to the idea that Russia not only is a besieged fortress surrounded by enemies, but also that there are groups within the country who seek to destroy it. As these post-Soviet discourses explored here suggest, such groups are usually the liberal intelligentsia and the progressive ruling class. Russian authors, including Dugin and Platonov, are quick to label anyone that disagrees with their views as being part of the "fifth column", and accusing such people of being conspiring with the West.

In his article, "Russia Re-Defines Itself and Its Relation with the West", published in 2007, Trenin explains the increase of anti-Western sentiments in post-Soviet Russia with the fear of globalisation seen as a phenomenon that will deprive Russia of its unique national identity. There was no coherent domestic ideology after the dissolution of the USSR, as Trenin explains it. Thus, there was a lack of resistance to questionable values flooding in from the West, and this resulted in deep fear. In a similar vein, Lilia Shevtsova (2007), a renowned Kremlinology expert, suggests that in recent times anti-Westernism has been turned into the national idea used to consolidate the post-Soviet Russian society. In her view, it is manifested, for instance, in Putin's aggressive foreign policy rhetoric and political elites who argue that there is the need to protect Russia from external enemies and establish "a new global order to replace the one that humiliated Russia in the 1990s". This view is also shared by Iver B. Neumann, a political scientist and author of *Russia and the Idea of Europe: A Study in Identity and International Relations* (1996), who argues that anti-Westernism in post-Soviet Russia serves not only to consolidate the society, but also to compensate for the lower economic output, standard of living, and military capability in contrast to the West. Facing a higher level of welfare in the Western countries, Russian conservative authors tend to contrast the materialistic approach to life in the West with the "moral superiority" of Orthodox Russia.

Many researchers specialising in post-Soviet Russia associate the growing "dislike" of Western Europe and the United States with the "conservative turn". Referred to also as a "conservative revolution", it is an ideological trend, which occurred in the Russian Federation in the early 2000s, and coincided with Putin's rise to power. The "conservative turn" in Russia not only marks the symbolic shift in the post-Soviet discourses of art, literature, and philosophy, but also is noticeable in Russian politics, both on internal and external levels. It is characterised by an extreme anti-Westernism, a strong division between "us" and "enemies", and often refers to traditions of the Russian Messianism (Akopov 2016). Among the so-called godfathers of this intellectual and political movement, there are well-known and influential Russian intellectuals and media figures, including Dugin, Shafarievich, and Filimonov, whose names repeatedly come up in this study. Many of them are members of the Izborsky Club, established in 2012, and headed by Alexander Prokhanov, a writer and the editor-in-chief of a radical newspaper *Zavtra*. A community of well-known conservative experts, the Izborsky Club is closely related to the Kremlin and acts as its "advisory board" (Engström 2014, Laruelle 2016).

Vladimir Ilyin (2016), a Russian sociologist, argues that the post-Soviet "conservative turn" was a response to the failure of the liberal-democratic reforms marking a decade after the breakup of the Soviet Union. As he insists, in the face of the social, political, and economic crisis, both political elites and public opinion turned to conservative values. This view is shared by Serguei Oushakine (2009), an anthropologist researching contemporary Russian culture, who sees the positive reception of revived conservatism and patriotic values that took place in the Russian Federation in the 2000s as an expression of "patriotism of despair". He defines it as an "emotionally charged set of symbolic practices called upon to mediate relations among individuals, nations, and states and thus to provide communities of loss with socially meaningful subject positions" (2009b: 5). Oushakine insists that the acceptance of patriotic and conservative values is a symbolic practice aimed at not only dealing with the trauma of the breakup of the Soviet Union, and what many see the savage transformation, but also resolving the sense of a break with historical continuity and disintegration of identities, both individual and collective. In his view, the fact that at that time the oil prices increased, and provided the society with relative prosperity, only strengthened the positive attitude to the revived conservatism. Although post-Soviet Russia is no exception, and we can observe the conservative backlash in other countries, including the United States, Hungary, and Poland, the Russian "conservative turn" has its unique traits. As Vladimir Ilyin argues, on the moral level it is shaped by the values promoted by the Russian Orthodox Church and patriotic education, and, on the political level, it is characterised by the glorification of the Russian imperial past and strong anti-Americanism.

Even though in post-Soviet Russian discourses the West is portrayed as the Kingdom of the Antichrist, it is not the only political formation described in such a way. According to conservative and religious authors, the Soviet Union was yet another incarnation of the anti-Christian empire. Due to its materialistic and atheistic character, the Communist regime is seen by many, specifically religious people, as the Kingdom of the Antichrist. This apocalyptic perspective is fuelled by the fact that during the first years of their rule, the Bolsheviks conducted a fierce anti-religious campaign, including the mass destruction of churches, persecutions of hierarchs of the Russian Orthodox Church, and official rhetoric of state-promoted atheism. Following the Russian thinkers and writers like Dmitry Merezhkovsky and Vasily Rozanov, who lived through the Bolshevik Revolution, and perceived the new regime as the Kingdom of the Antichrist, post-Soviet writers tend to perceive the USSR as a violent Leviathan state, hostile towards the Orthodox Church. In such a perspective, what was supposed to be the Communist utopia based on freedom, equality, and justice, turned out to be the anti-Christian dystopia, where the true Russianness, identified with Orthodoxy, was supposed to be destroyed.

Mikhail Nazarov (1999) insists that the Bolshevik Revolution was, indeed, a profoundly anti-Christian phenomenon. As he argues, by replacing the will of God with the will of people, the new regime not only removed state power from the sphere of *sacrum*, but also led to the reversal of orders: it replaced good with evil. Alluding to the Scriptures, and, especially, the Book of Revelation, Nazarov suggests that the leaders of the Revolution were not merely false prophets and servants of the Antichrist, but the embodiment of the Antichrist himself. Nazarov supports this claim with the fact that Soviet Russia was ruled by seven General Secretaries, and the apocalyptic Beast foretold by John in the Book of Revelation had seven heads. Moreover, Nazarov argues, the Soviet Antichrist gained power over the Russian nation not only thanks to blasphemy and dictatorial power, but also due to imposing the full nationalisation of property. By cancelling cash flows and introducing the socialist system of ration cards, Nazarov claims only supporters of the new anti-Christian regime could have survived. In short, Nazarov depicts the Soviet system as a seven-headed Beast imposing seals on the foreheads and right hands of people and turning them into "Homo Sovieticus".

So, how did the Holy Rus', ruled by the Romanovs in symphony with the Orthodox Church, get turned into its metaphysical pole, the Kingdom of the Antichrist? It was due to the wicked intervention of Russia's enemies, as Oleg Platonov (2010) explains. According to him, the Bolshevik coup was financed and conducted by the Judeo-Masons from outside. Platonov insists that turning Orthodox Russia into an atheistic state was the first step on their way to seize power over the world and establish the anti-Christian Paradise on Earth. This view is echoed by Metropolitan Ioann Snychev (1994), who suggests that by gradually infecting the Russian Orthodox soul with sinful Western ideas, the creators of the Revolution capitalised on people's everlasting longing for establishing the "Kingdom of universal brotherhood and justice". Consequently, Snychev insists, deceived and bewildered Russians surrendered to the anti-Christian temptation to build the Godless Paradise on Earth where international solidarity, building Communism, and the triumph of the world revolution would be preached.

However, as Snychev warns in the book *Overcoming the Time of Troubles: The Word to the Russian Nation* (1995), a decline of the Communist regime did not cease the anti-Christian danger Russia was confronting. He argues that even though the fall of the Soviet Union enabled the Russian Orthodox Church to resurrect itself after seventy years, just like Christ resurrected after the three days, it did not end the suffering of Orthodox people. Snychev believes that the "times of troubles continue" as the world is permeated with anti-Christian ideas of democracy and freedom that are leading to greater demoralisation in Russian society. Nazarov (1999) and Platonov (2010) add that the democratic experiment is not much different from the Soviet regime. According to them, since both democracy and Communism are attempting to build an "earthly paradise" inhabited by the multinational, yet unified, materialistic society, they belong to the same symbolic order: they both represent the Kingdom of the Antichrist.

Post-Soviet Russian discourses that allude to the Kingdom of the Antichrist portray the world outside of Russia not only as profane, but also extremely threatening, on both political and moral levels. From this perspective, Russia appears to be a fortress besieged by hostile forces which, in order to survive, needs to preserve its traditional Orthodox values (Yablokov 2018). According to political scientist David Campbell, the boundary-producing practices, dividing the social space into inside/outside, often result in emerging of a "conception of divergent moral spaces". Consequently, he argues, "the social space of inside/outside is both made possible by and helps constitute a moral space of superior/inferior, which can be animated in terms of any number of figurations of higher/lower" (Campbell 1991: 85).

Subsequently, good is positioned against evil, rationality against emotions, civilisation against chaos, and the sacred against the profane. By portraying the outside as sinful and immoral space, the discussed discourses emphasise the uniqueness and moral superiority of Orthodox Russia. Characterised as "good and sacred", it is often recognised as the Katechon, and the last force restraining the Antichrist's arrival. The Other, in turn, be it Catholicism, Western Europe, or the United States, is always profane and evil. Such narratives are, in fact, an example of an exceptionally conservative worldview. Moreover, by establishing firm boundaries within the community and excluding those who do not share the same values, this approach is a strategy to construct a collective identity.

As historian William McNeill points out, the exclusion of Others has always been one of the most important factors consolidating a community. He writes:

> Belonging to a tightly knit group makes life worth living by giving individuals something beyond the self to serve and to rely on for personal guidance, companionship, and aid. But the stronger such bond, the sharper the break with the rest of humanity. Group solidarity is always maintained, at least partly, by exporting psychic friction across the frontiers, projecting animosities onto an outside foe in order to enhance collective cohesion within the group itself. Indeed, something to fear, hate, and attack are probably necessary for the full expression of human emotions; and ever since animal predators ceased to threaten, human beings have feared, hatred and fought one another (McNeill 1986: 7).

In McNeill's view, establishing a group identity has always required the Other, and the more evil, terrifying, and disgusting this Other was, the better. Just as important, all these negative characteristics were projected on an outside foe to strengthen the bond within a community.

In this regard, the Other serves as a "constitutive outside", in a manner suggested by political theorist Chantal Mouffe in her book *The Return of the Political*

(1993). In it, alluding to Carl Schmitt's theories, Mouffe refers to politics as being based on the friend/enemy distinction and argues that politics comes down to the question of who belongs to a political community and is one of "us", and who does not; who is the excluded "them". Unlike Schmitt, however, Mouffe admits that this excluded Other does not necessarily have to be positioned outside of a community. Within different political systems, including democracy, Mouffe (1993:3) claims, there are external as well as internal Others. In whatever place the enemy is positioned, to serve his consolidative role, the values he represents have to be utterly foreign to those accepted by a given collective. Also, when the Other embodies all the worst features, he may be easily turned into the enemy (Schmitt 1985, Baumann and Gingrich 2004). It happens especially in the times of crises or social disasters when, as George Schöpfin (1997: 209-210) explains, communities tend to rely on "more and more heavily on myths of collective existence". As a result, the Other starts to be viewed as dangerous, and even diabolic, as in the case of post-Soviet Russian discourses identifying a political enemy with the apocalyptic image of the Antichrist.

Essential factors in the process of constructing a collective identity in opposition to the Other are time and space. According to Campbell (1992: 86), "identity is a condition that has depth, is multi-layered, possesses texture, and comprises many dimensions", and, thus, cannot "be reduced to any single spatial or temporal source". Despite this, as Campbell argues, the role of the spatial difference in constructing a collective identity cannot be diminished. This view is shared by Akhil Gupta and James Ferguson (1992:6), who suggest that the special division into "us" and "them" leads to creating frontiers, which are spaces of "contact, conflict, and contradiction between cultures and societies". Indeed, Space plays an idiosyncratic role in constructing the "imagined communities" and maintaining a clear division between the superior self/us and the devalued them/Other.

Importantly, a crucial aspect of the discursive demarcation of space is a danger. In the book, *Writing the Security. The United States Foreign Policy and the Politics of Identity* (1992), Campbell argues that portraying the "outside" as hostile and threatening is an example of "evangelism of fear", often employed to legitimise the role of the ruling political entity by claiming to keep its citizens safe from facing diverse dangers. Campbell suggests that such a strategy can be used by both the state that commits to providing security to its citizens and the Church that promises salvation to its faithful. Moreover, as Campbell insists, imposing a rigorous self/Other dichotomy in the context of geopolitics can lead to creating the imaginary "geography of good and evil", in which the boundaries between inside and outside are practically unremovable. Even though Campbell focuses on constructing identity and security in the United States, analogical mechanisms can be observed in post-Soviet Russia. An example is Dugin's notion of "sacral geography", in which the political Other is portrayed as inherently evil and fearsome.

The discord between morally superior "us" and the immoral and evil "them" is a reaction to discursively constructed, yet often imagined, dangers and threats. Therefore, since what "we" fear is immanent to what we are, the Other not only is perceived as a constant threat, but also embodies the anxieties of a given community. The excluded negativity, which represents everything we are not, organise a social antagonism based on the interplay of "logic of difference" and "logic of equivalence", as suggested by Ernesto Laclau and Chantal Mouffe (1985) in their theory of politics. As they see it, whereas "logic of equivalence" operates by dividing social space and accumulating meanings around the two antagonistic extremes, the "logic of difference" has an opposite function – it "weakens and displaces a sharp antagonistic polarity" and relegates "that division to the margins of society".

The interplay of these two logics creates antagonism and relegates the negative identity that cannot be integrated into the system of differences accepted within a given community to its frontiers (Howarth et al. 2000). As a result, what is excluded as negativity constitutes the positive identity within the system. Following this logic, the Antichrist ideomyth, employed to demarcate the "outside", is a reflection of the "inside". Thus, the Antichrist figure, as discussed in these discourses, not only serves as a limit of the Russian collective identity in relation to which all internal differences are abolished, but also is the embodiment of social fantasies, fears, and anxieties (Dolińska-Rydzek 2016).

Notably, the discussed post-Soviet writings fit into the specific geopolitics of the Apocalypse, in which current political events are portrayed not so much as the rivalry between the Russian Federation and the West, but as the earthly manifestation of the struggle between Christ and the Antichrist. The discursive strategy of interpreting political phenomena in an eschatological way is an attempt to make sense of historical events and to capture increasingly complex political and social processes. Consequently, as theologian Robert Bultmann (1975) concluded, "history is swallowed up in eschatology", and the end of the world is perceived as imminent.

In consequence, in many discourses, the contemporary world is seen as unreliable and permeated with the spirit of the Antichrist. The crises, social experiments, national catastrophes, and utopian reforms are described in apocalyptic terms. Modernisation and progress, in turn, are perceived as the continuous destruction of the world and gradual isolation from the ontological foundation of history, the sense of which may be revealed only through the Apocalypse. Following this logic, post-Soviet Russian authors depict the contemporary world as a scene of the apocalyptic drama. Phenomena such as secularisation, globalisation, and modernisation are considered to be not only the signs of the Antichrist's imminent arrival, but also the proof that, thanks to the spiritual evil, the Antichrist has already begun building his earthly Kingdom. By situating contemporary politics within the eschatological paradigm, discussed authors employ the Antichrist ideomyth as a mental shortcut that explains what is otherwise inconceivable. In their texts, the Antichrist ceases to be an abstract idea, and, indeed, becomes the "real political possibility of our times".

V. The Antichrist: New Incarnations

Throughout the centuries, the Antichrist ideomyth in Russia has undergone numerous historical and semantic transformations. Russian historiosophy has seen him not only in historical figures such as Ivan the Terrible, Peter the Great, and Lenin, but also in political and social systems, including the Russian autocracy, Bolshevik regime, and liberal democracy. Moreover, the Russian Antichrist has been portrayed as an enemy of God, the grand deceiver, and a usurper of the power of Tsar. However, the most fundamental reading of the ideomyth has been determined by the apocalyptic historiosophy of the Old Believers, put forth in the 17th century. Consequently, in many Russian discourses, an image of the Antichrist oscillates between him being described as a spiritual evil unlocked in the world or a tangible being, whose arrival will herald the approaching Apocalypse. When portrayed as a tangible being, the Antichrist is believed to be a vicious individual, who is not only the adversary of Christ, but also a false Messiah attempting to replace him. The Antichrist is viewed not so much as a supernatural Beast or the embodiment of evil forces, but as the anthropological agent of Satan.

In post-Soviet Russian fiction, the Antichrist is mostly portrayed as a sinful man empowered by Satan, who will gain power over humanity by deluding people with false miracles and silver-tongued blasphemies; and when the right time comes, he will reveal his true nature of the merciless Endtime tyrant. Portraying the Antichrist as a reflection of Christ and his evil twin alludes to the ambiguity embedded in the very word "antichrist": the prefix ἀντί means both "against" and "in opposition to" and "instead of". Much of this is illustrated in the iconographic tradition, with Ilya Glazunov's painting *Christ and Antichrist* (1999) being one of the best examples.

However, portraying the Antichrist as an evil twin of Christ is not the only way of how this apocalyptic figure is depicted in the post-Soviet Russian fiction. Some works often go far beyond this interpretative framework and offer a much more complicated and nuanced portrait of this apocalyptic figure. The analysed writings not only use an entire repertoire of postmodern stylistic devices, including intertextuality, fragmentation, and metafiction, but also situate the Antichrist figure in various, sometimes surprising, contexts. Indeed, in the post-Soviet Russian fiction, the Antichrist is portrayed in many different ways: as an individual, who cannot decide whether he wants to be good or evil; a young erotomaniac who believes that he has a special mission in the world; a serial killer who kills in the name of a "higher idea"; and, finally, a trickster who turns the world as we know it upside down. Moreover, the Antichrist figure appears in the novels and short stories of all genres: crime and detective stories, thrillers, science fiction and fantasy novels, as well as a variety of postmodern works.

In this chapter, I discuss how the post-Soviet Russian fiction continues to deconstruct and reinterpret the Antichrist ideomyth. Referring to selected examples, I focus on the most unusual and exploratory ways of portraying the Antichrist, both in popular fiction distributed through official channels and ultimately niche self-published fanfiction circulated mostly on the internet. Among the authors analysed, there are relatively well-known and often quite controversial writers, including Alexander Prokhanov and Pavel Krusanov; authors assigned to specific genres, such as a science fiction writer Alexander Kashanskiy; as well as less established writers such as Dmitriy Lugovoy and Alexander Tumanov. Even though their works differ in authors' literary status, popularity, and audience (both intended and real), what connects them is employing the Antichrist ideomyth and offering new approaches to this apocalyptic figure.

The main criteria used when choosing the works for analysis is that they are written in Russian and published after 1991. Also, they should employ apocalyptic motifs with the Antichrist figure among them, either as the protagonist or one of the characters. However, in the two novels included in the study, there are no characters explicitly named "the Antichrist": Alexander Prokhanov's *Mr Hexogen* (2002) and Pavel Krusanov's *The American Hole* (2005). Although the exact term "antichrist" is not used in them, in both novels there appear characters modelled on this apocalyptic figure. Overall, as I will demonstrate, the chosen Russian novels and short stories offer a wide range of new incarnations of the Antichrist ideomyth in various post-Soviet Russian contexts.

V.1. I, the Antichrist or the Antichrist in Me

> *I was born at night*
> *The hour of the wolf's prayer*
> *(...)*
> *My name is the Antichrist.*
> Aria, "Antichrist" (1999).

The epigraph above is a fragment of the song "Antichrist" written by the lyricist Margarita Pushkina and performed by the band Aria on the album *Blood for Blood*. Formed in Moscow in 1985, Aria was one of the first Soviet heavy metal bands that managed to reach out to a broader audience. To this day, it remains one of the most famous Russian rock music bands and is often equated with its Western counterparts, such as Iron Maiden and Black Sabbath. Over time, Valeriy Kipelov, the band leader, refused to perform the song "Antichrist" at concerts. He disliked how fans loudly sang out the last lines of the song: "My name is Antichrist, my sign is six six six/ My name is Antichrist/ Cry for the soul". As well, he feared that because the lyrics were written in the first person, many people could associate him with the Antichrist.

Aria's song "Antichrist" is a kind of a soundtrack of Alexander Tumanov's novel, *Temptation: The Book About the Eternal Love* (2016), which was put out through the Ridero e-publishing system. Written as a confession of the Antichrist, Tumanov's novel is a meta-narrative record of how the protagonist and alter ego of the author continues to write a book about the search for eternal love and Paradise on Earth, which is supposed to become the New Gospel. Blending various religious motifs, different cultural myths, references to Russian literature, excerpts from the 1980s and 1990s Russian rock, as well as speculations about evolution, GMO, yoga, and automotive industry, it is an interesting example of a postmodern hybrid novel that cannot easily be assigned to any literary genre. In general, it can be situated somewhere between a memoir, parable, and esoteric treaty. Although relatively obscure, readers on the various literary portals have given Tumanov's novel different reviews, varying from total admiration to calling it the work of a talentless hack.

The narrator and protagonist of Alexander Tumanov's novel is a young man with an unsatisfied sexual desire named Alexander. As he reveals in the prologue, he is the Antichrist, who, after a life-changing illumination, understood that the ultimate goal of his mortal life is to seek immortal love. It is fair to assume that *Temptation*'s protagonist is the author's alter ego since the novel's main character not only shares the same name with the author, but, as with Tumanov, the protagonist also lives in Krasnoyarsk. It can also be indicated by the author's Twitter account – @Antichrist666t – which is full of matrimonial announcements, apocalyptic motifs, and song lyrics by legendary Russian rock bands, such as Aria, Alisa, and Kino, and suggest that the novel is based on the author's real-life experiences.

The novel's plot centres on the protagonist's search for the perfect woman. While looking for true love, which will be the embodiment of Margarita from the Bulgakov's novel *Master and Margarita* (1966-1967) and the Biblical Mary Magdalene, Alexander-Antichrist gets involved in countless love affairs with various women, each of whom has a profoundly symbolic name referring to either religious themes or pop culture. In addition to vivid descriptions of his sexual conquests with women named Eve, Barbie, and Lilith, the narrator devotes many pages to describing alcohol libations, smoking marihuana, and strange encounters with the Serpent, who symbolises Satan, as described in the Old Testament when tempting Eve to eat the fruit from the Tree of Knowledge of good and evil (Gen 2-3).

Alexander-Antichrist believes that he is destined to establish Paradise on Earth which, unlike Paradise promised by Christ, should be based on love and created in the here and now. The love that will be the basis of the Earthly Paradise created by the Antichrist, however, will not be like the love present in the teachings of Jesus. Instead, it should be a lustful love between a man and a woman. In this context, the novel's title acquires additional meaning. It represents both the temptation of Christ by the Devil as described in the Scriptures and the sexual temptation, which is the driving force of the protagonist's life in the novel.

One of the reasons the narrator of *Temptation* rejects love offered in the teachings of Christ is the belief all misery in the world happens because of Christianity. This kind of criticism of Christianity, as well as naming oneself the Antichrist, have roots in Nietzsche's philosophy, expressed in his book *The Antichrist* (1888). As he argued, Christianity is a religion devoid of true morality, created to keep slaves under control. An equally critical approach to Christianity was represented by Vasily Rozanov, whom Dmitry Merezhkovsky called the Russian Nietzsche. Another slightly less known example of this kind of discourse is the novel by Valentin Sventsiskiy *Antichrist: Notes of a Strange Man* (1908), in which the main character, disappointed with the emptiness of his life and the surrounding world, decides to become the human opponent of God – the Antichrist (Isupov 1996). Nevertheless, the Antichrist, as described in Tumanov's novel, is much more than a mere adversary of Christ. Tempted by the Snake, the protagonist becomes the dark shadow and a doppelganger of Christ, whose aim is to establish Paradise on Earth. In one of the climactic scenes of the novel, the Serpent-Satan, who reveals that he is the father of Alexander-Antichrist, explains his complex relationship with Christ. According to the Serpent, Christ and the Antichrist share one self, and, thus, they have a common "matrix of faith". In other words, everything that is experienced by Christ, including crucifixion, has to be experienced by the Antichrist as well.

Such an understanding of the Christ/Antichrist entanglement echoes the conception of the self as put forth in Carl Gustav Jung's book *Aion: Researches into the Phenomenology of the Self* (1970). Jung argued that Christ and the Antichrist are complementary aspects of human consciousness. As he explained it, whereas Christ represents the good side of the self, the Antichrist is the embodiment of a dark side – he is an evil reflection of Christ. Furthermore, as Jung suggested, since the Antichrist "is not just a prophetic prediction", but the "inexorable psychological law", the whole archetype of the self "must express both good and evil, the conscious as well as the unconscious" (Jung 1970, McGinn 1994).

What is more, in his novel, Tumanov creates specific mystical geography, which, contrary to Dugan's notion of sacral geography (see 4.2.), does not have a political character. Instead, it is a blend of esoteric ideas characteristic for the New Age movement that echo here and there throughout the book. In the Book of Revelation, according to Tumanov, when St. John employed metaphors such as the Tower of Babel and the harlot of Babylon, he was writing about Russian statehood and Moscow. Hence, as Tumanov insists, it is evident that Moscow not only is the "city of cities", where the Tsars have ruled, but also it is the apocalyptic metropolis, where the end of the world will begin. Seeing Moscow and Russia playing an integral role in the Endtime is deeply rooted in the Russian messianic tradition, based on the conviction that God chose the Russian nation to accomplish a special mission for the sake of all humanity when the doomsday comes. It also alludes to the apocalyptic prophecies by Seraphim of Sarov, who argued that the Antichrist would be born in Russia in the Jewish community, in an enormous city named "Moscow-Petrograd" that will be formed right before the Apocalypse (see 2.2). Overall, Tumanov offers a rather bizarre novel which, by blending various literary genres, is, in many regards, an attempt to write the New Gospel more suitable for the present-day. Tumanov not only makes the Antichrist his alter ego, but also alludes to the richness of the Russian culture, including the philosophy of the Silver Age, modern Russian rock music, and classic works of Russian literature. Also, by situating the action of the novel in contemporary Russia, Tumanov refers to the Russian messianic tradition, according to which Russia has a crucial role to play in the Endtime. What Tumanov adds to the Russian Antichrist ideomyth is his human character which is manifested primarily in the sexual desire and need for love. Tumanov's Antichrist is at first an ordinary contemporary Russian man, who, due to the occult revelation, begins to identify himself as the son of Satan. To oppose the human suffering and falsehood of Christianity, he decides to redeem humanity and create Paradise on Earth.

Another novel written in the first person from the perspective of the Antichrist, which was also published in 2016 on Ridero, is *Antichrist* by Ilya Alekseyev. As with Tumanov, Alekseyev portrays the Antichrist as an individual, whose life is parallel to that of Christ. However, rather than situating the action in Russia, Alekseyev sets the story in Jerusalem, where Christ lived. As the author states in the lead of the novel, "we are all familiar with the history of Christ, but who knows what the fate of the Antichrist was? After all, he was born on the same day, but the Bible is silent about it" (Alekseyev 2016). In this regard, *Antichrist* is stylised as a missing piece of the Bible, an Apocrypha. In addition, The novel employs a rich repertoire of literary strategies, including a memoir approach, reinterpretations of myths and biblical parables, as well as rewriting historical chronicles. Alekseyev's protagonist turns out to be a complex character that embodies flaws and virtues characteristic for the human condition. Through the novel, we observe the Antichrist wander from town to town, fall in love, and change incarnations.

The Antichrist in Post-Soviet Russia: Transformations of an Ideomyth 159

Even though at times the main character may seem like an ordinary person entangled in the crushing machine of history, it quickly turns out that he is the dark shadow of Christ, responsible for evil happening in the world for more than two millennia. This is how the Antichrist narrator begins his story:

> Today I decided to break the silence and tell my story. Some people will be surprised that after two thousand years of silence, I suddenly started talking. I have been through a lot: from the crucifixion to Adolf Hitler's concentration camps. In my memory, one bloody millennium has replaced another. In my mind, there are so many answers, but the modern man is not ready for all of them, and while exposed to all of these secrets, he will take them as the madman's delusions. For this reason, I will answer only a small part of all your questions (Alekseyev 2016: 6).

Despite the promise, the first-person protagonist does not give readers the answers about the two millennia of his existence. The narrator limits his story to the time from his birth, which coincided with the birth of Christ, and, thus, is the beginning of the Christian era, to the fall of the Roman Empire, conventionally considered to be the end of Antiquity. This time frame seems to allude to the general belief that, whereas Western Christianity has been from the very beginning permeated with the Antichrist's influences, Orthodoxy has remained the only genuinely Christian faith. In the last scene of the novel, when the decline of the Roman Empire is apparent, the Antichrist sets forth to Constantinople, which – along with the tradition of *translatio imperii* – has become the Second Rome and the centre of Christianity. However, the Antichrist never reaches Constantinople, which means that Orthodox Christianity has remained untouched by the evil influences of Christ's adversary.

Before leaving the Roman Empire, the Antichrist goes through numerous transformations and oppressions, including beatings, diseases, and long-lasting starvation. In the first part of the novel, which describes how Christ's and the Antichrist's lives are intertwined, the Antichrist follows Jesus, persecutes, and imitates him. To get closer to Christ, the Antichrist not only turns into the devil tempting Jesus with the earthly goods on the desert, and Judas, who deceives Jesus for the thirty shekels of silver, but also, at some point, begins to claim that he is Christ himself. In one of the most important scenes of the novel, while observing the crucifixion of Christ, the Antichrist undergoes a temporary transformation and has an impression that it is he hanging on the cross. Convinced that he has become Christ, he appropriates the power of God and considers himself to be the true Messiah.

In this regard, Alekseyev alludes to presumably the most popular way of portraying the Antichrist as that who not only is the adversary of Christ, but also tries to take his place. Unlike in numerous traditional interpretations and prophecies based on the exegesis of the Scriptures, the Antichrist does not take the place of Christ for good. After the short transformation, he returns to his true nature and sets out on a journey during which he joins the brotherhood that aims to liberate Israel from Rome. As well, he finds a wife, who gives him a son, Lucifer, a demon that is as immortal as the Antichrist himself.

The second part of the novel is based on the ancient Greek myth that describes Jason's adventurous expedition to obtain the fleece of the gold-haired sheep, which symbolises power and authority (Guirand 1963). In a postmodern manner, Alekseyev reinterprets the well-known myth and gives the main part to the Antichrist who, just like Jason, had to go on a long journey to gain wealth that will allow him to convince the parents of a little girl named Eva to let her marry him. During the expedition, he is helped by demons that are a personification of Medea from the myth about Argonauts, who was abandoned by Jason and killed their sons in despair. Just like Jason abandons Medea for Creon's daughter Glauce, the Antichrist does not remain faithful to the demons and falls in love with Eve. In revenge, the demons kill Eva's little brother. Filled with despair, Eva notices the true nature of her fiancé and breaks the engagement.

When the marriage with Eva does not take place, lonesome and deprived of everything, the Antichrist distances himself from the world. Not for long, however, as his son Lucifer, who became Satan, offers him the opportunity to take power in the Roman Empire. After the initial refusal, the Antichrist decides to sit on the emperor's throne. During his reign, not only does he build churches, libraries, and orchards, but he also kills without mercy those, who do not recognise his authority. In this part, Alekseyev portrays the Antichrist as an autocratic and charismatic ruler. This interpretation has its roots in the Book of Revelation, considered by many to be a metaphoric picture of Nero's reign and his persecutions of Christians. In the Russian context, such an image of the Antichrist has been perpetuated by figures such as Dostoyevsky's Grand Inquisitor and Solovyov's Apollon. In Alekseyev's novel, the image of the Antichrist as a relentless tyrant is not always apparent. Over time, the main character decides to free the slaves. Since freedom and equality for all are associated with Christ's teachings, the outraged Satan forces the Antichrist to give up the power. Consequently, the Antichrist is getting closer to God, and finally recognises his superiority and power.

In his novel, Alekseyev not only sheds a different light on the Biblical representation of the life and teachings of Christ, but also attempts to answer the question of who the Antichrist really is. Interestingly, instead of describing the Antichrist from the outside as Tumanov did, Alekseyev gives him his own voice. Throughout the novel, the readers observe internal dilemmas, numerous contradictions, and dramas of the protagonist, who is burdened with absolute freedom and immortality. Even though the author does not give the final answer about the nature of the Antichrist, a whole new image of Christ's opponent emerges from the novel. Portrayed not only as a false Messiah and the ruler of demons, but also as an ordinary man, the Antichrist here is not unequivocally evil. Despite his evil deeds, he is still able to repent his sins and try to reconcile with Christ.

Furthermore, being the observer of tragic historical events, he resembles the protagonist of the novel *The Psalm* (1975) by Fridrich Gorenstein, in which the Antichrist named Dan is not the enemy of Christ, but God's emissary, who, together with his brother Jesus, was sent to Earth to fulfil the will of God. Such a way of portraying the Antichrist brings up a few important questions: what if the Antichrist does not want to be the Antichrist? What if he chooses to be good? The answer Gorenstein and Alekseyev provide is quite simple: it is not possible. As they suggest, only being the evil other and dark shadow of Christ can the Antichrist make salvation happen as foreseen in the Scriptures.

However, in post-Soviet Russian fiction, the Antichrist is not necessarily portrayed as a malicious individual. He can be depicted as both a tangible individual and presence in the human soul. The internal character of the Antichrist understood as being an evil element in each human stems from the exegesis of the Scripture put forth by Origen of Alexandria (ca. 185-253). In his view, until the illumination by the Word of God, in every human soul, there are only false wisdom and lies. This evil can be overcome only by recognising Christ as the Messiah and accepting the teachings of God. If it does not happen, a person slips over to the side of the Antichrist and is excluded from the community of the redeemed.

A similar reading of what is anti-Christian was suggested by one of the greatest thinkers of early Christianity, St. Augustine (ca. 354-430). In his classic *The City of God*, Augustine argues that "whatsoever is contrary to the Word of God is in the Antichrist" (as quoted in Emmerson 1981: 64). Thereby, he views the Antichrist not as a "supernatural agent who would appear outside the political and social borders of Christianity", but as a permanent struggle between good and evil, both on the Church level and that of the human soul (Fuller 1995: 32). In the subsequent centuries, the internalised understanding of the Antichrist as suggested by Origen of Alexandria and St. Augustine has inspired numerous thinkers, philosophers, and writers, including Nietzsche and Dostoyevsky.

In post-Soviet Russia, such an interpretation of the Antichrist ideomyth can be found in the short story collection *The Temptation-2* by Sergey Mavrodi. The book, published in 2012, is a series of stories involving conversations between Lucifer and his son. *The Temptation-2* is, in fact, the current edition of Mavrodi's book *The Son of Lucifer* written during one of his terms in prison. Mavrodi, whom the Russian media called the greatest Soviet and Russian crook, and a financial genius and adventurer, was the founder of the MMM joint-stock company, considered the largest pyramid scheme in Russian history. In August 1994, he was arrested for tax fraud. A month later, he was released from prison and elected as the deputy of the State Duma of the Russian Federation. After a year, however, he was removed from office. Undeterred, he established the Party of the National Capital, and, again, participated in the Duma election, but failed. This also did not cool his political ambitions. In 1996, Mavrodi intended to run for president of the Russian Federation, but the Central Election Commission refused to register him. Since the 1990s, three criminal cases were filed against Mavrodi: for using a false passport, for financial fraud, and tax evasion. In 2003, he was found guilty and sentenced to 13 months in prison. Four years later, in April 2007, while still in jail due to the protracted process, he was sentenced to four and a half years for financial fraud, and after serving the remaining months, he was released from prison in May 2007. Prison apparently did not reform Mavrodi, and, in 2011 and 2012, he created two new pyramid schemes, which, again, duped people out of huge amounts of money. Mavrodi also announced his participation in the presidential elections in March 2018. However, his start in the election did not happen, and a few days later, on March 26, 2018, Mavrodi died of a heart attack. Due to his popularity as a public figure, one can assume that his book reached a wider audience than Tumanov's and Alekseyev's works. Adding to the popularity of Mavrodi, his collection of stories has very good reviews on various portals, including one of the biggest Russian online bookstores, Labirynt.ru.

The title of Mavrodi's book refers to the temptation of Christ in the desert. However, the temptation by Satan involves not only scenes described in the Gospels in the New Testament, as invoked in Tumanov's and Alekseyev's novels, but also everyday temptations imposed by Satan on ordinary people. In Mavrodi's stories, characters are tempted with infinite wealth ("The PyraMMMid"), changing the reality, and controlling other people's feelings ("The Game"), as well as false miracles ("The Sect"). A common theme of losing a loved one and loneliness connects the stories, a theme also found in Alekseyev's novel, in which the immortal Antichrist witnesses the deaths of all his relatives.

Each story in *The Temptation-2* is introduced and summarised by a fragment of the conversation between Lucifer, the omniscient narrator, and his son. In their dialogues, they not only comment on behaviours and motivations of the characters, but also give general remarks on the human condition in the contemporary world. Interestingly, Lucifer also appears as one of the characters in Tumanov's and Alekseyev's fiction. However, while Lucifer is portrayed here as the son of the Antichrist, in Mavrodi's book the roles are reversed: the Antichrist is the son of Lucifer, who educates him about human weaknesses and the nature of evil.

Although apocalyptic motifs can be traced in all the stories in *The Temptation-2*, the Antichrist appears explicitly in only two. In the first story, "The Satanist" written as a recording of a television programme, based on a dialogue between the nameless Host and C., a mysterious man in his forties, who turns out to be the guru of a Satanist sect. In his lengthy speech, with rhetorical flippancy, C. argues that people have been tricked into believing that the Parousia indicates the second arrival of Christ. In his opinion, the truth is that it will be the Antichrist who will come to Earth to redeem humanity. Further, in freely interpreting the Scriptures to support his controversial opinions, C. insists that since Christ came to the world as a human, he could not avoid the struggle of choosing between good or evil. In this regard, C. suggests, Christ is not much different from the Antichrist.

As C. points out, by not choosing to help people and refusing to turn stones into bread, while being tempted by Satan in the desert, Christ actually did even more harm to humanity than the Antichrist, who offers people freedom and the Earthly Kingdom that emanates a golden age of progress, advancement, and independence in civilisation. The rhetoric C. uses, resembles arguments expressed by the Grand Inquisitor in the parable told by one of the brothers in Dostoyevsky's *The Brothers Karamazov*. In the parable, Ivan tells his younger brother, the seemingly merciful cardinal accuses Christ of leaving people puzzled and suffering. For this reason, the cardinal decides to improve God's work and satisfy the greatest needs of humanity: the need for bread and miracles. The Grand Inquisitor entrusts Satan, and, just like a false Messiah, preaches Christianity detached from God.

The Antichrist also appears in Mavrodi's short story, "The Sermon". Written as a prophecy, it consists of three complementary parts describing the relationship between God and Lucifer, the life of Christ, and the fate of the Antichrist. In his story, Mavrodi not only rewrites quotes from the Bible and recontextualises them, but, also provides the reader with an interesting interpretation of the Scriptures. The narrator, who is probably Lucifer, argues that when God noticed that people became tired of their misery and started to drift away from him, he decided to "wed them to the good husband", and sent Christ to the Earth. However, contrary to God's intentions, Christ's arrival brought even more suffering to people, just to mention the Massacre of Innocents. Moreover, the narrator accuses Christ of not wanting to eliminate hunger in the world and argues that God's Son decided not to turn stones to bread when tempted by Satan in the desert, because he was afraid that if people did not have to fight for food, progress would have accelerated too quickly, and, subsequently, they would become too much like God.

What is more, according to the narrator, the reason Christ agrees to die on the cross is not to redeem humanity, but to create a religion, which is the "top of shamelessness, bigotry, and hypocrisy" (Mavrodi 2012: 339). From this perspective, Christianity, based on Christ's preaches of mercy and forgiveness, is seen as the religion of the weak, and equated with stagnation and "sleep of reason". Lucifer, in turn, is portrayed not as the fallen angel of evil, but a symbol of progress and the enlightenment, what is actually suggested by his name. Such an argument against Christianity dates back to 1888 when Nietzsche deemed the religion as being immoral, established to enslave people and to limit their greatness.

In his prophecy, the narrator in "The Sermon", admits that it is difficult to state when exactly the Antichrist will come to the world. He argues:

> The Antichrist has not yet appeared in the world, and therefore I will not deal here with speculations about this. Just because neither I, nor anyone else, know anything about Him. Not who He is, not how He will act. Not when He will arrive. It is possible that He is already among us. It is possible. But I do not know this (Mavrodi 2012: 347).

The narrator, in expressing doubts whether the Antichrist is here or not, alludes to one of the most recurring questions regarding this apocalyptic figure. Boris Molchanov, one of the most influential figures of the Russian Orthodox Church Outside of Russia in the 20th century, attempted to tackle this subject in his writing. In his view, since the Antichrist's life will be a mirror image of that of Christ's which means that he will reveal himself to the world at the age of thirty. Mavrodi follows this line of thought and, in his story, suggests that there is the possibility that the Antichrist is here and waiting for the right moment to come out.

In his story collection, Mavrodi portrays the Antichrist in two ways: either as an individual or as a metaphor of evil present in the human soul. When portrayed as a human, the Antichrist is seen as the saviour of humanity, who, contrary to Christ, really cared for people and wanted to offer worldly goods and freedom. In this regard, Mavrodi's perspective is similar to that of Tumanov, who depicted the Antichrist as being human, and wants to make humanity happy by establishing Paradise on Earth, based on the erotic love between a man and a woman. Moreover, as in the case of Tumanov's novel, it would not be an overinterpretation to state that the Son of Lucifer/Antichrist in Mavrodi's stories symbolises the author himself. He also was a crook and deceiver, who broke the law repeatedly. Interestingly, author's features can be found in the main character of the first story "The PyraMMMid", Sergey Kondratevich Pautov, who not only is the namesake of Mavrodi, but also creates the huge pyramid scheme, for which he ends up in prison.

Nevertheless, the most interesting aspect Mavrodi adds to the post-Soviet Antichrist ideomyth is the emphasis on his internal character. By referring to Origen of Alexandria's interpretations of the Scriptures, Mavrodi suggests that the Antichrist does not have to be an evil individual, aiming to destroy the world. Since evil can be internalised and quite universal, there is a little bit of the Antichrist in each of us, he suggests. Here, the Antichrist is seen as evil slumbering in the human soul that leads to immoral deeds and misery.

Overall, discussed post-Soviet Russian are grounded in the traditional interpretations of the Antichrist ideomyth, deriving from ancient prophecies, early-Christian writings, the historiosophy put forth by Old Believers, and literature of Russian Silver Age. Even though discussed authors apply the entire repertoire of postmodern stylistic devices, including intertextuality, fragmentation, and metafiction, the image of the Antichrist they create remains relatively conventional. Although situated in more contemporary contexts, in their works the Antichrist still represents either the adversary of Christ or evil forces unlocked in the mundane world. Nevertheless, many authors of post-Soviet Russian fiction do not limit themselves to portraying the Antichrist in one of these two ways. It is interesting to look at authors, who go far beyond interpretative frameworks traditionally applied the Antichrist ideomyth.

V.2. (Not Only) Postmodern Variations: From Scientist and Serial Killer to Politician and Trickster

Post-Soviet Russian authors often employ literary devices rooted in postmodernism, which entered Russian literature after the collapse of the Soviet Union. Mikhail Epstein (1993), a renowned literary critic, argues that after the decades of censorship, ideological manipulation, and lack of freedom of speech, postmodernism became the dominant trend in the post-Soviet Russian fiction of the 1990s. According to him, the post-Soviet Russian postmodernism was not only a response to its Western counterpart that reigned in literature for almost the entire 20th century, but it was also an attempt to reinterpret and reconsider the principal aspects of the Russian cultural tradition. Moreover, as argued by Mark Lipovetsky (2010: 9), post-Soviet Russian postmodernism has often led to the emergence of surprising literary hybrids as it repeatedly collided and intertwined with other post-Soviet discourses, many of which were the response to a cultural trauma triggered by the collapse of the Soviet Union.

In his essay collection, *Post-Soviet Literature and the Search for Russian Identity* (2016), Boris Noordenbos suggests that in the late 1990s and early 2000s, the postmodernism fashion gradually declined, and post-Soviet Russian culture has undergone a so-called "neo-imperialist turn". Consequently, there appeared numerous novels that overflow with concerns about Russia's "unique national character" and "its cultural place in the world". By either idealising the past or placing the action in a better future, these narratives not only offer visions of former Russian glory, but also emphasised the distinctiveness and uniqueness of the Russian culture by putting it in opposition to what is generally seen as the morally degraded West (Noordenbos 2016: 1-26). According to Rosalind Marsh (2010), a professor of Russian Studies at the University of Bath, the neo-imperialist turn resulted in the emergence of a so-called "imperial novel" that, in turn, is an example of a New Political Novel. As she argues, this kind of narrative not only addresses the most current political problems, but also, being a critical response to postmodernist literature associated with the liberal cultural elites, represents the nationalist worldview.

It is important to note that the "neo-imperialist turn" this is not limited to one literary genre. Rather, represented by authors such as Pavel Krusanov, Alexander Prokhanov, Dmitry Bykov, and Eduard Limonov, it embraces novels and short stories that not only contain elements of the thriller, romance, and dystopia, but also refer to mythology, Russian folklore, conspiracy theories, as well as biblical and apocalyptic motifs. According to Noordenbos (2016: 24), "imperial novels", deeply immersed in the Russian messianic tradition, serve as a reservoir of compelling stories. As he points out, they not only tackle questions of identity, memory, and self-knowledge, but also, by offering comforting fantasies about alternative worlds, heal the "cultural wounds" caused by rapid political, social, and economic changes triggered by the dissolution of the USSR.

In this context, a genre of particular importance is science fiction that has its roots in the Soviet *nauchnaya fantastika*. Based on interdisciplinary connections between the history of science and technology, political and economic development, as well as cultural history, it not only blurs the border between classic and popular literature, but also has an uncanny communicative power (Suslov 2016b, Khagi

2013). Drawing upon Slavic mythologies, utopian legends, and compelling visions of the future technological developments, science fiction often serves as modern mythology that imposes an unequivocal cosmological order on reality and explains what is otherwise incomprehensible.

The post-Soviet Russian science fiction often employs and reinterprets apocalyptic motifs, including the Antichrist figure. An excellent example of using this literary strategy is the novel *The Antichrist* (2000), a debut work by Alexander Kashanskiy, who, since 1994, has been the director of the Zelenogorsk branch of the Krasnoyarsk Regional Medical Insurance Company. Kashanskiy, tired of being a civil servant, became a literary star with that first novel, especially among conservative and radical circles. Interviews with the author have appeared in media outlets linked to Dugin's neo-Eurasian movement, including the main website of the International Eurasian Movement.

Interestingly, in recent years, Kashanskiy became active with the School of Common Sense, established in 2008 by Alexey Nazarevskiy, a poet, philosopher, and interpreter. A part of the Military Institute of Foreign Languages, the school aims to educate the new elite of a rapidly changing world. According to the description on the website, the main purpose of this institution is, among other things, to tackle political, economic, and religious "issues related to our life", "reveal the true background of received information", and "explain the provisions of worldview system and ideologies". In addition to Kashanskiy, among people associated with the School, there are public figures, academics, and politicians, including Alexander Nagornyy (a secretary of the Izborsky Club), Dmitry Trenin (the director of the Carnegie Moscow Centre), and Shamil Sulmanov (a former deputy and member of the Islamic Revival Party). Interestingly, the school's activities are not limited to the Russian Federation. It also has branches in many countries, including the United States and Israel.

Kashanskiy's *The Antichrist* describes the fate of Ivan Sviridov, an outstanding mathematician who invents a complicated system of modelling the universe. The action of the novel takes place on two intertwining narrative plans: in a small provincial Russian town, where Ivan lives, and a spiritual space, which is the place of the ultimate conflict between God and Satan. The only way of resolving this

The Antichrist in Post-Soviet Russia: Transformations of an Ideomyth 169

metaphysical conflict and saving the world from the ultimate destruction is for Ivan to decide whether he wants to establish the system he invented or not.

Satan does everything in his power to drag Ivan to his side and to use the system to steal God's title of being the only Creator; God, curiously, allows Ivan to decide for himself what to do. Ivan must then decide for himself whether he will stand on the side of good or whether he will become the Antichrist. If Ivan chooses the good, he will be redeemed, even though he does not possess an eternal soul. However, if he decides to create the system and write the new "Book of Life", people will lose their souls and become subordinates of Satan. As Satan unfolds before Ivans's eyes early in the novel, the "Biblical Sodom will seem like a kindergarten" and people will be led to self-destruction by "overflow[ing] each other with the melted greyness of nuclear explosions and sprinkl[ing] with salt from the sewage of their filthy civilisation" (Kashanskiy 2000:2).

Although a crucial role in human history is assigned to Ivan, for most of his life, he is not aware of his mission. He leads an everyday life in Moscow and works on developing his complicated mathematical system. Nevertheless, despite his ordinary existence and a popular, even banal, Russian name, Ivan is no everyman. He is a brilliant, talented, and charismatic genius whose knowledge overwhelms and frightens his superiors. Consequently, Ivan loses his job and is forced to return to his hometown. Upon his return, he meets all of his old friends, including Natasha, an unusually beautiful woman, who has been in love with him since they first met as teenagers. Yasnitskiy, an influential businessman, becomes jealous and angry at Natasha's attraction to the mathematician, and, subsequently, orders some henchmen to attack Ivan. Ivan almost dies from the attack. In a state fluctuating between life and death, Ivan meets God, who gives him the Liyil, a magical feather that not only enables him to perform miracles, such as showing Christ's resurrection to the doubtful or turning water into wine during a party, but also allows him to travel back in time. Ivan uses this power to meet his ancestors, talk to Zarathustra and Christ, as well as to become the protopope Avvakum and participate in the turbulent events of 17th century Russia.

As with the other novelists examined, Kashanskiy alludes to the biblical narrative about Christ being tempted by Satan in the desert. Satan and his assistant, Riikoy, offer money, sex, and fame, but Ivan resists; they then plan an encounter with

Ivan. Right before heading out to meet Satan in the deserted mountains, Ivan decides to be baptised. However, it does not protect him from doubts regarding creating the system he invented as it would not bring happiness to anyone. Ivan is exhausted and hungry after forty days of waiting, and, yet, he is on the verge of endurance when Satan appears, imitating the biblical scene of tempting Christ in the desert, and offering Ivan earthly bread, immortality, and unlimited power. The only thing Satan requires of Ivan is to prove that he is the Anointed One by bringing the Liyil to Earth. Ivan refuses, and Satan leaves him in the mountains; after a few days, he is found and brought safely home. Now, Ivan distances himself from Natasha, who is now his fiancée, but he also loses interest in working on his mathematical system. Exhausted with being the chosen one, he tries to return to everyday life.

It is important to note that in his novel, Kashanskiy not only employs the religious motifs, including the Apocalypse and Temptation, but also refers to classic Russian literature, pop culture, and conspiracy theories. Conspirological themes, combined with the biblical motifs, are particularly present in the second part of the novel, in which Ivan, together with his friend Sergey, establish a company called Legion Id. Its name refers to the story from the New Testament about Jesus healing a man possessed by numerous demons under a collective name, Legion. Another demonic name appearing in *The Antichrist* is Samael, which derives from the Talmud and denotes the accuser, seducer, and destroyer; it is also the name of the supercomputer that controls human behaviour and enables building a new financial system. In many regards, Kashanskiy's Samael resembles the Computer named Beast believed to track every action of every person in the world from a conspiracy theory popular in post-Soviet Russian conservative discourses (see 3.1.).

Since the supercomputer Samael is not only capable of modelling biological, physical, economic, and social processes, but also can display the future, it turns out to be indispensable for Ivan's and Sergey's company. Thus, they fly to the United States where the supercomputer is based and meet its creator, the incredibly wealthy Jew Zilbert, whose aim is to create a "new world order" that will overcome the ideology crisis in the contemporary world. Interestingly, the figure of an old Jew Zilbert brings to mind yet another self-proclaimed saviour of humanity: the Grand Inquisitor from Dostoyevsky's novel. As with the Grand Inquisitor, the creator of the supercomputer aims at introducing the new political system based on false values of democracy, freedom, and human rights. Moreover, being of Jewish descent, the Zilbert figure evokes antisemitic prejudices present in the New World Order conspiracy theory based on the conviction that it will be controlled by wealthy and powerful Judeo-Masons (see 3.2.).

Although Zilbert does not believe that Ivan is the Forerunner of the Apocalypse, whose mission is to change the fate of the world, he allows Ivan to use Samael to generate the "instrument of creation". He has, however, one condition: Ivan has to become a Jew to guarantee that even if Satan seizes power over humanity, there will not be another holocaust. After agreeing to Zilbert's condition, Ivan has three and a half years to establish his system. Kashanskiy portrays Ivan as a Jewish Antichrist and implicitly refers to the writings of Irenaeus of Lyon, who argued that, coming from the Tribe of Dan, the Antichrist will be a false Jewish Messiah. Contrary to the traditional depiction of the Antichrist figure, in the final scene, Ivan chooses to be good. Just before the system is launched, he stops the supercomputer and leaves unlimited power to God. As a reward, God turns the Liyil into Ivan's soul, but Kashanskiy's novel does not have a happy ending. Ivan is brutally killed after his best friend Sergey betrays him; Sergey acts like Judas and sells information about the system to Yasnitskiy.

Kashanskiy's novel, which the reading portals often classify as a "philosophical thriller", has many features of the science fiction genre. Although based in contemporary Russia, it describes a speculative futuristic reality of the Endtime. The protagonist is capable of travelling in time and visiting parallel universes, and the system he works on leans on the newest digital technologies. In *The Antichrist*, scientific and technological development serve cosmological purposes: they are supposed to be used to create a new order of the universe. From this perspective, Kashanskiy's novel is a profoundly religious critique of our world today and post-Soviet Russia as steeped in consumption, economic progress, and atheism. By referring to the biblical motifs, popular myths, and conspiracy theories, Kashanskiy builds a new universe of meanings and a specific cosmology, in which the protagonist is torn between good and evil. By choosing good and sacrificing himself for humanity, Ivan-Antichrist becomes, in a sense, the new incarnation of Christ. As with the biblical Jesus, he subordinates to the power of God, and is betrayed and brutally killed in the name of redemption.

In yet another work called *The Antichrist*, the 2017 science fiction novel by Dmitry Lugovoy, the protagonist also faces a dilemma of choosing between good and evil. In 2014, Lugovoy tragically died at age 26. Thanks to his father, the author's fiction, ranging from fantasy and adventure novels to horror and sci-fi, have been published by Kompaniya, through the Ridero portal. *The Antichrist*, written in the third person from the position of an omniscient narrator, tells the story of a mysterious man who arrives in the United States around the year 2050 with a distinctive, yet very controversial, mission of killing ten people. Who are the ten people the Antichrist has to kill? These are extremely intelligent and talented children who, in the future, will contribute to the destruction of the world. As adults, they will work for a US government secret project aimed at creating a portal that can turn fictional characters into real people, and, consequently, will blur the boundaries between fiction and the real world.

Lugovoy's novel is a record of the Antichrist's journey which is supposed to end when the world is saved. It is, indeed, not an ordinary journey, as both the Antichrist and his nemesis, James Montgomery, can travel between various media that generate narratives, including radio, television, and books. As the novel unfolds, the Antichrist follows his victims, and, at the same time, escapes Montgomery, a former police officer and the husband of the Antichrist's first victim, who was a talented biologist involved in the secret project. Another person who follows the Antichrist is Kate, a young detective assigned to investigate the case. After one of the murders, when the Antichrist accidentally teleports himself to her apartment through a TV set, Kate discovers that he is not a cold-blooded murderer, but a man who wants to fulfil his mission by all means. Subsequently, going against common sense and professional conduct, she decides to follow the Antichrist in his mission, and, along the way, she falls in love with him.

In his novel, Lugovoy puts forth a complex universe, based on the universal competition between good and evil. As with Kashanskiy, he blends various motifs and literary strategies characteristic for science fiction, including futuristic visions of the technological developments, the interpenetration of parallel universes, and scientific vocabulary. Lugovoy does not limit himself to one literary genre or literary strategy. In *The Antichrist*, the reader can find elements of a detective novel, romance, and even memoir, as well as references to various motifs from popular culture, including the classic sci-fi B film *The Eight Plague* (2011) and the New World Order conspiracy theory.

Lugovoy's protagonist, who is similar to Ivan from Kashanskiy's novel, is not merely Christ's evil twin, but a man who is pressed to make a tragic choice. Unlike Ivan, the Antichrist's mission is not to rewrite the history of the universe, but to protect the old order by killing ten outstanding scientists, whose cooperation with the US authorities will lead to the Apocalypse. In other words, even though Lugovoy's protagonist is a serial killer named Antichrist, he is not unequivocally evil. There is an interesting paradox embedded in this character: whereas his mission is to save the world, he can achieve it only by killing children, who, of course, are associated with innocence and purity. Here, Lugovoy's Antichrist resembles Mephistopheles that appears in *Faust*, Johann Goethe's 1833 play, and is described as "... a part of that power which constantly wills evil, and constantly creates the Good". Also, since the Antichrist does not kill for pleasure, but to prevent the anticipated catastrophe, even against his will, he becomes a part of the divine order.

What is particularly interesting in Lugovoy's novel, the Antichrist serves as a symbol of opposition against the excessive globalisation, technological progress, and artificial interference in the human body. By killing ten future geniuses, the Antichrist aims to prevent a portal that not only will mingle reality with fantasy, but also blur the difference between good and evil. The narrative echoes post-Soviet Russian conservative and religious authors, including Alexander Dugin, Olga Chetverikova, and – above all –Patriarch Kirill, who equate blending good and evil with postmodernism, which they consider the ideology of the Kingdom of the Antichrist (see 4.2). Another similarity between Lugovoy's work and the conservative and religious community is the steady criticism of the United States. In the novel, America is depicted not only as the centre of the globalised world, but also the core of all darkness from which evil will spread to other parts of the globe.

Logovoy is not alone in his critique of the US. According to literary critic Boris Noordenbos, anti-American positions also characterise novels of the "neo-imperialist turn" in post-Soviet Russian fiction. An interesting example of such a novel, which also involves apocalyptic motifs, is *The American Hole* (2005) by Pavel Krusanov. *The American Hole* is the part of a trilogy that also includes *The Angel's Bite* (2001) and *Bom-Bom* (2002). Loosely related to each other, all three novels were published as one book entitled *Triada*, in 2007. Although each volume of the trilogy tells a different story, what connects them is absurd humour, tenacious anti-Westernism, and alluding to messianic ideas of the unique mission Russia allegedly has in the world. As Noordenbos points out (2016: 125), Krusanov's trilogy not only oscillates around the idea of the "apocalyptic destruction and revival of the Russian Empire", but also blends an ironic sense of humour with a radical neo-Eurasian worldview. The United States is portrayed here as the metaphysical antipodes of Russia. Krusanov depicts it as the capitalistic hell penetrated with greed and falseness, and deprived of morality and fundamental spiritual values.

The American Hole foretells the events of the near future – the years 2010-2011 – which, for today's readers, is already the past. It is the story of Evgraf Malchik, a young man who starts working for a mysterious Captain also named Abarbarchuk. Malchik immediately recognises him as his youth idol, Sergey Kuryokhin, who was an artist and musician and died of a heart attack, in 1996. Kuryokhin was a real man, very active in the Saint Petersburg arts community, who, in 1995, became a member of the National Bolshevik Party, and died one year later due to a rare heart condition. The novel by Krusanov describes Kuryokhin's "afterlife" as the owner of the company that specialises in "practical jokes" aimed at punishing the United States for its greediness, spiritlessness, and spaciousness. Kuryokhin-Abarbarchuk's aim is achieved: with the help of Malchik and his girlfriend Olga, he convinces the American government that there are vast deposits of gold in the Kola Peninsula. When greedy Americans start to drill, they wake up demons frozen in the ground that, out of revenge, cause a severe economic crisis in the US. As a result, conflicts between ethnic groups arise, some of the American states declare independence, and banks go bankrupt. Finally, the US falls apart.

The Russian Federation, in turn, becomes rich and flourishes as the "great continental empire".
As with Krusanov's other works, *The American Hole* is permeated with the nostalgia for Russia's status as a superpower that opposes the political and cultural hegemony of the West. It echoes Dugin's neo-Eurasian geopolitics and the Kremlin's political direction adopted in the 2000s. Interestingly, in 2001, Krusanov became famous for the letter he wrote to Putin, in which he expressed a deep concern that Russia had lost its imperial status. He suggested if Russia wanted to regain its superpower status, the newly appointed leader of the Russian Federation should initiate the annexation of Istanbul, once known as Constantinople, which for centuries was the cradle of Orthodoxy. Although the takeover of Constantinople "may seem absurd from a pragmatic point of view", Krusanov insisted in the letter, "from an aesthetic point of view, this idea is impeccable", and Russia needed to become the only Orthodox empire (Krusanov as quoted in Mørch 2008: 128). This certainly sounds particularly incongruous after the annexation of Crimea, in 2014. Five years later, Krusanov claimed in an interview the letter was "a funny joke", yet, according to Audun Mørch, who conducted the interview, this was, indeed, an expression of the author's real views.
It is impossible to state with certainty whether Krusanov's suggestion to take over Constantinople was a joke, a provocation, or an expression of his actual views. This is what would be called *stiob*, according to Alexei Yurchak (2006: 249-250), a professor of anthropology at the University of California, Berkeley. In his book, *Everything was Forever, Until it was No More: The Last Soviet Generation* (2005: 249-250), he defines the term as "a peculiar form of irony that differed from sarcasm, cynicism, disdain, or any of the more familiar genres of absurd humour. It required such a degree of overidentification with the object, person, or idea at which this *stiob* was directed that it was often impossible to tell whether it was a form of sincere support, subtle ridicule, or a peculiar mixture of the two". In the late Soviet era, *stiob*, a strategy of making fun of the hegemonic discourse, was used mostly by artists and repressed groups. However, in time, it moved to the mainstream and became an important part of the post-Soviet culture. Noordenbos (2011: 149) notes that, together with the legacy of the "sots-art", *stiob* has been

an important means of artistic expression for authors, whom he classifies as "imperialists writers", such as Pavel Krusanov, Eduard Limonov, and Alexander Prokhanov. As he argues, they "often balanced on the very borderline between irony and ideological militancy" to such an extent that determining whether what they write is a malicious mockery and pastiche or their real views has become virtually impossible.

Stiob was also a vital element of the work of Sergey Kuryokhin, whom Krusanov used as the prototype for Abarbarchuk. Born in 1954 in Leningrad (now Saint Petersburg), Kuryokhin was a Russian musician, actor, and writer. Not only was friends with Krusanov, who immortalised him in *The American Hole*, but he was also closely associated with the National Bolshevik Party, established by Eduard Limonov and Alexander Dugin. Together with the latter, he even wrote a radical esoteric *Manifesto of New Magicians*, preaching the need to build metaphysical bridges between Russian politics and art. The most considerable provocation staged by Kuryokhin was his appearance in a popular TV show *The Fifth Wheel*, broadcasted in 1991 by the 5th Channel of Leningrad television, in which he impersonated a historian and claimed in all seriousness that Lenin was a mushroom. Interestingly, many viewers took this obvious *stiob* for the truth, and the Leningrad Regional Committee of the Communist Party of the Soviet Union received so many letters that they decided to issue the statement that "Lenin could not have been a mushroom because a mammal cannot be a plant" (Yurchak 2011: 310). Noordenbos (2016: 125), argues that Kuryokhin is a "well-chosen symbol for Krusanov's ambiguous 'imperialism'". As Krusanov suggests in his novel, Kuryokhin was not only a hoaxer and provocateur, but also he returned from the dead. As a result, Kuryokhin's death and resurrection symbolise the fall and subsequent revival of the Russian Empire. However, even after returning to the world of the living and "transcending all states of human existence", Kuryokhin-Abarbarchuk still belongs to the underworld, which is the demonic realm of deathly devils (Krusanov 2005:491). For this reason, even though he is not once explicitly named the Antichrist, Capitan is clearly the embodiment of this apocalyptic figure. Just as the Antichrist was portrayed in various interpretations throughout history, he is an omnipotent leader, who, like a false prophet, always turns out to be someone else than he claims to be.

Nevertheless, Kuryokhin-Abarbarchuk is not only the charismatic and smart Capitan, who manages to restore the Russian Empire, but he is also "a trickster who tricks the US into another civil war" (Mørch 2008: 134). The trickster figure derives from folk and popular culture and symbolises an archetypal joker-deity, who crosses boundaries and opposes the dictated norms (Hyde 2017). As literary critic Alla Latynina (2006) sees it, that is exactly what the Captain is like: he continuously lies, cheats, changes his form, and travels between the worlds. Furthermore, being an eternal antagonist, whose domain is the destruction, he does not recognise the difference between good and evil. When attempting to destroy what he deems the embodiment of evil, the US, Captain uses lies and provocations. In his twisted logic, evil is considered good, and good becomes evil. Consequently, genuine values lose their meaning, and a trickster and jester appear like the Antichrist. Another novel, in which no character is explicitly named the Antichrist, but the plot of which is inscribed in the apocalyptic drama, is the novel *Mr Hexogen* (2002) written by Alexander Prokhanov, whom Marina Aptekman (2006: 669) names "one of the most prominent writers of the Red-Brown camp". Prokhanov is not only a writer, but also editor-in-chief of the extreme right-wing newspaper *Zavtra*, and an active supporter of the pro-Russian separatism in Eastern Ukraine. Known for his ultranationalist and anti-capitalist views, he entered the literary scene in the early 1970s. Although he has since published numerous novels and short story collections, it was not until 2002 when his literary career experienced a "meteoric rise" when he won the National Bestseller Prize for *Mr Hexogen* (Marsh 2010: 161).

This win provoked a passionate debate among Russian literary critics. The controversy erupted because the novel was put out by the Ad Marginem publishing house, considered an intellectual publisher known for promoting postmodernist philosophy and literature. Whereas some literary critics perceived *Mr Hexogen* as a postmodern parody of the trashy nationalist writing, others argued that his "poor writing style and unconventional imagery should not be mistaken for postmodernist experimentation" (Noordenbos 2016: 7). Curiously, the debate about the novel has gone beyond literary circles – the book was also discussed by politicians. Criticised by representatives of the more liberal wing, such as Boris

Nemtsov and Alexander Nevzorov, it was praised by others, including the leader of the Communist Party of the Russian Federation, Gennady Zyuganov.

Set in Moscow in 1999, *Mr Hexogen* is a surreal political thriller about the conspiracy set up by Russian secret services aiming at removing the ruling elites of the Russian Federation. The plot revolves around mysterious bombing attacks on apartment buildings in Buynaksk, Moscow, and Volgodonsk, something that actually happened in Russia, in 1999. Since Chechen fighters were accused of the attacks, they served as a direct pretext for the Second Chechen War. Shortly after these events, there appeared speculations that the explosions were indeed caused by hexogen bombs planted by the FSB agents. These speculations were confirmed by Boris Berezovsky, who, in exile, produced[26] the film *The Assassination of Russia* (2002), directed by Jean-Charles Deniau and Charles Gazelle, and based on the book *Blowing Up Russia: Terror from Within* (2002) by Alexander Litvinenko and Yuri Felshtinsky. Right after its premiere, the film was banned in the Russian Federation.

In his novel, leaning on the real political events, Prokhanov describes behind-the-scenes power games between the two camps: the KGB (state intelligence) led by Beloseltsev, the dedicated Stalinist and the author's supposed alter-ego, who wants to replace the current president nicknamed Idol with Chosen One, and the GRU (military intelligence) that wants to prevent this change. As it turns out, contrary to what the plot's mastermind wants, the KGB, in general, is quite liberal in its approach and aims to stabilise Russia's political and economic situation by establishing good relations with the West. At the same time, the GRU strives for Russia to be an independent and powerful empire. It is the GRU's opinion that only through their plan can the Russian state save the collapsing world.

According to Anastasia Mitrofanova, a researcher at the Federal Centre of Theoretical and Applied Sociology of the Russian Academy of Sciences, the conflict between KGB and GRU depicted in *Mr Hexogen* is, indeed, a symbolic image of the struggle between good and evil. While Beloseltsev believes that the conspiracy he participates in is an "ordinary" plot aimed at restoring the Soviet Union, it

---

[26] Whether Boris Berezovsky actually produced the film is still unclear. There are allegations that he only bought the rights for screening the Russian version.

The Antichrist in Post-Soviet Russia: Transformations of an Ideomyth 179

turns out that his adherents are "agents of Satan planning the unification of humankind under the power of the Antichrist" (Mitrofanova 2005: 92-93). The GRU, in turn, is portrayed as a group of people who want to prevent Russia from giving in to the liberal West and strive to restore Russian superiority as the spiritual capital of the Christian world.

As the story in *Mr Hexogen* unfolds, there is a series of explosions in apartment blocks in Moscow and other Russian cities, thanks to which the KGB wins the power struggle, and secures their preferred man in the presidential seat. However, their triumph is not secure. In the final scene, when Chosen One, now the president of the Russian Federation, flies with Beloseltsev and other KGB officers to Sochi, he suddenly, and mysteriously, disappears from the cockpit, and turns into a transparent rainbow, "into the blueness, into a void" (Prokhanov 2002: 474). What happened? Was it the result of the conspiracy controlled by the GRU, or maybe the GRU controlled the conspiracy of the KGB? We will never know. As Andrew Baruch Wachtel (2006: 117), a researcher at the University of California, argues, the Prokhanov's "Chinese box of conspiracies" remains unopened.

For many readers and critics, *Mr Hexogen*, which alludes to the real events, is the roman a clef. It not only is highly topical, but, as Marsh suggests (2010: 162), also contains "biting satires of many of Russia's leading politicians of the past decade". While Idol can be easily deciphered as Boris Yeltsin, who at the end of his political career was not capable of performing the presidential duties, Zaretskiy, the incredibly rich and influential oligarch, represents Berezovsky. Chosen One, in turn, is often equated with Putin, who became the president of the Russian Federation in 1999, believed by religious radicals to be the year of the Antichrist's arrival. However, Chosen One does not represent the Antichrist. Instead, he is supposed to be the redeemer, who will save Orthodox Russia. As such, he is portrayed in opposition to the protégé of Mayor Luzhkov, a devilish and beautiful man of Jewish origin, whose presidency would mean turning Russia into a "New Khazaria" (Aptekman 2006). After taking advantage of Luzhkov in overthrowing Idol and positioning Chosen One as the president, the mission of making Russia a Jewish state and colony of Israel is thwarted.

Luzhkov's protégé, portrayed in the novel as a "dazzling black-haired beauty, dressed in crimson clothes and the diamond-encrusted crown with horns" (Prokhanov 2002: 94), can, indeed, be identified as the Antichrist. He represents the demonic anti-Russian Jewish conspiracy, the goal of which is to turn Moscow into the centre of the Semitic world. As with other authors who believe in the anti-Russian Judeo-Masonic plot, in *Mr Hexogen*, Prokhanov blends conspiratorial narratives, apocalyptic motifs, and utopian imagery. Moreover, he depicts Moscow under Idol's rule as an apocalyptic city penetrated by evil forces. Like in the historiosophy of the Old Believers, the city, which once was supposed to be the Third Rome and the Katechon where the Antichrist's arrival will happen, becomes the centre of the apocalyptic drama. Interestingly, Prokhanov's Moscow in the late 1990s and early 2000s, in many regards, resembles the Moscow ruled by numerous devious devils in Mikhail Bulgakov's classic novel *Master and Margarita* (1966).

What is more, in *Mr Hexogen*, Prokhanov refers to the popular conspiracy theory about the Judeo-Mason plot aimed at destroying Russia. Apparently inspired by the *Protocols of the Elders of Zion*, Prokhanov attempts to expose the hidden ties and secret links that allegedly hinder Russia's efforts to becoming the strong Orthodox empire. As Boris Noordenbos (2016) and Dariya Slesaryeva (2013) suggest, *Mr Hexogen* is an example of a "conspiratorial novel", which is simultaneously modern and postmodern. Whereas, on the one hand, it leans on the "grand style" in literature, on the other hand, it features many genres, including the fairy tale, dystopia, as well as the Gothic and detective novel. Even though Prokhanov creates a world "in which the Church of St. Basil changes its place on Red Square every night (...); in which a dead Lenin guards the Kremlin against the underground beast that disguises itself as the Moscow metro system; (...); and in which Boris Nemtsov is transformed into a dog and Putin becomes a rainbow" (Aptekman 2006: 672), these amusing literary images are richly seasoned with the extreme anti-Westernism, zealous antisemitism, and the nostalgia for the Soviet Union. Thus, many critics and readers maintain that *Mr Hexogen* is, in fact, a "reactionary, antiliberal, and antisemitic political pamphlet" (Livers 2010: 486).

Apocalyptic motifs, including the Antichrist's arrival, often appear in post-Soviet Russian fiction. The majority of authors I discuss in this chapter, depict the Antichrist as an individual, whose life mirrors Christ's life. Whether he is a seemingly ordinary man (Alekseyev), young artist and erotomaniac (Tumanov), outstanding scientist (Kashanskiy), serial killer (Lugovoy), perverse trickster (Krusanov) or anti-Russian conspirator (Prokhanov), the Antichrist in the post-Soviet Russian fiction is always involved in the battle between good and evil, which takes place simultaneously in two dimensions – at the level of the human soul and the metaphysical level. It should be noted that the Antichrist ideomyth appears particularly often in the books that can be classified as "new political" and "new imperial" novels, which not only depict the political reality in apocalyptic terms, but also tend to represent the nationalist worldview.

Although these works differ in terms of the author's publishing status, popularity, and the audience (both intended and real), the majority of them significantly transcend the traditional interpretative framework of an image of the Antichrist. By employing various literary strategies and situating this apocalyptic figure in new, often unexpected, contexts, the novels and short stories create their own Antichrist ideomyth. In them, the ideomyth not only is grounded in the traditional exegesis of the Scriptures, early-Christian patristic writings, and Nietzschean philosophy, but also it alludes the Russian traditions such as historiosophy of the Old Believers, the literature of the Silver Age, and Russian folklore. As well, many of these novels imitate other post-Soviet discourses that employ the Antichrist figure, including conspiracy theories and political concepts, the examples of which were discussed earlier. Drawing upon a rich tradition and tackling contemporary social and political issues, post-Soviet fiction adds new dimensions to the Antichrist ideomyth and makes it even more multidimensional and complex.

VI. Ultimate Fight: Orthodox Russia Against the Antichrist

First, the Lamb of God opens seven seals securing the scroll "with writing on both sides". The opening of each subsequent seal is accompanied by catastrophic events happening on Earth, including the arrival of the Four Horsemen of the Apocalypse. Portrayed as the plague, war, famine, and death, they personify all the ills afflicting humanity in the Endtime. When the last, seventh seal, is opened, the roar of seven trumpets is heard, and the mundane world is plunged into chaos and destruction: there are numerous earthquakes, the sun turns black, the stars fall to Earth, and the sea swells with blood. A Woman "clothed with a white robe, with the sun at her back, with the moon under her feet, and on her head, a crown of twelve stars" gives birth to a baby boy, who is raised to God and His throne. When the Dragon, symbolising Satan, attempts to devour the child, he is defeated by Archangel Michael. Before being thrown into the abyss, the Dragon passes power to the Beast, which in the subsequent centuries has been recognised as the Antichrist. The Beast-Antichrist, with the help of the second beast, named 666 and described as a false prophet, gains power over humanity. However, after the three and a half years of their rule, Christ appears on a white horse and defeats both beasts, throwing them to hell. The defeat of the Antichrist is followed by the Last Judgment and the rise of New Jerusalem, in which the Parousia and the redemption of humanity take place (Rev 1-22).

This is the vision of the end of the world as articulated in the Book of Revelation, which to this day remains the most canonical apocalyptic narrative. Written in the 1st century by a mysterious St. John[27] and packed with metaphorical, sometimes incomprehensible, images, the last book of the Bible not only is considered a reaction to persecutions of early Christians in the Roman Empire, but also is viewed as the basis of the majority of subsequent prophecies and speculations about how the world will end (Barr 2006).

---

[27] The Book of Revelation is attributed to John the Apostle. However, due to significant differences detected in writing styles, many scholars insist that the Gospel and the Apocalypse were written by two different authors (Barr 2003).

What is more, the Book of Revelation serves as the foundation for what Nikolai Berdyaev, the Russian philosopher of the Silver Age, calls the "eschatological myth". As he argues in his book *The Russian Idea* (1948), even though there is no specific nationality assigned to apocalyptic writings, the "eschatological myth" has for centuries inspired Russian intellectual and social life. In times of chaos and distress, Russian intelligentsia, as well as Russian folk culture, have turned to apocalyptic discourses, which not only put a narrative onto the inconceivable, but also gave hope that after the end of the world they knew, a new better world would be established. This "eschatological orientation" of Russian culture meant that the present had been perceived rather as a time of waiting for utopia, whether religious or political (Epstein 1994, Sadowski et al. 2014). After all, as St. John envisioned it, after the doom and catastrophe, there comes New Jerusalem where humanity will be redeemed and ruled by Christ.

Based on the Book of Revelation and other early-apocalyptic narratives, in the subsequent centuries, the Antichrist was portrayed as a false Messiah, whose life will mirror that of Christ. It has been believed that the Antichrist will Christ's evil twin, who will reveal his true nature as the Endtime tyrant only after seizing power over humanity. He will establish his Kingdom, based on total subordination, where good will not differ from evil, people will not differ from each other, and everyone will receive the seal of the Antichrist on their foreheads and right hands. Similar scenarios of the end can be found in numerous post-Soviet Russian discourses. Interestingly, they are not limited to literary images, but also appear in conspiracy theories and political concepts, especially in the writings of authors associated with religious and conservative milieus, such as Julia Voznesenskaya, Anatoliy Zabolotnikov, Oleg Platonov, and Mikhail Nazarov. What connects these discourses is the role assigned to Russia – whether it is portrayed as the place where the Antichrist will be born, or the Katechon, where he will ultimately be defeated, Russia always plays a crucial role in the apocalyptic drama. As this study moves forward, not only is it important to focus on how the Antichrist ideomyth is constructed in contemporary Russian discourses, namely, religious, political, and literary texts, but also how various post-Soviet Russian authors describe the Apocalypse drama.

VI.1 The Role of Russia in the Endtime Drama: The Katechon or Not?

> Even now Russia performs the function of the Katechon. For this reason, Russian statehood is potentially mystical and sacred regardless of who is the head of it, and the Russian nation remains a God-bearer regardless of its today's somewhat miserable position
> (Dugin 2009b).

The biblical concept of the Katechon, invoked by Alexander Dugin in the epigraph above, derives from the Greek word κατέχω that can be translated as "that which withholds" and "the one that restrains". It appears in the Scriptures, in the Second Epistle of St. Paul to the Thessalonians, in which the apostle warns the early Christian community that "the mystery of lawlessness is already at work" and the one "who now restrains it will do so until he is out of the way" (2 Thess 2: 7). As St. Paul insists, when the one that withholds is removed, lawlessness will prevail. The Son of Perdition, who, as the interpretations suggest, will be identified as the Antichrist, will arrive and seize power. As long as the Katechon exists, the Antichrist's arrival, followed by the Apocalypse drama, will be hindered.

Even though St. Paul does not explicitly name the Katechon, in the Christian tradition, "that which withholds" has been for centuries interpreted as the eschatological state, the existence of which restrains the advent of the Antichrist. This interpretation has its roots in the writings of the Church Fathers, including Tertullian and St. Jan Chrysostom. While Tertullian identified the Katechon as the Roman Empire, St. Jan Chrysostom argued that the Katechon is linked to the power of the Emperor, whose authority restrains Anomia, understood as socio-political chaos equated with the Antichrist and the lawlessness that comes with him. Over the years, following this tradition, the notion of the Katechon has appeared primarily in the writings of conservative thinkers and has been interpreted as the "apocalyptic space of politics". The Katechon/Antichrist relationship, in turn, has been viewed as the "driving force within history and politics, continually threatening to end them" (Fornari 2010).

Carl Schmitt, the controversial German lawyer, thinker, and the supporter of the Third Reich, contributed to the development of the Katechon concept in politics. In his view of the political theology, presented in his essays "Political Theology" (1922) and "The Concept of the Political" (1932), not only did he suggest that politics is based on the friend/enemy dichotomy, but he also transferred the religious notion of the Katechon to the political philosophy. In the subsequent years, his writings have inspired numerous political and cultural theorists, representing different worldviews: from conservatives (Leo Strauss, Eric Voegelin) and leftists (Giorgio Agamben, Walter Benjamin, Jacques Derrida, and Slavoj Žižek) to liberals (Raymond Aaron, Norberto Bobbio). What is more, after the dissolution of the Soviet Union, Schmitt's political views became popular in the Russian Federation, especially within conservative and religious circles. Among the followers of his ideas are, for instance, Alexander Filippov, who translated Schmitt's works to Russian in the early 1990s and Alexander Dugin, who not only introduced Schmitt's concept of the Katechon in his article "The Katechon and Revolution" (1997), but also, on many occasions, describes himself as a follower of the Schmittean political theology (Akopov 2016).

The political theology Schmitt put forth was based on the approval of strong state power in the Hobbesian sense. Referring to the concept of a Leviathan[28], Schmitt (1938) insisted that the strong empire is the only political entity capable of opposing the chaos of Anomos, which he equated both with the movements denying the existence of the state, such as anarchism and Communism, and the reign of the Antichrist. Schmitt perceived democracy as the expression of secularism and atheism, based on the rejection of the true Christian faith and the role of the Church as a moral guardian for the nation. In his view, unlike the strong empire, democracies are not capable of resisting the apocalyptic chaos and participating in international relations on equal footing with other countries.

---

[28] Leviathan refers not only to the multifaceted biblical sea monster which, by the principle of metaphor, can be associated with the domain of evil (Frye and Macpherson 2004), but it is also the semantic sign of a state-Leviathan, which – just like myth – over the centuries has undergone various metamorphoses and transformations. For instance, according to the Jewish tradition, a Leviathan symbolised a power hostile towards Jews, whether it be the Babylonian, Assyrian or Egyptian empires. For the early Christians, it was the Roman Empire that was viewed as the devilish Leviathan, cruelly persecuting people of true faith. Interestingly, whereas in the Western Christian tradition the image of state-Leviathan lost its demonic meaning around the 16th century, in Orthodox Russia it was the other way around. After the *Raskol*, the Old Believers claimed that the Holy Rus', betrayed by the Tsar and the Patriarch, had turned into the Kingdom of the Antichrist. To avoid his evil power, they turned away from the state, which, for them, was embodied by the omnipotent Leviathan that controls people through money, passports, and population censuses (Crummey 1970).

As Schmitt argued, facing the constant danger of the approaching Apocalypse, people need stability, order, and security, which may be provided only by the stable Christian state, the Katechon being the final emanation. This view was based on his criticism of the Weimar Republic, which he perceived as a compromised and corrupt country that had embezzled its values. Even though, as he saw it, the pragmatic claims about parliamentary democracy might be correct, democracy turned out to be aimed at manipulating the masses through media and strengthening inequalities. Therefore, as Schmitt suggested, the only way to create a new and better reality is the "conservative revolution" that will result in the rule of a strong all-powerful sovereign, whose decisions would be above the law.

According to Schmitt (1985), there are no realms of pure politics and pure theology, and political concepts are, in fact, secularised translations of theological ones. Therefore, as he insisted, the concept of the Katechon, even though it comes from the Bible, should be applied to the political realm. Therefore, he described the Katechon as a "historical power to restrain the appearance of the Antichrist and the end of the present aeon" (Schmitt 1950: 59-60). For Schmitt, the Katechon was not only the intellectualisation of the Christian Empire, but also the bridge between history and eschatology (Hell 2009). Schmitt, as well as his life-long intellectual adversary, Jacob Taubes[29], viewed history not so much as constant progress, but, rather, as a postponed sentence. Hence, the existence of the Katechon meant the possibility of "buying time". Both Schmitt and Taubes believed that an effort at putting off the arrival of the Antichrist should last as long as possible so that non-believers could convert to Christianity and join the community of the redeemed.

The Katechon, Schmitt explained, was an old myth of an empire that – translated, renewed, and reinterpreted – found its realisation in the Third Reich. He perceived Hitler as an entity sent by God to perform miracles, and "the miracle was the recovery of a this-world transcendence to sovereignty and thus the human realm of the political" (Schmitt 1950: xxx). As well, Schmitt emphasised the unique role of Germany in the development of world history. Since the condition restraining the arrival of Antichrist was the very existence of the Roman Empire, after its fall,

---

[29] Jacub Taubes (1923-1987) was a philosopher, religion sociologist, and Jewish studies expert. In his works, he focused on subjects of religion, eschatology, and messianism.

he foresaw that the Katechon's mission had to be continued – first by Byzantium, and, after the crowning of Charlemagne as the Emperor of the Romans, by the Holy Roman Empire. The notion that Charlemagne's Empire might be both a political and eschatological continuity of Rome derives from the historiosophic concept of *translatio imperii*, discussed by Jacques le Goff in his book *La Civilisation de l'Occident Medieval* published in 1964.[30] Based on Daniel's prophecy about the four kingdoms following one another (Dan 2: 34-44), the idea of *translatio imperii* assumes the linear succession of the status of *imperium* (empire) understood as the supreme power embedded in the ruler: the emperor. In other words, having no established spatial or temporal characteristics, the status of the Katechon could have been inherited by any Christian state (Engström 2014).

Following this logic, numerous post-Soviet Russian discourses also appeal to the idea of *translatio imperii*. It shows how all this is expected to come about, and the belief the only legitimate successor of the Christian Empire is Moscow. This conviction has its roots in the messianic concept of Moscow the Third Rome, put forth in the 16th century by the monk Philotheus of Pskov. In his letter to the Grand Prince of Moscow, Vasily III Ivanovich, he argued that the First Rome (the Roman Empire) fell due to heresy and the Second Rome (Constantinople) declined due to a betrayal of faith. As a result, Russia had remained the only genuinely Christian (Orthodox) Empire capable of protecting the world from the Antichrist and his power (see more in 1.1.). Arguing that Moscow is the Third Rome, is the same as believing that Russia is already the full-fledged Katechon. Indeed, post-Soviet Russian authors, including Metropolitan Ioann Snychev, Alexander Dugin, and Mikhail Nazarov, often insist that Russia is the only heir to the Byzantine Empire and the spiritual and ecclesiastic continuation to Jerusalem.

What is more, discourses portraying Russia as the Katechon lean on a specific cliff-hanger: hovering between the former glory and the bright future, they abolish the separation between the "divine" history of the Holy Rus' and the history of the Russian Federation as the "worldly power". It follows from what literary critic Mikhail Epstein (1995) calls the "eschatological orientation" of the Russian culture, in which the present is often seen as the time of transition and waiting for the

---

[30] The English translation of *The Medieval Civilization* was published in 1988.

realisation of another, better world. According to Epstein, the present in Russian culture is often perceived as a point between the former splendour and the bright future, in which Russia will regain empire status with world importance. This, and the fight with the Antichrist, are viewed not as some distant and vogue image, but as the imminent historical possibility. It should be emphasised that in such a perspective, the Apocalypse does not necessarily have to be associated with doom and catastrophe. Along with the millenarian tradition, it can be seen as the end of the world as we know it, resulting in the emergence of the Kingdom of God on Earth, which will last for at least a thousand years. Thus, Apocalypse can indicate the doomsday and catastrophe, as well as the beginning of a new utopia, both religious and political (Sadowski et al. 2014).

According to post-Soviet conservatism and right-wing intellectual milieu expert Marie Engström (2014: 362), the katechonic rhetoric can be found in Putin's speeches, including the Valdai speech in 2013 and the Crimea speech in 2014. Its elements are also present in the new Concept of Foreign Policy of the Russian Federation, announced in 2013. In these texts, Russia is portrayed as "an important military, economic, and ideological pole" and a unique civilisation that restrains the increasing chaos of the contemporary world. While in the Schmittean understanding the Katechon is the state that "holds the power of chaos beyond the borders of the world by its inner order", in the Russian context, the one that withholds is to be a "military force that resists a metaphysical enemy", which "takes different shapes in different historical periods: the Tatars, the Turks, freemasons, Napoleon, Hitler, and nowadays American agents, Ukrainian fascists, and the Kiev junta", as Engström argues (2014: 364).

Engström insists that the ambition of many right-wing intellectuals is to make the concept of the Katechon the basis for Russia's new state ideology, as well as foreign and security policy. Their idea of creating new empire mythology, based on this concept, that would mobilise both Russian state structures and citizens, is connected with the post-Soviet "conservative turn", commonly associated with Putin rising to power. Its roots, however, reach much deeper in Russian history. The discourses referring to the "golden past" and traditional values, which swarmed Russia after the fall of the Soviet Union, were already present in nationalist milieus during the Soviet era, in the late 1970s and 1980s.

Post-Soviet Russian conservative discourses that employ the idea of the Katechon not only hark back to Schmitt's political theology and the messianic idea of Moscow the Third Rome, but they are also deeply immersed in 19th-century Russian conservatism. One of its recognisable representatives was Konstantin Leontiev (1831-1891), a philosopher and active supporter of imperial monarchism. In his writings, similar to that of Nikolay Danilevsky and Fyodor Dostoyevsky, Leontiev sharply criticised Western civilisation and its values, such as democracy, liberalism, materialism, and technological development. Equating the West with the Anomos and the actions of the Antichrist, he believed that only the Byzantine civilisation, based on Christian values, has the right to survive. He developed a specific Orthodox political theology based on the Byzantine idea of the "symphony of powers", assuming that sacral and secular powers are complementary to each other and should never be separated. Leontiev argued that the union between Orthodoxy and Tsardom is, in fact, "the best form of keeping the peoples from the path of unbelief, in order to delay the advent of the last time" (as quoted by Engström, 2014: 367). This approach coincides with Schmitt's claim that the Katechon is a fusion of the "sacerdotium" (sacral power) and an empire (strong secular power).

In post-Soviet Russian conservative discourses, the idea of the Katechon is often accompanied by the concept of "symphony of powers". For instance, Nazarov and Dugin argue that Russia can fulfil its eschatological mission of being the shield protecting the world from the Antichrist's arrival only as a strong Orthodox empire, in which the power of the Orthodox Patriarch is harmonised with the power of the Orthodox Tsar. Here, the autocratic Tsar is viewed not so much as the authoritarian ruler and a bearer of temporary power, but as a spiritual and eschatological pillar of all of Christianity.

The tradition of glorifying the autocratic Tsar is, indeed, deeply rooted in Russian culture. It has its roots not only in the medieval sacralisation of power, but also in the Byzantine idea of the "last (Orthodox) Tsar", who will cede his kingdom to God, and the earthly power will be taken over by the Antichrist (de Lazari 1995). The concept of complementary sacral and secular authorities is present also in official Russian Orthodox Church rhetoric. Enthroned in 2009, the Patriarch of Moscow and all Russia Kirill often refers to the idea of "symphony of powers", which he understands as a lack of interference between the Church and secular authorities. In his view, whereas the role of the Russian Orthodox Church is the spiritual education of the human soul, the state should cooperate with the Church and protect Russian people from enemies (Strelchik and Kirill 2009).

The conviction that Russia will be able to accomplish its mission of the Katechon only as an autocratic state ruled by the Orthodox Tsar is especially popular among religious and nationalist circles. Supported by right-wing media, such as Radio Radonezh and the Orthodox news agency Russian National Line, the idea of restoring Orthodox monarchy in Russia is an example of the "Russian revisionism", based on the conviction that Russia is "doomed" to be the powerful empire ruled by the autocratic Tsar (Trenin 2002:212). According to Russian studies specialist Mikhail Suslov (2016a), even though the Orthodox monarchism is of minor political importance in today's Russia, it "possesses great potential for growth and emergence from the 'grey zone' of political marginality". As with many possibilities, being a response to the disillusion with liberal democracy and imperfections of the current regime, it can quickly move from the fringes of political debate to the mainstream.

The conviction that Russia can serve as the Katechon only as the Orthodox empire ruled by the Tsar is present also in the post-Soviet fiction. For instance, it is expressed by Aleksey Sukharenko, an author of the unfinished apocalyptic trilogy of novels *The Mystery of the Course* (2012), *The Antichrist and the Russian Tsar* (2013), and *The God's Fool: The Doomsday*. Set in the near future in Moscow and London, Sukharenko's novels depict the world on the verge of the Apocalypse. As it turns out, the Antichrist is not an abstract figure of a false Messiah, but an individual of flesh and blood: he is Harold Davis Windsor, the son of Prince Charles and a luxury companion lady, and the third grandson of Queen Elisabeth. However, his spiritual father is Satan, to whom Harold swears absolute loyalty in return for the help in seizing power over the world.

The evil plans of Harold-Antichrist can only be thwarted by Yurodivy, the incarnation of an attorney named Alexander Sobolev. Being a young boy, Sobolev rejected Satan's offer to become the Antichrist, and, for punishment, was cursed and turned into a disabled "God's fool", who could transform his body into other people and animals. The crippled body of Yurodivy has remained his main point of reference, and, with time, changing into other people, has become more and more painful for him. Despite his deteriorating physical conditions, Alexander tries to stop Harold from gaining power over the world. When Russia decides in a referendum that the monarchy should be restored and the ruler of Russia will be the Orthodox Tsar, Sobolev takes the side of Mikhail Georgevich Romanov, who, as the rightful successor of the Romanovs, represents the continuity of power. Together, they do everything to prevent Harold Windsor from sitting on the Russian throne, as it would mean the catastrophe and the victory of evil.

Interestingly, Sukharenko's trilogy ends with the second novel, right before the climax. The readers do not learn whether Russia has fulfilled its eschatological mission of the Katechon, and successfully opposed the powers of evil, nor what the result of the ultimate fight between the Antichrist and the Orthodox Tsar is. In the afterword, Sukharenko explains why he did not publish the third novel: the two novels carry a persuasive power, and many people considered the works to be true prophecy. To avoid the responsibility of depicting the real Apocalypse, the author leaves the readers in a situation similar to where the Scriptures leave each doubtful Christian: not knowing anything. Consequently, the ultimate fight between good and evil remains in the sphere of imagination, which makes it even more suggestive.

Author Julia Voznesenskaya, who is also a journalist and poet, also depicts Russia as the Orthodox monarchy facing the same challenges: In the Soviet era, Voznesenskaya was active in Leningrad's underground arts community and repeatedly convicted of anti-Soviet activities. In 1980, she fled to Germany, where for many years she worked for Radio Liberty. In 2003, she was named "Best Author of the Year" in the Orthodox Book of Russia competition. Although her books are deeply embedded in the Orthodox Christian tradition and filled with post-apocalyptic and dystopian motifs, Voznesenskaya managed to reach out to a broad readership of both religious people and non-believers. Her works have been translated into many languages, including English and Polish, and, subsequently, she is well known out of Russia.

In her duology *The Journey of Kassandra or Adventures with Pasta* (2003) and *Lancelot's Pilgrimage* (2004), Voznesenskaya describes a world devastated by the Catastrophe and World War III. Much of the Western world is under water, but the advanced technology now allows people to live in specially adapted ships. Dressed in identical uniforms and eating artificial "energens", they live simultaneously in the reality of the so-called Planet and the "Reality", to which they connect through their laptops named "personniks". Each planet citizen has a personal code on their hands, and this is how they made everyday purchases. However, the codes have one more function most of the people are not aware of: they track and record everything the people do. Those who do not have a personal code live outside the society.

It is interesting to note that the individual codes in Voznesenskaya's novels are a reinterpretation of the mark of the Beast as foretold by St. John in the Book of Revelation. As well, they evoke a more contemporary phenomenon that occurred in the Russian Federation: the introduction of the INN (tax identification numbers), which, at the beginning of the 2000s, triggered a real apocalyptic panic among the most radical circles of the Russian Orthodox Church. Literary critic Mariya Akhmetova (2010) suggests that by modelling personal codes on the INN, Voznesenskaya draws parallels between the contemporary world and the totalitarian state ruled by the Antichrist anticipated in the Scriptures.

Voznesenskaya's world is ruled by the World Government with the Messiah at the head. The only state that did not recognise the Antichrist as the world ruler is Orthodox Russia, where, contrary to the rest of the world, the traditional way of life has prevailed. Not only is the monarchy restored, but also there is no euthanasia nor access to the "Reality". Moreover, Russian people are profoundly religious and live in large and loving families. Also, Orthodoxy has somehow survived outside of Russia. There are a few small Orthodox communities that remain scattered around the European mountains. Separated from the world which they consider to be permeated with the anti-Christian spirit, and protected from the eyes of the Messiah, these communities resemble those established by the Old Believers in the outskirts of the Russian Empire after the *Raskol* in the 17th century. Kassandra Sakkos, the protagonist of the first part of Voznesenskaya's duology, undergoes a spiritual transformation and joins one of the Orthodox communities, where she finds shelter during the Apocalypse.

According to post-Soviet conservative and religious authors, the only way to defeat the Antichrist is to be faithful to Orthodoxy. Thus, the greatest threat to the fulfilment of Russia's eschatological mission is the breaking of the "symphony of powers" and gradual apostasy. With the dissolution between the Church and the State, along with the mounting spiritual power of the Antichrist and people falling into heresy and blasphemy, these writers often associate such breakdowns with what had happened in the West after the East-West Schism in the 11th century. Dugin and Metropolitan Ioann argue that Russia has also entered the path of gradual moral decline, which has deepened with each tragic historical event, including the *Raskol*, reforms introduced by Peter the Great, and, above all, the Bolshevik Revolution. That last event was particularly tragic, as it was the Bolshevik coup that led to the collapse of the Russian Empire and the rise of the anti-Christian Soviet Union. According to both authors, the dissolution of the USSR did not end the drama of Russia. On the contrary, Russia's attrition to the West contributed to an even more profound crisis of religiosity, moral corruption, and departure from Orthodoxy.

Interestingly, Mikhail Nazarov insists that since the Antichrist did not appear to the mundane world after the Bolsheviks destroyed the Russian Orthodox monarchy, there is still hope that Orthodox Russia will resurrect itself and serve its role of the Katechon. In his book *The Mystery of Russia*, Nazarov argues:

> The withholding of Orthodox statehood collapsed, bringing the last days, but the coming of the Antichrist has not yet occurred. So, even afterwards, there was something that has been restraining him, and most likely, it is connected with Russia; in the world, there have not appeared any other Restraint ever since. Of course, Divine powers might defend the world from the coming of the Antichrist, however, only through the worldly carriers with such a purpose; otherwise, such withholding would be nothing (Nazarov 1999).

Nazarov is convinced that even after the gradual departure from Orthodoxy, Russia is still morally healthier than the West. Thus, God postpones the end of the world and gives Russians a chance to understand how important the role of Orthodox Russia is, atone for their sins through continuous suffering, and, finally, rise against the "mystery of lawlessness".

Less optimistic attitudes towards Russia can be found in a novel *The Child: The Apocalypse by Ivan the Antichrist (2012)* by Anatoliy Zabolotnikov, written as an apocryphal biblical parable set in early post-Soviet Russia. The novel tells the story of Ivan, better known as The Child, born in the early 1990s, in Moscow,

The Antichrist in Post-Soviet Russia: Transformations of an Ideomyth 195

whose mother is reportedly Jewish, or she has a Jewish background. In time, Ivan turns out to be the Antichrist. Zabolotnikov evokes not only the early-Christian exegesis of the Book of Revelation and end-of-the-world narratives so characteristic of Russian culture, but also blends various mythological motifs with real historical events. The novel, subsequently, is riddled with ant-Semitic overtones, with suggestions the Antichrist's mother is Jewish, that Jews were responsible for the atheist Communist state, then responsible for the spiritless capitalism, all leading to Russia's destruction. In this regard, *The Child* resembles Prokhanov's *Mr Hexogen.*

In Zabolotnikov's novel, a nun named Svetlana, together with a nurse, Stalina, decide to take care of The Child when his mother dies in childbirth. Svetlana then has a vision in which Russia is the place of the coming of the Antichrist. Svetlana sees Russia as a modern counterpart of the ancient Rome, where the Antichrist first arrived in the flesh as Nero at the beginning of the Christian. In her vision, all evil in the world is caused by Jews, who rejected Christ as the true Messiah and, thus, became the collective Antichrist. After all, as she argues, St. Paul warned in his Letters to the Thessalonians that those who reject God and Christ are Satan's emissaries. The accusation that all evil comes from the Jews is shared by Stalina, who claims that the Soviet Union, established by people of Jewish origins, was the Kingdom of the Antichrist. Though she acknowledges that Stalin saved Russia during World War II, his former followers betrayed him, called him the Antichrist, and blamed him for the Soviet state's failures. She insists that the same people introduced Gorbachev's Perestroika and, of course, she deems Gorbachev to be the real Antichrist because of the birthmark on his forehead. Her name, surely no accident, and views appear to illuminate the Stalinist nostalgia, and, at the same time, a critique of the Soviet Union, viewed as a traitor to true Stalinism.

In his work, Zabolotnikov criticises both the atheistic Soviet Union and what Russia became after the dissolution of the USSR. Above all, he condemns greed, capitalism, moral corruption, as well as the uncritical submission to Western influences. He portrays Yeltsin's Russia as a place ruled by corrupt politicians, where, as a result of capitalist and Western influences, people abandoned Orthodoxy, in consequence of which the state plunged into moral decay, and good was replaced with evil. As he sees it, what was once the Third Rome gradually became a centre of anti-Christian spirit. In other words, Zabolotnikov argues that Russia, breaking with its Orthodox tradition, betrayed its mission of being the Katechon and transformed into the Kingdom of the Antichrist. Zabolotnikov invokes the Old Believers' historiosophy: by betraying true Christianity, Russia became an evil habitat; the author then goes on to refer to Seraphim of Sarov, who insisted the Antichrist would be a Jew born in Russia. According to this Russian saint, canonised by the Russian Orthodox Church in 2015, the Antichrist's arrival in the world would be preceded by a protracted war accompanied by a terrible revolution. Subsequently, Orthodoxy would lose its purity, rivers of blood would flood Russia, and the great disaster will prevail on Earth.

As mentioned, Russia is believed to have the idiosyncratic role to play during the Apocalypse. It is portrayed either as the Katechon that restrains the arrival of the Antichrist and the place where he will be defeated or as the venue where the Antichrist will be born. In both cases, Russia is portrayed as the eschatological empire and a unique civilisation harassed by demonic powers, on both external and internal levels. Russian history is full of forewarnings of an apocalyptic catastrophe and gains a universal, cosmic significance. The Russians, in turn, are believed to have the seal of the Third Rome in their souls and are viewed as the apocalyptic nation. In addition, Russia is seen in two dimensions: as the political entity, the Russian Federation, and, at the same time, the spiritual Kingdom of the Holy Rus', where the Antichrist will be defeated, and humanity will be redeemed. This daunting and important role in what is deemed Russia's remaining days ripples through these post-Soviet Russian works. The eschatological character of many Russian messianic discourses is threaded also through the fiction, all based on a belief that the Russian nation has been chosen to accomplish a special mission for the sake of all humanity.

VI.2. Apocalypse Now!

According to the apocalyptic vision put forth by Boris Molchanov, the Antichrist's arrival will mark the start of the end of the world. Alluding to the early-Christian patristic writings and exegesis of the Book of Revelation, Molchanov argued that the Antichrist's life would mirror that of Christ. Molchanov portrayed the Antichrist as a clever, decisive, and ecumenical ruler, who, with the help of false miracles, will solve all crises and misfortunes haunting humanity. Only after gaining total power, he will reveal his true nature as the merciful tyrant, who hates Christianity. It will be followed by the end of the world, as described in the Book of Revelation.

The more radical post-Soviet Russian authors argue that the Antichrist is already in the world, yet not revealed. For this reason, the Apocalypse and the end of the world are only a matter of time. Authors such as Metropolitan Ioann Snychev, Mikhail Nazarov, and Oleg Platonov insist that Russia will soon take part in the final battle against the forces of evil which will decide the fate of the world. Perhaps the best representation of all this is Platonov's *The Battle for Russia*, released in 2010 by the Algoritm publishing house, which, as its website advertises, specialises in books tackling acute and relevant socio-political and historical issues. Platonov, who is the director of the conservative Institute of History of Russian Civilisation, a famous antisemite and a pusher of Metropolitan Ioann's preachings, shares a vision of Russian history as a constant struggle with anti-Christian forces in the West. As he argues in his book:

> What has been happening before our eyes over the past quarter of a century cannot be called anything else like the Battle for Russia. Against our Fatherland, against Great Russia, all the evil forces have turned the world against us, all external and internal enemies, because our country is the last obstacle on the West's path to world domination. In the battle for Russia, should participate all Russian patriots, all Russian citizens, who are aware of themselves as part of it, and its spiritual values that are their own values (Platonov 2010: 5).

According to Platonov, the only guarantee of Russia's victory over the Antichrist is Russian people uniting against the forces of evil, represented by liberalism, democracy, technological progress, and globalisation. In his view, Russia has a chance to defeat hostile forces only as a conservative monarchy, faithful to its spiritual and metaphysical ideas, based on Orthodoxy. In other words, Platonov portrays Russia as a separate civilisation that has different metaphysical foundations and is the last bastion of Christianity in the world dominated by the morally degenerate West.

The visions of the Apocalypse present in post-Soviet fiction are no different than political conceptions offered by Platonov and other conservative and religious authors. Drawing on the same cultural codes and narrative traditions, writers such as Sukharenko, Voznesenskaya, and Zabolotnikov, describe the end of the world as the apocalyptic struggle between Christ and the Antichrist that is reflected on in the struggle between Russia and the Western hemisphere. In this context, the most political narrative is Sukharenko's unfinished trilogy, in which the eschatological and political conflict over who will become the Tsar of Orthodox Russia and the ruler of the world takes place between Harold Davis Windsor, the servant of Satan, and Mikhail Georgevich Romanov, the rightful descendant of the Romanovs, supported by Alexander Sobolev – Yurodivy.

Prince Harold, one of the protagonists of Sukharenko's novels can easily be recognised as the Antichrist. In one of the scenes, he gives an oath of allegiance to Satan in exchange for world power. He then becomes the head of the New Order, an international foundation established by the wealthiest and most influential people and organisations in the world, intending to eliminate wars, environmental disasters, and famine on the planet. Sukharenko describes the New Order, which invokes the concept of a global government as articulated in conspiracy theories about the New World Order, believed to rule the world behind the scenes. As with the alleged global government controlled by Judeo-Masons, the fictional organisation prepares the world for the Antichrist's arrival by promoting liberalism, democracy, globalisation, and ecumenism. When prince Harold becomes the leader of the foundation, he says:

> Now I am in charge of the "New Order", I am the Messiah, who came to you and revealed his divine mission – establishing the new, rightful world order on the planet Earth. All those who will interfere with the reign of justice in the world will be defeated by me (Sukharenko 2012: 35).

In his speech, Harold presents himself as the redeemer, whose role is to save humanity and introduce a new righteous order in the world. As with other such fictional characters, Harold has the makings of the long-established Antichrist figure, wrapped with the false Messiah element, and plays the Endtime tyrant role well known in the Christian tradition. Once he is crowned as the Head of One

Absolute Church and the God of all Nations in Solomon's rebuilt Temple in Jerusalem, he announces a cashless system, which will involve personal civil codes. In addition, all borders are eliminated, and Christianity is replaced with the Church of Absolute, the only religion allowed.

Sukharenko's unfinished work is a daring blend of various literary genres, including political thriller, science fiction, and romance. By intermingling numerous apocalyptic prophecies with battle scenes, and elements of family drama, Sukharenko creates a specific literary world, in which everything has a determined meaning, and each decision between good and evil has serious consequences. With this literary approach, Sukharenko's novels resemble parables that conventionally end with a moral. The author also richly refers to the Christian, and especially Orthodox, symbols.

An example of such symbols is Yurodivy, a character that evokes a specifically Russian tradition, *yurodstvo*, the foolishness in Christ. In the Russian tradition, so-called "holy fools" were the people who imitated Christ and resigned from earthly goods to dedicate their lives to God. Wandering across Russia, they often behaved in shocking and unconventional ways, challenging accepted norms. As well, they delivered prophecies and preached the imminent coming of the Kingdom of God (Wodziński 2000). Such a character includes Alexander Sobolev, who, after refusing to become the Antichrist, is cursed by Satan. Having the possibility to transform his body, he finds himself in the ambiguous position between two worlds: the tangible and the spiritual.

As stated, the duology consisting of the novels *The Journey of Kassandra or Adventures with Pasta* (2003) and *Lancelot's Pilgrimage* (2004), written by Julia Voznesenskaya, is also full of religious motifs. Both novels are set in the near future, in a world devastated by the Catastrophe and World War III, provoked by the Americans despite the peace-making efforts of Russia and its allies. After the war, the Western states are united into one state, named the Planet, and ruled by the World Government with the Messiah being the leader. As with Sakharenko's Harold, the incredibly beautiful and charismatic Messiah in Voznesenskaya's duology presents himself as the redeemer of humanity, but, in fact, strives for unlimited power over the world. The only state that opposes the Messiah's rules is Russia, ruled by the Orthodox Tsar and separated from the Planet with a wall.

Under the totalitarian World's Government, people have three survival strategies to choose from: they can play according to the rules imposed on them, confront the Antichrist, or flee to an Orthodox community hidden in the woods and await the Second Coming of Christ. Kassandra Sakkos, the protagonist in Voznesenskaya's first novel, chooses the third option, and undergoes a spiritual revival; as a result, she abandons her previous life, rids herself of the personal code, and lives in an Orthodox monastery. The disabled fisherman, Lars, the protagonist in *The Lancelot's Pilgrimage*, also experiences a spiritual transformation. When Lars loses his job, he decides to travel to Jerusalem to be healed by the Messiah. He is accompanied by a young woman, Jennifer, her donkey Patti, and doctor Vergelann, who refused to carry out euthanasia on one of his patients, and now has to flee persecution. All of them block their personal codes and set off on an adventurous and challenging route.

The world through which they travel to Jerusalem is immersed in decay and deterioration, all foreseen in the Book of Revelation. People are beleaguered with floods, droughts, plagues of locusts, and famine. Meanwhile, out of revenge, Russia attacks the Antichrist's rockets; then all electrical devices, except for special Tesla batteries, stop working. Along the way, as a result of various events, Lars decides to be baptised. Although he is initially sceptical of the new Orthodox faith, he becomes increasingly religious over time. When Lars reaches Jerusalem, he suddenly loses faith in the Planet and its ruler. Nevertheless, he decides to participate in a race, in which the winner will be healed by the Messiah. What no one realises is that the race is a way to remove disabled people from society: those who drop out become euthanised. The individual healings, in turn, are only false miracles that work only for a short time.

Lars wins the race and meets the Messiah at the top of the Tower of Babel. Waiting to be healed, he discovers the true nature of the world's leader:

– You are not the Messiah – said Lancelot. – The Messiah is another person, and He has already come into this world. You are the Antichrist, the murderer of people and the destroyer of the world. I refuse your healing and spit on you! (Voznesenskaya 2005: 623).

Lancelot, indeed, spits on the Messiah, who immediately ignites in blue flame. Black claws grow from his fingers, and his arms are suddenly covered with thick red hair. Furious, the Antichrist orders his minions to crucify Lars on one of the lanterns. Before they do, however, a thunder hits the Tower of Babel that begins to collapse. The Antichrist falls, and, as he is hit by the crucifix that dropped from the wall, he goes up in flames, and turns into a pile of ashes. Now that the Antichrist is ultimately defeated, the Second Coming of Christ takes place. In Voznesenskaya's novel, the image of Parousia is relatively canonical: Christ comes to Earth, and the Kingdom of God originates. By employing such an extensive vision of the Second Coming of Christ, Voznesenskaya not only intends to calm down eschatological moods, but also to emphasise the importance of moral values represented by Christ (Khoruzhenko 2017).

Another post-Soviet novel that offers a doomsday description is *The Child: The Apocalypse by Ivan the Antichrist* (2012) by Anatoly Zabolotnikov. The novel tells the story of a boy named Ivan born in Russia in the early 1990s, who, from the moment he is born, spreads evil and extinction. As is common with such a character, he appears innocent and good, seduces people, then leads them astray.The two women, Stalina and Svetlana, who decide to adopt the Child, are no exception. His apparent innocence deceives them, and they fall in love with him.

Interestingly, both women represent the two opposing orders. Whereas Stalina symbolises the secular order, Svetlana represents religiosity and unshakable faith in God. Even their names are emblematic: whereas the name Stalina is a direct reference to Stalin, the name Svetlana derives from the Slavic word *svet*, meaning "light", "pure", and "holy". The name of the Child is also significant. Not only is it the most popular name in many Slavonic countries, but also it invokes the Russian folklore. The most famous hero of the Russian folklore is Ivan Tsarevich – the Tsar's valiant son, who, after many adventures and struggles with Koschey the Deathless, finally defeats the evil antagonist, and marries the beautiful Tsarina. By referring to the Ivan Tsarevich figure, Zabolotnikov emphasises The Child's royal charm and charisma.

As Ivan grows up mysterious things of devilish nature happen around him; only Father Ioann, the monk staying in one of the Western monasteries who witnessed his birth, suspects The Child might come from the Tribe of Dan, and, indeed, be the Antichrist. Zabolotnikov, thus, uses the centuries-old belief about the Antichrist and the Jewish connection (see 3.1. and 3.2.). What is more, portraying the

Antichrist as a seemingly innocent child that spreads disasters and destruction, Zabolotnikov uses pop cultural patterns, particularly present in the movie *Omen* (1976).

When the Apocalypse starts, Ivan leaves his two mothers and joins his friends, who got lost in the "labyrinth" built by the Black Angel. The labyrinth symbolises the greediness and modern lifestyle, which seduced many young people in post-Soviet Russia. In the farewell conversation with Semen Matveyevich, who supported Stalina and Svetlana in raising The Child, Ivan discloses himself as the ultimate enemy of humanity, and announces the imminent end of the world:

> I am not even a man of the Earth, and because of this, at least regarding the mind, any community seems stupid. It all takes place due to our urge for a cage, which is our innocent starting position, as all have started in the cage, about which we have already talked. Forget, grandpa; all these boundaries will soon be washed away with waters of the flood which is continuously shown to you on television, even though it was known much earlier (Zabolotnikov 2012: 185).

Ivan's nature, however, turns out to be much more complicated. Towards the end of the novel, a symbolic disintegration of the protagonist takes place: he breaks up into Ivan and The Child. Here, The Child symbolises Satan, who was a part of Ivan from the very beginning but had been waiting for the right moment to reveal himself to the world as a separate being. Ivan is seen as being human, and, at the same time, he is the habitat of malicious powers. In other words, keeping with the traditional interpretations of the Antichrist ideomyth, Ivan is the human agent of Satan.

It is finally disclosed that Ivan is the absolute evil, and he confronts Father Ioann. They participate in a television debate, in which the fate of the world is decided. Despite Father Ioann's attempts to convince the viewers that Ivan is just a false prophet, who presents himself as the avenger and the saviour of the world, people vote for Ivan to become the new leader of the united world. On election day, mysterious viruses infect all the world's processors, programs, and information systems. As a result, all historical, political, and religious websites disappear from the Internet. It happens because all ideologies and philosophies had reached their limits of absurdity, and the world reached the edge of the abyss. At this time, people tired of chaos and disorder want a strong ruler to restore justice, even if by questionable means. To Father Ioann's surprise, Ivan-Antichrist wins. At the novel's end, good, evil, and death are abolished, and the world as we know it reaches its end.

The discussed authors tend to employ a whole repertoire of apocalyptic and eschatological motifs. Thus, although deeply immersed in contemporary politics and popular conspiracy theories, their visions of how the Antichrist will come to power remain relatively traditional. As with the majority of ancient prophecies, the Antichrist is supposed to appear as the false Messiah, who will reveal himself as the Endtime tyrant. The Antichrist is portrayed as a "clever world" in "sheep's clothing", who deludes people with false miracles and silver tongue blasphemies. This image derives not only from early-Christian writings and various subsequent prophecies, but it also refers to different post-Soviet discourses which employ the Antichrist ideomyth. Crowned in the rebuilt Temple of Jerusalem, the Antichrist is believed to rule over humanity for three and a half years, after which the ultimate fight between good and evil will take place. After the victory of Christ, the new era of the Kingdom of God will begin.

Although discussed authors differ in terms of literary status, popularity and audience, what connects their writings, is employing apocalyptic themes and motifs, specifically the Antichrist figure. Leaning on traditional interpretations, many of these authors tend to go far beyond the designated interpretative frameworks regarding this apocalyptic figure. They achieve it primarily by blending various literary genres, such as science fiction, fantasy, thriller, romance, and detective novels with narrative traditions, including Christian prophecies, Russian folklore, and conspiracy theories. Consequently, the centuries-old Antichrist figure acquires new semantic dimensions and serves as the complex ideomyth that reflects current dilemmas of political and social life. Notably, these works were not created in a vacuum. They refer to various historical, philosophical, religious, and political discourses, as well as codes fixed in Russian culture, ranging from Orthodox prophecies to apocalyptic, antisemitic and anti-Western discourses. Moreover, the texts not only refer to concepts of the Holy Rus', Moscow the Third Rome, and Katechon, but also reinterpret them and situate them in a new, often political, context.

Conclusions

> O man; you have the signs of the Antichrist;
> and remember them not only yourself but impart them also freely to all
> (Cyril of Jerusalem).

"The kingdom of the Antichrist is approaching", "The Antichrist will soon seize power over humankind", "This is the Endtime!": these and other similar statements spread across various post-Soviet Russian discourses. They are present especially in the writings of conservative and religious authors, who seem to take to their hearts the call of Cyril of Jerusalem. Many post-Soviet Russian ecclesiastical writings, as well as political concepts, conspiracy theories, and literary works, are full of eschatological motifs and, specifically, references to the Antichrist ideomyth. According to Russian historian Aleksey Beglov (2014), discourses that describe the end of the world, the arrival of the Antichrist, and the final battle between forces of good and evil as the imminent historical possibility, are a result the "wave of eschatological expectations" caused by turbulent historical, political, and social changes. As Beglov insists, discourses that emerged after the dissolution of the Soviet Union are analogous to those present in Russia in the times of the *Raskol* in the 17th century, during the dynamic changes in the Russian Empire in the late 1800s and early 1900s, and after the Bolshevik Revolution.

Even though the Antichrist figure is mostly associated with the Beast from the Book of Revelation, over the centuries, it has acquired a whole range of meanings. In various prophecies, as well as philosophical and exegetical writings, the Antichrist has been portrayed not only as an individual who will arrive on the eve of the world's end, but also as a collective of heretics, religious dissenters, and non-believers. In the Russian context, the Antichrist figure was also given an additional spiritual dimension and perceived as the symbol of evil unlocked in the mundane world.

These varied interpretations of the apocalyptic Antichrist figure have two reasons. First, since the Antichrist appears in the Scriptures only once in the Epistles of St. John, in addition to a plural form, its features were seen in many other analogous wicked figures, including the Man of Wickedness, the Son of Destruction, and the Lawless One from the Second Epistle of St. Paul to the Thessalonians. Secondly, the interpretative freedom related to the Antichrist figure was ensured by the ambiguity embedded already in the word "antichrist", in which the prefix ἀντί means both "against'" and "in opposition to", as well as "instead of". Many commentators of the Scriptures have interpreted the Antichrist as both the antithesis and ultimate enemy of Christ, as well as his evil twin and usurper, who presents himself as the Saviour, and only after winning people's trust and world power, he reveals his true nature. The Antichrist is the personification of evil disguised as good, and, thus, practically impossible to recognise.

This study has scrutinised how and why the apocalyptic image of Antichrist transforms across diverse discourses in post-Soviet Russia. To thoroughly analyse the complexity, ambiguity, and polysemic character of this figure and its incarnations in the post-Soviet Russian context, I employed the analytical tool of the ideomyth. The name of this category is borrowed from Konstantin Isupov's introduction to a book *Antichrist: Anthology* (1994) and Vardan Bagdasaryan's article "The Image of the Antichrist in the Russian Historiosophic Thought'" (2004). Even though both authors use the word "ideomyth" several times, neither of them defines this notion. Therefore, I took the liberty to put forth my own definition and approach to the ideomyth as an analytical tool combining critical perspectives embedded in the Russian idea and myth. In this context, the Russian idea is viewed as a traditional category of self-knowledge and a reservoir of Russian cultural myths; and myth, in turn, is understood as an ideologically driven narrative that mirrors thoughts, words, and values underlying a given culture (Liszka 1989, Barthes 1957, Veraksa 2013). Such a perspective enabled me to grasp all semiotic implications of the multidimensional Antichrist apocalyptic figure in various post-Soviet discourses.

Describing the contemporary world as a stage of the Apocalypse and situating geopolitical phenomena in religious and eschatological contexts is a narrative strategy eagerly used by the representatives of Russian Orthodox and conservative communities. Among the adherents of the belief that the Antichrist is approaching and Russia will play an important role in the apocalyptic drama, one should mention the prominent post-Soviet Russian public figures such as Ilya Glazunov, Metropolitan Ioann Snychev, Alexander Dugin, Mikhail Nazarov, Oleg Platonov, Konstantin Dushenov, Olga Chetverikova, Tatyana Gracheva, Vladimir Osipov,

Julia Voznesenskaya, and Alexander Prokhanov. Since they are political scientists, journalists, writers, ecclesiastics, and academics, who have many possibilities to reach their audience through utterances, publications, and media presence, one can assume that they shape to a large extent the public debate in post-Soviet Russia. However, it should be noted that their writings and utterances, being only a part of all post-Soviet discourses, are used here only as a synecdoche. They represent not only prevailing tendencies and potential motivations behind any use of the Antichrist figure, but also show various transformations this ideomyth undergoes, depending on cultural, social, and political needs it has to fulfil. The chosen texts demonstrate the diversity of voices, discourses, problems, and functions related to the Antichrist ideomyth in post-Soviet Russia.

The Antichrist ideomyth did not appear in post-Soviet Russian discourses out of the blue. Deeply rooted in Russian cultural imagery, the Antichrist figure has for centuries been a significant part of Russian historiosophic concepts such as Moscow the Third Rome or the Holy Rus'. Also, it has served as a constitutive Other and the final enemy against whom Russian national identity has been constructed. For this reason, it can be argued that the Antichrist ideomyth not only encapsulates the most important features of Russian culture, but also serves as the constitutive part of Russian auto-stereotypes, and a response to social, political, and cultural change.

Being an essential part of what Russian religious thinker and philosopher Nikolai Berdyaev names the Russian "eschatological myth", over the centuries, the Russian Antichrist has undergone numerous historical and semantic transformations. He was viewed not only as the false Messiah, the enemy of God, and the grand deceiver, but also a usurper of the Tsar's power, religious dissenter, and the embodiment of evil forces. He was also recognised in historical figures such as Ivan the Terrible, Peter the Great, Napoleon, and Adolf Hitler, as well as political and social systems including Russian autocracy, the Bolshevik regime, and liberal democracy (Isupov 1995). As Russian historian Vardan Bagdasaryan (2004) insists, "each epoch of Russian historiosophy created its own Antichrist, who has little in common with the Beast from the Revelation of John", and post-Soviet Russia is in this regard no exception. Reinterpreting and reworking various narratives, such as early Christian ecclesiastical texts, Russian writings of the Silver Age, and occult and New Age eschatological discourses dominant among Soviet underground nationalist and religious milieus of the 1970s and the 1980s, post-Soviet authors gave the Antichrist ideomyth an entirely new life.

Nevertheless, the most common way of presenting the Antichrist in post-Soviet Russian discourses is to portray him as the mirror image and twin of Christ, whose diabolic nature is revealed only through references to Masonic and Satanic symbols. The Antichrist is seen as the false Messiah, who will present himself as the Saviour and only after seizing the absolute power over humanity, he will reveal his true, evil nature. An example of the post-Soviet Russian visual illustration of such an interpretation is Ilya Glazunov's painting *Christ and Antichrist*. Imagining Christ and the Antichrist as an almost identical handsome man with long hair, eyes wide open, and tightened lips concealed in bushy beards, Glazunov's painting shows that in today's complicated world, it is increasingly difficult for people to distinguish between good and evil. The reason for this is believed to be both the departure from what is traditional religious values and the growing importance of postmodernist ideas that disperse grand narratives and claim that everything is relative. The negative attitude towards postmodernism, considered to be a wicked and valueless philosophy, is, indeed, relatively widespread in post-Soviet religious and conservative circles, and can be found in the writings and utterances of public figures such as controversial thinker and political scientist Alexander Dugin, and the Patriarch of Moscow and all Rus' Kirill.

Portraying the Antichrist as someone who presents himself as Christ and deceives humanity is not limited to iconographic representations. The canonical example of an image of the wicked individual, who claims to be the saviour of humanity, but, in fact, is the embodiment of evil and the enemy of Christianity, is the Grand Inquisitor from Dostoyevsky's novel *The Brothers Karamazov* (1880). In the parable which Ivan Karamazov tells his younger brother Alyosha, the Grand Inquisitor is the seemingly compassionate and merciful cardinal ruling 16th-century Seville. When Christ finally arrives in the earthly world after one and a half centuries after his death and resurrection, the Grand Inquisitor identifies him as the Messiah and, threatened by his power, accuses him of leaving people in confusion and agony. By usurping the right to save humankind, the Cardinal entrusts Satan and attempts to improve God's work and satisfy people's most significant needs that include the need for bread and miracles. Although the Grand Inquisitor is never named the Antichrist throughout Dostoyevsky's parable, it is evident that his power is of devilish origin. In other words, preaching values detached from Christianity, the cardinal turns out to be a false Messiah and the antithesis of Christ.

Another image of a false Messiah is Apollon from Vladimir Solovyov's *The Short Tale of the Antichrist* (1899-1900). He is a thirty-three years old pacifist, philanthropist, and humanist, who becomes the ecumenical leader of the universal state that unifies all nations. He then reveals himself as a false Messiah who wants to seize unlimited power over the world and even replace God. Due to its prophetic acuity, Solovyov's parable is in many ways consistent with Dostoyevsky's *Grand Inquisitor*. The image of Apollon as an autocratic ruler preaching progressive, humanistic ideals under the guise of Christian values not only alludes to Dostoevsky's vision, but also situates the Antichrist figure in the historical context. The Antichrist is not a mere religious concept, nor a rhetorical figure anymore. Instead, he becomes a real historical threat (Walicki 1979).

Antichrist-like figures created by Dostoyevsky and Solovyov have significantly influenced Russian interpretations of who Christ's adversary would be, and how he would attempt to seduce humanity. Nevertheless, this was not the only way of portraying this apocalyptic figure. From the very beginning, the Antichrist ideomyth eluded straightforward and unambiguous interpretations. Neither in the Scriptures nor other early-Christian eschatological narratives such as the writings of Church Fathers and subsequent prophecies about the end of the world, was it possible to clearly determine whether the Antichrist would be spiritual or tangible, if he would be an individual, a duo or a collective, and, finally, when and where he would be born, and how long he would rule before the ultimate Apocalypse. The discussed post-Soviet Russian authors also did not reach consensus on most of the issues related to the nature and arrival of the Antichrist.

Despite interpretative difficulties, or rather thanks to them, the post-Soviet Russian Antichrist ideomyth remains a polyvalent symbol, which acquires different meanings in different contexts. In discussed discourses, the Antichrist most often serves as an image of the archenemy, whose aim is to weaken and then destroy Russia. Depending on the ideological needs, he is blamed for all misfortunes that have plagued Russia for centuries, with the Bolshevik Revolution and the dissolution of the Soviet Union among them. Such events are perceived not as a result of historical contingency, but as the consequence of a complex multi-level plot orchestrated by the Antichrist and his minions. In these conspiratorial narratives, Russia is portrayed as a besieged fortress surrounded by all sorts of enemies, from demonic Jews and Masons to power-hungry oligarchs and westernised liberals, who aim at gaining world power at the expense of ordinary Russians.

Conspiracy theories that depict the Antichrist and his minions as the greatest Russophobes, who will not rest until they destroy Russia, are an example of explanatory models that "arise out of radical doubt about how knowledge is produced", and may serve as a tool of political manipulation (Birchall 2006, Yablokov 2018). Not only do they explain complicated and puzzling historical, political, and social phenomena, but also they consolidate a given community (Piirsalu and Panchenko 2017). Conspiracy theories popular in post-Soviet Russia tend to employ various eschatological motifs, with the Antichrist figure among them. Interestingly, based on a promise of "unveiling" what is hidden and disclosing the truth, conspiracy theories spread similarly to apocalyptic fears. They impose the Manichean view on politics and history, in which the place of deities is taken over by omnipotent individuals and groups governing politics and economics. Miracles, in turn, are replaced by "secrets" and the truth is considered to be hidden from the "ordinary man in the street" behind the "superficial and misleading veil", through which only the chosen ones – "seers, prophets, apocalyptic thinkers" – can see (Hagemeister 2006: 252).

It is important to emphasise that conspiracy theories discussed in this study do not emerge in the void. Present in various post-Soviet Russian discourses, they are not only permeated with eschatological fears, but also they are full of antisemitic and anti-Western attitudes. Moreover, they appropriate narratives coming from other cultures, as in the case of the theory about the evil computer-Beast based in Brussels, or from the past, as with rumours of the Dulles Plan and the Judeo-Mason plot aimed at destroying Russia. By combining conspiratorial and eschatological motifs and imagining enemies of Russia as minions of the Antichrist, these discourses situate the contemporary political situation in the context of the final struggle between good and evil. As a consequence, events such as World

War II, the Bolshevik Revolution, dismantling of the Soviet Union, and attempts to democratise and liberalise the Russian Federation are perceived as steps on the path to its destruction. Actualised and reinterpreted according to the existing political situation, conspiracy theories in post-Soviet Russia often use societal anxieties and fears to convey a specific ideological message and elevate the responsibility for state failure from the authorities.

Interestingly, numerous post-Soviet Russian discourses perceive the Antichrist not only as the great conspirator, who, for centuries, has been striving to destroy Russia, but also as the real political possibility. Indeed, portrayed as a religious dissenter, ideological opponent or representative of an alien socio-political system, the Antichrist figure was transferred to the realm of politics. This discursive strategy coincides with political theology put forth by Carl Schmitt, who gained considerable popularity in Russia after the breakup of the USSR, especially among nationalist and religious circles. Based on the assumption that there are no realms of pure politics and pure theology, and that political concepts are, in fact, secularised translations of theological ones, Schmitt's theory of politics organised reality around the dichotomous tension between the community and its political Other. Politics was perceived as a result of an inevitable conflict between "us" and "them", in which "them" represent everything that "we" are not. Since in these discourses the Antichrist is believed to represent values contradictory to that characteristic of Orthodox Russia, he serves not only as the ultimate political enemy, but also the constitutive Other against whom the Russian collective identity is constructed.

The strategy of constructing Russian identity in relation to the Antichrist is characteristic predominantly among radical circles. It is based on the universal assumption that the more the enemy differs from what a given community believes to be representing, the more intense are the processes of the identity formulas, and the more inevitable is the legitimation of power of the leaders of a given group (Achkasov 1997). When the enemy is seen as the ultimate antithesis of a group, it becomes easier to project on him the dissatisfaction and aggression of the masses. These processes are quite ironic in the context of the Antichrist ideomyth, which, in the majority of post-Soviet discourses, is interpreted as Satan's human actor and the antithesis of Christ. Dehumanising the Antichrist turns him back into the

Apocalyptic Beast embodying all possible evil. In these discourses, the Antichrist figure represents both personified evil and dehumanised enemy. Such an approach allows not only to exclude the Other from the community, but also provides tools for ideological violence and violent behaviours toward him. In other words, once our enemy is the enemy of Christ, the Antichrist, no holds are barred in fighting him and those associated with him.

As mentioned in this study, the West, as a homogenous entity, is considered to be the political scene of the Antichrist's activities. Portrayed mostly as the contractor of the United States that wants to maintain their hegemony at all costs, the West is usually described in terms of Anomia, as the chaotic and morally depraved space. Moreover, authors such as Metropolitan Ioann Snychev, Alexander Dugin, and Olga Chetverikova argue that the West, being the traitor to true Christianity, uses globalisation and ecumenism to establish the Kingdom of the Antichrist in the world. In their view, the only obstacle to creating a totalitarian space, where there are no nations and people are persecuted for believing in Christ, is Orthodox Russia. Unlike the West, as these discourses argue, Russia is the last bastion of morality and a defender of genuine Christian values.

This perspective is deeply rooted in Russian messianism based on the belief that Russia has a crucial role to play in world history. Whether as the place where the Antichrist will come to the world or as the Katechon that is the last force restraining his arrival, in these discourses, Russia plays an idiosyncratic role in the apocalyptic drama. In this perspective, human history acquires an additional, otherworldly aspect, and the political conflict between Russia and the West is believed to take place simultaneously in the two dimensions: mundane and metaphysical. Whereas on the mundane level, it is an ordinary fight for influences on the international arena, on the metaphysical level it is the ultimate fight between good and evil as foreseen in the Book of Revelation.

It is worth noting that the Antichrist figure also appears in a more entertaining context as one of the themes of contemporary Russian fiction. Invoked in novels representing various literary genres, such as detective stories, thrillers, science fiction, and dystopian novels, the Antichrist ideomyth goes far beyond interpretative frameworks assigned by the traditional exegesis of the Scriptures, early-Christian writings, and apocalyptic prophecies. Post-Soviet Russian writers draw inspiration also from the centuries-old Russian tradition of naming the Antichrist. Referring to Old Believers' historiosophy, Silver Age literature, and Russian folklore, they transcend the image of the Antichrist as the enemy of Russia and the false Messiah, who only with time will reveal his true evil nature.

Indeed, post-Soviet Russian authors portray the Antichrist in numerous diverse ways: as internalised evil present in each human being (Mavrodi), an individual who cannot decide whether he wants to side with good or evil (Alekseyev), a young erotomaniac who is convinced of his special mission in the world (Tumanov and Zabolotnikov), a serial killer (Lugovoy), a talented scientist (Kashanskiy), a cunning politician (Prokhanov), and, finally, a trickster who turns the world upside down (Krusanov). Practically all these works can be classified as examples of so-called "new political" and "new imperial" novels, which not only depict the political reality in apocalyptic terms, but also tend to represent the nationalist worldview in contemporary political concepts, and conspiracy theories.

According to political scientist Valeriy Achkasov (1997), the popularity of traditionalist ideology following the Soviet Union break-up was the result of seeking an adequate response to the crisis of self-identification. A strategy that many post-Soviet circles chose was turning to the past and invoking values considered traditionally Russian, such as Orthodoxy, patriotism, and family values. It resulted in the so-called "conservative turn", which is commonly associated with Putin's rise to power. Its roots, however, reach back much deeper. Discourses referring to the "golden past" and the need to protect traditional values existed in one form or another since the late 1970s and 1980s. Interestingly, contemporary Russian culture expert Sergei Oushakine (2009b), interprets the positive reception of the revived conservatism and patriotic values that took place in the late 1990s and early 2000s as an example of the "patriotism of despair". As he argues, it was the response to savage transformation and corrupt privatisation, as well as the sense of a break with historical continuity and disintegration of identities, both individual and collective.

An attempt to deal with the disintegration of the world as people knew it also resulted in the proliferation of eschatological fears, which resonated particularly among post-Soviet nationalist and religious milieus. In the face of turbulent social, political, and economic changes, rumours about Armageddon, the Parousia, and the arrival of the Antichrist, have become a widely used discursive strategy aimed at grasping the rapidly changing reality. For the post-Soviet Russian society, affected by the cultural trauma of the dissolution of the Soviet Union, apocalyptic discourses, like contemporary myths, were employed as "healing narratives". Elevating the fear of the unknown and familiarising the unknowable, they consolidated the community confronted with rapid and severe changes that irrevocably modified the social and political structures. Apocalyptic discourses were often used to explain why Russian society and, in fact, the entire world, found themselves in a state of a permanent crisis, or, rather, numerous consecutive crises, after 1991. Ambivalent and multidimensional, the Antichrist ideomyth turned out to be not only a great source of fear used to consolidate the community, but also it made it possible to explain all the misfortunes experienced by the Russian state in the 20th century and beyond.

Nevertheless, the post-Soviet Antichrist ideomyth cannot simply be reduced to the image of the enemy and a healing narrative. Being a subject to ceaseless changes and metamorphoses, mostly in the wake of specific historical events and ideological disputes, this ideomyth has become a polyvalent symbol. As it grew away from the religious context and diffused into secular narratives; it became an act of linguistic transgression. This semantic translocation is symbolised by the inner logic of the Antichrist, which resembles that of the trickster and often is a masquerade, a reversal, and turning the world upside down. Thus, the Antichrist can simultaneously be a wolf in sheep's clothing, the grand deceiver, and the archhypocrite, intending to destroy Christianity, as well as a distorted imitation of Christ and an erotic provocateur. It can symbolise the anti-human character of the state-Leviathan, the Tsars' autocracy, the Bolshevik regime, and what is deemed the callous democracy. In addition, as suggested by the philosopher Konstantin Isupov (1995), in some contexts, the Antichrist ideomyth signifies the history of Russian statehood: social experiments, utopian initiatives, defeats, plagues, and catastrophes. Closely related to anti-liberal, antisemitic, and anti-Western attitudes, it is a discursive rebellion against overwhelming rationalism, the source of which is the Enlightenment, associated with the West. Although often equated with the godless chaos of postmodernism, in specific contexts, the Antichrist ideomyth can be approached as a symbol of the departure from Cartesian philosophy and the definiteness of the ultimate truths.

Overall, sculpted from early Christian exegesis of the Scriptures, eschatological fears, and apocalyptic prophecies, the Antichrist ideomyth has for centuries served as the mirror in which Russian culture has viewed itself. Ideologically driven, it has not only reflected thoughts, words, and values underlying Russian culture, but also, being Russia's constitutive Other and a significant part of concepts such as Moscow the Third Rome and the Holy Rus', it has constituted an important element of the Russian self-knowledge.

Moreover, since the Antichrist figure has no fixed meaning assigned to it, the ideomyth has served as a hermeneutic tool, embracing what is not apparent, and what escapes established interpretative frameworks. It has been transformed across time and discourses, blurring the boundaries between *the signified* and *the signifier*. At the same time, the Antichrist ideomyth in post-Soviet Russian discourses has evoked all previous interpretations and traditions, adding to them some entirely new dimensions. Consequently, the Antichrist ideomyth not only serves as a compelling narrative, predominantly referring to the image of the arch-enemy, but also as a kind of overarching narrative, explaining complex reality in an accessible way. It is the word at the intersection of discourses that adapts itself to various contexts, namely, ecclesiastical, philosophical, historical, political, and literary ones.

Bibliography

Primary Sources

Akurochkin (2012). Lzhe-Antichrist Barack Obama. Available at: https://akurochkin.livejourn al.com/65646.html [Accessed 31 August 2020]. [The False Antichrist Barack Obama].
Alekseyev I. (2016). *Antikhrist*. Moskva: Izdatelskiye Resheniya. [The Antichrist].
Chetverikova O. (2015). Rech Idet o Sozdaniy Antitserkvi. *Pravoslavnyy Krest* 3 (123). Available at: https://3rm.info/publications/54560-olga-chetverikova-rech-idet-o-sozdanii-anticer kvi.html [Accessed 31 August 2020]. [The Discussion About Establishing the Anti-Church].
Chetverikova O. (2016). Geopolitika. Mir i Prikhod Antikhrista. Available at: https://www.yout ube.com/watch?v=5TGL0tHjPYE [Accessed 31 August 2020]. [Geopolitics: The World and the Antichrist's Arrival].
Chetverikova O. (2017). Vatikan Vstrechayet Antikhrista. Available: https://www.youtube.co m/watch?v=ZMtPSr5xtkA [Accessed 31 August 2020]. [The Vatican Meets the Antichrist].
Dugin A. (1990). *Puti Absolyuta*. Moskva: Arktogeya. [Ways of the Absolute].
Dugin A. (1991). *Misterii Evrazii*. Moskva: Arktogeya. [Mysteries of Eurasia].
Dugin A. (1993). *Konspirologiya*. Moskva: Arktogeya. [Conspirology].
Dugin A. (1996). *Metafizika Blagoy Vesti*. Moskva: Arktogeya. [The Metaphysics of the Good News].
Dugin A. (1997). Katekhon i Revolutsiya. *Elementy, № 8*. Moskva: Arktogeya. [The Katechon and Revolution].
Dugin A. (2000). *Osnovy Geopolitiki*. Moscow: Arktogeya. [Foundations of Geopolitics].
Dugin A. (2001).Vozrashchenye Begunov. In: Dugin A. (2001) *Russkaya Veshch': Ocherki Natsionalnoy Filosofii*. Moskva: Arktogeya. [The Return of Beguny, In: The Russian Thing: Essays on the National Philosophy].
Dugin A. (2004). *Filosofiya Politiki*. Moscow: Arktogeya. [The Philosophy of Politics].
Dugin A. (2009a). *Chetvyortaya Politicheskaya Teoriia*. Moskva: Amfora. [The Fourth Political Theory].
Dugin A. (2009b). *Radikalnyy Subyekt i Ego Dubl*. Moskva: Evraziyskoye Dvizhenye. [The Radical Subject and His Double].
Dugin A. (2010). *Logos i Mifos*. Moskva: Arktogeya. [Logos and Myth].
Dugin A. (2011). K Kontseptu „Radikalnogo Antikhrista": Ontologiya i Opyt. Available at: http://dugin.livejournal.com/1799.html [Accessed 31 August 2020]. [To the Concept of "Radical Antichrist": Ontology and Experience].
Dushenov K. (2015). Antikhrist kak Politicheskaya Realnost Nashikh Dney. Available at: https://www.youtube.com/watch?v=PF0EmWUF6wc [Accessed 31 August 2020]. [The Antichrist as the Political Reality of Our Times].
Faid R. (1988). *Gorbachev! Has the Real Antichrist Come?*. Tulsa: Victory House Publishers.
Filimonov V. (2016). Kogda Pridet Antikhrist. *Odigitria*. Available at: http://www.odigitria. by/2016/02/11/kogda-pridet-antixrist-valerij-filimonov/ [Accessed 31 August 2020]. [When the Antichrist will Arrive].
Fokin S. (2015). Mirovye Prorochestva ob Antikhriste ("Rukami i Nogami Chelovecheskimi" Privedennogo na Tsarstvo). Sbornik. *Logoslovo.ru*. Available at: http://www.logoslovo.ru

/forum/all/topic_13377_3 [Accessed 31 August 2020]. [World Prophecies About the Antichrist (the Kingdom Brought "With Human Hands and Feet"). Collection].
Gaydar M. (2007). *Dyavol.* Available at: https://www.youtube.com/watch?v=Y0EofQr9dr4 [Accessed 31 August 2020]. [The Devil].
Glazunov I. (1999). *Khristos i Antikhrist.* Oil on canvas.114 x 141 cm. Moscow State Art Gallery of Ilya Glazunov. [Christ and Antichrist].
Gorenstein F. (1975). *Psalom.* Moskva: EKSMO-Press. [The Psalm].
Gracheva T. (2009). *Sviataya Rus' Protiv Khazarii: Algoritmy Geopolitiki i Strategiy Taynykh Voyn Mirovoy Zakulisy.* Ryazan: Zerna. [The Invisible Khazaria: Algorithms of Geopolitics and Strategies of Secret Wars of the World's Backstage].
Gracheva T. (2011). *Pamiat Russkoy Dushi.* Ryazan: Zerna. [The Memory of the Russian Soul].
Gracheva T. (2013). *Posledneye Iskusheniye Rossii: K Kakoy Voyne Dolzhna Gotovitsya Rossiya.* Ryazan: Zerna. [The Last Temptation of Russia: To Which War Russia Should Prepare Itself].
Ilyashenko A. (2004). Ekumenizm i Globalizatsiya (Chast 3). *Pravoslaviye i Mir.* Available at: http://www.pravmir.ru/ekumenizm-i-globalizaciya-chast-3/ [Accessed 31 August 2020]. [Ecumenism and Globalisation (Part 3)].
Irbulatova A. (2017). Informatsionnyy Zagovor Protiv Rossii. *Russkoye Agentstvo Novostey.* Available at: http://tiny.pl/g43bl [Accessed 31 August 2020]. [Informational Conspiracy Against Russia].
Kara-Murza S. (2015). Rusofobiya Zapada: Kratkaya Istoriya. Available at: https://ru-kara-murza.livejournal.com/200622.html [Accessed 31 August 2020]. [Western Russophobia: Short History].
Kashanskiy A. (2000). *Antikhrist.* St. Petersburg: Olma-Press. [The Antichrist].
Kedrov K. (2001). *Parallelnye Miry.* Available at: http://ligis.ru/librari/2782.htm [Accessed 31 August 2020]. [The Parallel Worlds].
Krusanov P. (2005). *Amerikanska Dyrka.* Moskva: Amfora. [The American Hole].
Larkin S. (2018). *Putin – Antikhrist.* Available at: https://www.youtube.com/watch?v=llvpSPrLWAI [Accessed 31 August 2020]. [Putin is the Antichrist].
Liverinternet.ru (2010). Prints Wilyam - Antikhrist?. Available at: https://www.liveinternet.ru/users/samanta_black/post125231482?aid_refresh=yes [Accessed 31 August 2020]. [Is Prince William the Antichrist?].
Lugovoy D. (2017). *Antikhrist.* Moskva: Izdatelskiye Resheniya. [The Antichrist].
Mavrodi S. (2012). *Iskusheniye-2.* Moskva: Ves. [The Temptation-2].
Nazarov M. (1999). *Tayna Rossii: Istoriosofiya XX Veka.* Moskva: Russkaya Ideya. [The Mystery of Russia: Historiosophy of the 20th Century].
Nazarov M. (2005). *Vozhdyu Tretego Rima.* Moskva: Russkaya Ideya. Available at: http://apocalypse.orthodoxy.ru/vtr/ [Accessed 31 August 2020]. [To the Leader of the Third Rome].
Nekrasov S. (2014). Gematriya i Khristologiya M.S. Gorbacheva. *Nauka-Rastudent.Ru.* Available at: https://nauka-rastudent.ru/6/1559/ [Accessed 31 August 2020]. [M.S. Gorbachev's Gematria and Christology].
Nemenskiy O. (2014). Rusofobiya kak Ideologiya. *Russkiy Dom.* Available at: http://www.russdom.ru/node/7732 [Accessed 31 August 2020]. [Russophobia As an Ideology].
Oleynik B. (2003). *Knyaz Tmy.* Moskva: Centrpoligraf. [The Prince of Darkness].
Osipov V. (2012). *Vozrozhdenye Russkoy Ideologii.* Moskva: Algoritm. [The Revival of the Russian Ideology].

The Antichrist in Post-Soviet Russia: Transformations of an Ideomyth 219

Panarin I. and Kostenko B. (2017). Konservativnyy Klub. *Telekanal "SPAS"*. Available at: https://www.youtube.com/watch?=1727&v=jWRX-dtKPBI [Accessed 31 August 2020]. [The Conservative Club].
Patriarch Kirill (2010). Slovo Svyateyshego Patriarkha Kirilla Posle Vrucheniya Diploma Pochetnogo Doktora Natsionalnogo Issledovatyelskogo Yadernogo Universiteta "MIFI". *Patriarchia.ru*. Available at: http://www.patriarchia.ru/db/text/1106371.html [Accessed 31 August 2020]. [His Holiness Patriarch Kirill Speaks After Receiving the Honorary Doctor's Degree From the National Nuclear Research University "MEPHI"].
Platonov O. (1998). *Tayna Bezzakoniya: Yudaizm i Masonstvo Protiv Khristianskoy Tsivilizatsyi*. Moskva: Rus-Sky. Available at: http://www.rus-sky.com/history/library/plat5-1.htm [Accessed 31 August 2020]. [The Mystery of Lawlessness: Judaism and Masonry Against the Christian Civilisation].
Platonov O. (2010a). *Bitva za Rossiyu*. Moskva: Algoritm. [The Battle for Russia].
Platonov O. (2010b). *Russkoye Soprotivlenye: Voyna s Antikhristom*. Moskva: Izdatelstvo Stolitsa-Print. [The Russian Resistance: The War with the Antichrist].
Platonov O. (2011). *Rossiya i Mirovoye Zlo. Trudy po Istorii Taynykh Obshchestv i Pod Ryvnoi Deyatelnosti Sionizma*. Moskva: Algoritm. [The World's Evil and Russia. The History of Secret Communities and Jerky Actions of Zionism].
Potupin A. and Mazurkevich A. (2001). Vladimir Putin – Antikhrist?. Available at: http://apocalypse.orthodoxy.ru/letter/2001_12_19.htm [Accessed 31 August 2020]. [Is Putin the Antichrist?].
Proyekt Rossiya (2005-2010). Available at: http://www.proektrussia.ru [Accessed 31 August 2020]. [The Project Russia].
Prokhanov A. (2002). *Gospodin Geksogen*. Moskva: Ad Marginem. [Mr Hexogen].
Prokhanov A. (2007). *Svoy –Chuzhoy*. Moskva: Algoritm. [Us – Them].
Psyportal.net (2012). *Rusofobiya*. Available at: https://www.psyportal.net/5814/rusofobiya/ [Accessed 31 August 2020]. [The Rusophobia].
Pushkina M. (1999) *Antikhtist*. Moskva: Sintez Records. [The Antichrist].
Shafarievich I. (2005) [1989]. *Rusofobiya*. Moskva: Eksmo. [The Rusophobia].
Shafarievich I. (2013) [1991]. *Rusofobiya: Desyat Let Spustya*. Moskva: Alistrous. [The Rusophobia: Ten Years Later].
Shishova T. and Medvedeva I. (2009). *Spetsmissiya Antikhrista*. Moskva: Algoritm. [The Special Mission of the Antichrist].
Snychev I. (1992). Tayna Bezzakoniya. *Odigitria.by*. Available at: http://www.odigitria.by /2011/10/23/tajna-bezzakoniya-mitropolit-ioann-snychev/ [Accessed 31 August 2020]. [The Mystery of Lawlessness].
Snychev I. (1993). Bitva za Rossiyu, *Odigitria.by*. Available at: http://www.odigitria.by/ 2011/11/25/bitva-za-rossiyu-mitropolit-ioann-snychev/ [Accessed 31 August 2020]. [The Battle for Russia].
Snychev I. (1994). *Tvorcy Kataklizmov*. Moskva: Rus-Sky. Available at: http://www.rus-sky. com/history/library/tvor_kat.htm [Accessed 31 August 2020]. [Creators of Disasters].
Snychev I. (1995). "Odolenye Smuty". Slovo k Russkomu Narodu. *Golden Ship*. Available at: http://www.golden-ship.ru/knigi/8/ioann-snichev_OS.htm [Accessed 31 August 2020]. [*Overcoming the Time of Troubles: The Word to the Russian Nation*].
Snychev I. (1997). *Samoderzhavye Dukha*. Moskva: Rus-Sky. Available at: http://www.rus-sky.com/history/library/samoderj.htm [Accessed 31 August 2020]. [Autocracy of the Spirit].

Strelchik, E. and Patriarkh Kirill (2009). "Antikhrist Pridet, Kogda...". *Pravoslavye i Mir*. Available at: http://www.pravmir.ru/antixrist-pridet-kogda/ [Accessed 31 August 2020]. [The Antichrist Will Arrive When...].
Sukharenkó A. (2012). *Tayna Proklyatiya*. Moskva: Grifon. [The Mystery of the Course].
Sukharenko A. (2013). *Antikhrist i Russkiy Tsar*. Moskva: Grifon. [The Antichrist and the Russian Tsar].
Tkachev A. (2013). Obama Melkovat Chtoby Byt Antikhristom. *Russkaya Narodnaya Liniya*. Available at: https://ruskline.ru/news_rl/2013/04/04/obama_melkovat_chtoby_byt_antihrist om/ [Accessed 31 August 2020]. [Obama is Too Small to Be the Antichrist].
Tumanov A. (2016). *Iskusheniye. Evangeliye Antikhrista*. Moskva: Izdatelskiye Resheniya. [The Temptation: The Book About the Eternal Love].
Vorobevskiy Y. (1999). *Put v Apokalipsis: Tochka Omega*. Moskva: Rus-Sky. Available at: http://www.rus-sky.com/history/library/omega/ [Accessed 31 August 2020]. [The Path to the Apocalypse: The Omega Point].
Voznesenskaya J. (2003). *Put Kassandry, ili Priklyucheniya s Makaronami*. Moskva: Lenta. [The Journey of Kassandra of Adventures with Pasta].
Voznesenskaya J. (2004). *Palomnichestvo Lanselota*. Moskva: Lenta. [Lancelot's Pilgrimage].
Wright R. (1988). *Mikhail Gorbachev is Gog and Magog: The Biblical Antichrist*. Bloomington: AuthorsHouse.
Zabolotnikov A. (2012). *Malysh: Apokalipsis ot Ivana Antikhrista*. Riga: YAM Young Authors' Masterpieces Publishing. [The Child: The Apocalypse by Ivan the Antichrist].

Secondary Sources

Achkasov V. (1997). *"Vzyrivayushchayasya Arkhaichnost": Traditsionalizm v Politicheskoy Zhizni Rossii*, St. Petersburg: SPBGU. ["Exploding Archaism": Traditionalism in Russian Political Life].
Ageyeva E. (1997). Staroobriadicheskaya Polemika ob Antikhriste na Iskhode XX Veka. *Uralskiy Sbornik. Istoriya. Kultura. Religiya* 1: 9-16. [Old-Believers' Controversy about the Antichrist at the End of the 20th Century].
Akhmetova M. (2008) Knowledge, Science and the Scientist in Contemporary Mythology: A Study of Quasi-Scientific Narratives Collected from People Involved in Russian Religious Organizations. *Folclorica*, 13: 1-24.
Akhmetova M. (2010). *Konec Sveta v Odnoy Otdelno Vziatoy Strane*. Moskva: Obedinennoye Gumanitarnoye Izdatelstvo. [The End of the World in a Single Country].
Akopov S. (2016). *Ideas of Carl Schmitt? An Analysis of Russian Conservative Discourse in the 21st Century*. Speech at the First Annual Conference "Europe under Stress: The End of a Common Dream?". Tartu, 12-14 June, 2016.
Aptekman M. (2006). Kabbalah, Judeo-Masonic Myth, and Post-Soviet Literary Discourse: From Political Tool to Virtual Parody. *The Russian Review*, 65 (4): 657-681.
Bagdasaryan V. (2004). *Obraz Antikhrista v Russkoy Istoriosofskoy Mysli*. Available at: http://www.pravaya.ru/faith/11/74 [Accessed 31 August 2020]. [The Image of the Antichrist in Russian Historiosophical Thought]
Baldwin J. (1955). Everybody's Protest Novel. In: *Notes of a Native Son*. Boston: Beacon: 20–21.

Ball A. (2003). *Imagining America: Influence and Images in Twentieth-Century Russia.* Lanham: Roman & Littlefield.
Barkun M. (2003). *A Culture of Conspiracy: Apocalyptic Visions in Contemporary America.* Berkeley: University of California Press.
Barr D. L. (2003). *Reading the Book of Revelation: a Resource for Students.* Atlanta: Society of Biblical Literature.
Barr D. L. (2006). *The Reality of Apocalypse: Rhetoric and Politics in the Book of Revelation.* Atlanta: Society of Biblical Literature.
Barthes R. (1957). *Mythologies.* Paris: Les Lettres Nouvelles.
Baumann G. and Gingrich A. (2004.) *Grammars of Identity/Alterity: Structural Approach.* New York: Berghahn Books.
Beglov A. (2014). Eschatological Expectations in Post-Soviet Russia: Historical Context and Modes of Interpretation. In: Tolstaya K. (Ed.) *Orthodox Paradoxes: Heterogeneities and Complexities in Contemporary Russian Orthodoxy.* Leiden: Brill: 106-133.
Berdyaev N. (1948). *The Russian Idea.* New York: Macmillan.
Berglund K. (2014). *The Vexing Case of Igor Shafarevich, a Russian Political Thinker.* Berlin: Birkhauser.
Bethea D.M. (1989). *Shape of Apocalypse in Modern Russian Fiction.* Princeton: Princeton University Press.
Betz H. D. et al. (2007-2013). *Religion Past and Present: Encyclopedia of Theology and Religion.* Leiden, Boston: Brill.
Billington J. H. (1966). *The Icon and the Axe: an Interpretative History of Russian Culture.* New York: Knopf.
Birchall C. (2006). *Knowledge Goes Pop: From Conspiracy Theory to Gossip.* Oxford: Berg Publisher.
Blumenberg H. (1985) *Work on Myth.* Cambridge, Mass: MIT Press.
Borenstein E. (2019). *Plots Against Russia: Conspiracy and Fantasy After Socialism.* Ithaca: Cornell University Press.
Bottici C. (2007). *A Philosophy of Political Myth.* New York: Cambridge University Press.
Bouveng K. R. (2010). *The Role of Messianism in Contemporary Russian Identity and Statecraft.* Durham theses, Durham University. Available at: http://etheses.dur.ac.uk/438/ [Accessed 25 May 2018].
Bowers K. and Kokobobo A. (2015). *Russian Writers and the Fin de Siècle: the Twilight of Realism.* Cambridge: Cambridge University Press.
Boym S. (1999). Conspiracy Theories and Literary Ethic: Umberto Eco, Danilo Kiš and The Protocols of Zion. *Comparative Literature,* 51 (2): 97-122.
Broda M. (2011). *Zrozumieć Rosję. O Rosyjskiej Zagadce-Tajemnicy.* Łódź: Ibidem. [Understanding Russia. About the Russian Mystery].
Bronnen S.E. (2000). *A Rumor About the Jews: Reflections on Antisemitism and the Protocols of the Learned Elders of Zion.* Basingstoke: Palgrave Macmillan.
Brown S. Bell J. and Carson D. (1996). *Marketing Apocalypse: Eschatology, Escapology and the Illusion of the End.* London: Routledge.
Bultmann R. (1975) [1957]. *The Presence of Eternity: History and Eschatology.* Westport: Greenwood Press.
Campbell D. (2008). *Writing Security. United States Foreign Policy and the Politics of Identity.* Minnesota: University of Minnesota.

Cassirer E. (1946). *The Myth of the State*. New Haven: Yale University Press.
Cassirer E. (1955). *The Philosophy of Symbolic Forms*. London Geoffrey Cumberlege: Oxford University Press.
Cherniavsky M. (1966). The Old Believers and the New Religion. *Slavic Review*, 25 (1): 1-39.
Chudo A. (2000). *And Quiet Flows the Vodka, or, When Pushkin Comes to Shove: The Curmudgeon's Guide to Russian Literature and Culture, with the Devil's Dictionary of Received Ideas, Alphabetical Reflection on the Loathsomeness of Russia, American Academia, and Humanity in General*. Evanston: Northwestern University Press.
Cohn N. (1970). *The Pursuit of the Millennium: Revolutionary Millenarians and Mystical Anarchists of the Middle Ages*. New York: Oxford University Press.
Cohn N. (1993). *Cosmos, Chaos, and the World to Come: The Ancient Roots of Apocalyptic Faith*. New Haven: Yale Nota Bene.
Cohn N. (2006). *Warrant for Genocide: The Myth of the Jewish World-Conspiracy and the Protocols of the Elders of Zion*. San Francisco: Harper & Row.
Collins J. (1979). *Apocalypse: The Morphology of a Genre*. Missoula: Scholars Press.
Crummey R. (1970). *The Old Believers & The World of Antichrist: the Vyg Community and the Russian State 1694-1855*. Madison: University of Wisconsin Press.
Cullman O. (1967). *Salvation in History*. London: SCM Press LTD.
Curanović A. (2014). *The Religious Factor in Russia's Foreign Policy*. New York: Routledge Tylor & Francis Group.
Czaja D. et al. (2015). *Scenariusze Końca. Zmierzch, Kres, Apokalipsa*. Wołowiec: Wydawnictwo Czarne. [Scenarios of the End: the Twilight, the End, and the Apocalypse].
De Lazari A. (1996). *Czy Moskwa Będzie Trzecim Rzymem?*. Katowice: Śląsk. [Will Moscow Be the Third Rome?].
De Lazari A. (2004). Skąd Przychodzi Antychryst?. In: T. Falęcki (Ed.) *Skąd Przychodzi Antychryst? Kontakty i Konflikty Etniczne w Europie Środkowej i Południowej. Fakty – interpretacje –refleksje*. Kraków: Wydawnictwo Naukowe Uniwersytetu Pedagogicznego: 139-145. [Where Does the Antichrist Come From? In: Where Does the Antichrist Come From? Ethnic Contacts and Conflicts in Central and Southern Europe. Facts – Interpretations – Reflections].
De Lazari A. (2014). Idea Rosyjska po Putinowsku, *Studio Opinii*. Available at: http://studioopinii.pl/andrzej-de-lazari-idea-rosyjska-po-putinowsku [Accessed 31 August 2020]. [The Russian Idea According to Putin].
Derevenskiy B. (2007). *Kniga ob Antikhriste*. St. Peterburg: Amfora. [The Book About Antichrist].
DeRoo N. and Manoussakis J. P. (2009). *Phenomenology and Eschatology: Not Yet is the Now*. Farnham: Ashgate.
Di Nola, A. M. (2000). *Diabeł*. Kraków: Universitas. [The Devil].
Dolińska-Rydzek M. (2016). Russia's Immoral Other: Moral Panics and the Antichrist on Russian Orthodox Websites. In: Suslov M. (Ed.) *Digital Orthodoxy in the Post-Soviet World*. Stuttgart: ibidem-Verlag: 53-82.
Doroszczyk J. (2016). Aleksandra Dugina Czwarta Teoria Polityczna jako antyzachodnia alternatywa wobec polityki liberalno-demokratycznej Zachodu. *Chorzowskie Studia Polityczne*, 11: 65-78. [Alexander Dugin's Fourth Political Theory as the Anti-Western Alternative Towards Liberal-Democratic Politics of the West].
Dostoyevsky F. (1955) [1880]. *The Brothers Karamazov*. Chicago: Encyclopædia Britannica.

Dostoyevsky F. (1861). *Obyavlenie o Podpiske na Zhurnal "Vremya" na 1861 God.* Available at: http://dostoevskiy.niv.ru/dostoevskiy/public/obyavlenie-o-podpiske-na-vremya-1861.htm [Accessed 31 August 2020]. [The Announcement about Subscription to the Magazine "Vremya" for the Year 1861].
Duncan P. J. S. (2000). *Russian Messianism: Third Rome, Holy Revolution, Communism and After.* London, New York: Routledge.
Duncan P. J. S. (2005). Contemporary Russian Identity Between East and West. *The Historical Journal,* 48 (5): 277-294.
Emmerson R. (1981). *Antichrist in the Middle Ages: a Study of Medieval Apocalypticism, Art, and Literature.* Seattle: University of Washington Press.
Engström M. (2012). Forbidden Dandyism. Imperial Aesthetics in Contemporary Russia. *Nordic Fashion Studies:* 179-199.
Engström M. (2014). Contemporary Russian Messianism and New Russian Foreign Policy. *Contemporary Security Policy,* 35 (3): 356-379.
Epstein M. (1993). *The Origins and the Meaning of Russian Postmodernism.* Washington: The National Council for Soviet and East European Research.
Epstein M. (1994). *From Anti-Socialism to Anti-Semitism: Igor Shafarevich.* Available at: https://www.ucis.pitt.edu/nceeer/1994-807-21-2-Epstein.pdf [Accessed 31 August 2020].
Epstein M. (1995). *After the Future: The Paradoxes of Postmodernism and Contemporary Russian Culture.* Amherst: University of Massachusetts Press.
Etkind A. (2011). *Internal Colonization: Russia's Imperial Experience.* Cambridge, Malden: Polity Press.
Fedotov G. (1960). *The Russian Religious Mind.* Cambridge: Harvard University Press.
Fenster M. (2008). *Conspiracy Theories: Secrecy and Power in American Culture.* Minneapolis: University of Minnesota Press.
Flood C. (1996). *Political Myth: a Theoretical Introduction.* New York: Garland Pub. Inc.
Fomin S. (1999). *Rossiya Pered Vtorym Prishestvem. Prorochestva Russkikh Sviatykh.* Moskva: Serda Press. [Russia Before the Second Coming of Christ. Prophecies of Russian Saints].
Fornari G. (2010). Figures of Antichrist. The Apocalypse and its Restraints in Contemporary Political Thought, *Journal of Violence, Mimesis, and Culture,* 17: 53-85.
Frye N. and Macpherson J. (2004). *Biblical and Classical Myths: The Mythological Framework of Western Culture.* Toronto, Buffalo: University of Toronto Press.
Fuller R. (1995). *Naming the Antichrist: The History of an American Obsession.* New York: Oxford University Press.
Golunov S. and Sminova V. (2016). Proliferation of Conspiracy Narratives in Post-Soviet Russia: The "Dulles' Plan" in Social and Political Discourses. *Acta Slavica Iaponica,* 37: 21-45.
Gudkov L. (2004). *Negativnaya Identichnost: Stati 1997-2002 Godov.* Moskva: Novoye Literaturnoye Obozrenye. [Negative Identity: Articles From the Years 1997-2002].
Guirand F. (1963). *Greek Mythology.* London: Hamlyn.
Gulyga A. (2003). *Russkaya Ideya i Eyo Tvortsy.* Moskva: Eksmo. [Russian Idea and Its Creators].
Gupta A. and Ferguson J. (1992). Beyond "Culture": Space, Identity, and the Politics of Difference. *Cultural Anthropology,* 7 (1): 6-23.

Hagemeister M. (2004). Anti-Semitism, Occultism, and Theories of Conspiracy in Contemporary Russia: the Case of Ilya Glazunov. In: *Anti-Semitism and Philo-Semitism in the Slavic World and Western Europe*. Haifa: 235-241.

Hagemeister M. (2006). The "Protocols of the Elders of Zion" and the Myth of a Jewish: Conspiracy in post-Soviet Russia. In: Brinks J.H., Timms E., Rock S. (Ed): *Nationalist Myths and Modern Media: Contested Identities in the Age of Globalization*, London: Palgrave Macmillan.

Hagemeister M. (2008). The "Protocols of the Elders of Zion": Between History and Fiction. *New German Critique*, 35 (1): 83-95.

Hagemeister M. (2010). Trilogie der Apocalypse. Vladimir Solovyev, Serafim von Sarov und Sergej Nilus über das Kommen des Antichrist und das Ende der Weltgeschichte. In: Brandes W., Schmieder F. (Ed.): *Antichrist: Konstruktionen von Feinbildern*. Berlin: de Gruyter Verlag: 255-276. [Trilogy of the Apocalypse. Vladimir Solovyov, Seraphim of Sarov and Sergey Nilus on the Coming of the Antichrist and the End of World's History, In: *Antichrist: Constructing the Ultimate Enemy*].

Harris P. (2012). One in Four Americans Think Obama May be the Antichrist, Survey Says. *The Guardian*. Available at: https://www.theguardian.com/world/2013/apr/02/americans-obama-anti-christ-conspiracy-theories [Accessed 31 August 2020].

Hell J. (2009). Katechon: Carl Schmitt's Imperial Theology and the Ruins of the Future. *The Germanic Review*, 84(4): 283-326.

Hellinger D.C. (2019). *Conspiracies and Conspiracy Theories in the Age of Trump*. Cham: Palgrave Macmillan.

Hofstadter R. (1966). *The Paranoid Style in American Politics and Other Essays*. London: Jonathan Cape.

Howarth D.R, Norval A.J., Stavrakakis Y. (2009). *Discourse Theory and Political Analysis: Identities, Hegemonies, and Social Change*. Manchester: Manchester University Press.

Hyde L. (2017). *Trickster Makes This World: How Disruptive Imagination Creates Culture*. Edinburgh: Canongate Books.

Ilyin V. (2016). Anatomy of the Russian Conservative Turn. In: F. Saccá, (Ed.) *Globalization and New Socio Political Trends*. Roma: Eurilink.

Isupov K. (1995) *Antikhrist (Iz Istorii Otechestvennoy Dukhovnosti): Antologiya*. Moskva: Vysh. Shk. [Antichrist (From the History of Russian Spirituality): Anthology].

Jenks G. (1991). *The Origins and the Early Development of the Antichrist Myth*. Berlin: de Gruyter.

Jung C. (1970). *Aion. Researches into the Phenomenology of the Self*. Princeton: Princeton University Press.

Kantor V. (2012). Liubov k Dvoyniku: Dvoynichestvo Mif i Realnost Russkoy Kultury. *Forum Noveyshey Vostochnoyevropeikoy Istorii i Kultury*, 9 (2): 186 208. Available at: https://iph-ras.ru/uplfile/root/biblio/pj/pj_11/8.pdf [Accessed 31 August 2020]. [Love for the Double. The Doublness: Myth and Reality of the Russian Culture].

Kantorowicz E. (1957). *The King's Two Bodies*: a *Study in Medieval Political Theology*. Princetown: Princeton University Press.

Khagi S. (2013). One Billion Years after the End of the World: Historical Deadlock, Contemporary Dystopia, and the Continuing Legacy of the Strugatskii Brothers. *Slavic Review*, 72(2): 267-286.

Khlebnikov M.V. (2012). *Teoriya Zagovora. Opyt Sotsiokulturnogo Issledovaniya.* Moskva: Kuchkovo Pole. [Conspiracy Theory. Sociocultural Research Experience].

Khoruzhenko T. (2017). Motiv Vtorogo Prishestviya v Sovremennoy Russkoy Fentezi. *Problemy Istoricheskoy Poetiki*, 15(2): 141-158. [The Motive of the Second Coming in Modern Russian Fantasy].

King A. (2017). Kremlin Spokesman: "Russia is Being Demonized". *CNN Politics*. Available at: https://edition.cnn.com/2017/03/12/politics/peskov-on-gps-cnntv/index.html [Accessed 31 August 2020].

Kocherov S. (2003). *Russkaia Ideya: Sushchnost i Smysl*. N. Novogrod: NGPU. [Russian Idea: Essence and Meaning].

Kostiuk K. (2002). Tri Portreta. Sotsialno-Eticheskie Vozzreniya v Russkoy Pravoslavnoy Tserkvi Kontsa XX Veka. *Kontinent*, № 113. Available at: http://magazines.russ.ru/continent/2002/113/kost.html [Accessed 31 August 2020]. [Three Portraits. Social and Ethical Views in the Russian Orthodox Church at the End of the 20th Century].

Kuleshov E. (2017). Chem Otlichayetsya Rusofobstvo Ot Rusofilstva. *Newsland.com*. Available at: https://newsland.com/community/4765/content/chem-otlichaetsia-rusofobstvo-ot-rusofilstva/5849603 [Accessed 31 August 2020].

Laclau E. and Mouffe C. (2001). *Hegemony and Socialist Strategy: Towards a Radical Democratic Politics*. London: Verso.

Landes R. and Katz S.T. (2012). *The Paranoid Apocalypse: a Hundred-Year Retrospective on the Protocols of the Elders of Zion*. New York: New York University Press.

Laqueur W. (1993). *Black Hundred: The Rise of the Extreme Right in Russia.* New York: Harper Collins Publishers.

Laruelle M. (2012). Conspiracy and Alternate History in Russia: A Nationalist Equation for Success? *The Russian Review*, 71 (4): 565-580.

Laruelle M. (2016). The Izborsky Club, or the New Conservative Avant-Garde in Russia. *Russian Review*, 75 (4): 626 644.

Laruelle M. (2017). *Eurasianism and the European Far Right: Reshaping the Europe-Russia Relationship*. Lahnam: Lexington Books.

Latynina A. (2006). Trikster Kak Spasitel Rossii. *Novyi Mir*. Available at: http://magazines.russ.ru/novyi_mi/2006/2/la11.html [Accessed 31 August 2020]. [Trickster as the Saviour of Russia].

Leontiev K. (1969) [1879]. *Against the Current: Selections from the Novels, Essays, Notes, and Letters of Konstantin Leontiev*. New York: Weybright and Talley.

Levada.ru (2020). Velikiy Post i Religioznost. Available at: https://www.levada.ru/2020/03/03/velikij-post-i-religioznost/ [Accessed 31 August 2020]. [The Lent and Religiosity].

Lincoln B. (1999). *Theorizing Myth: Narrative, Ideology, and Scholarship*. Chicago: University of Chicago.

Lipovetsky M. (2010). *Charms of the Cynical Reason: Tricksters in Soviet and Post-Soviet Culture*. Boston: Academic Studies Press.

Liszka J.J. (1989). *The Semiotic of Myth: a Critical Study of the Symbol*. Bloomington: Indiana University Press.

Livers K. (2010). The Tower or the Labirynth: Conspiracy, Occult, and Empire-Nostalgia in the Work of Viktor Pelevin and Aleksandr Prokhanov. *The Russian Review*, 69 (3): 477-503.

Lotman Y. (2005). On the Semiosphere. *Sign Systems Studies*, 33 (1): 205-229.

Lotman Y. and Uspensky B. (1985). Binary Models in the Dynamics of Russian Culture (to the End of the 18th Century). In: Nakhimovsky A.D. and Nakhimovsky A.S. (Ed): *The Semiotics of Russian Cultural History: Essays*. New York: Cornell University Press.
Lyotard J.F. (1979) *The Postmodern Condition: A Report on Knowledge*. Minneapolis: University of Minnesota Press.
Malia M. (2000. *Russia Under Western Eyes. From the Bronze Horseman to the Lenin Mausoleum*. Cambridge: Belnap Press of Harvard University Press
Marsh R. (2010). The "New Political Novel" by Right-Wing Writers in Post-Soviet Russia. *Forum für Osteuropäische Ideen und Zeitgeschichte*, 14(2): 159-188.
Matich O. (2005). *Erotic Utopia: The Decadent Imagination in Russia's fin-de-siècle*. Madison: University of Wisconsin.
Mazurek S. (2008). *Rosyjski Renesans Religijno-Filozoficzny: Próba Syntezy*. Warszawa: Wydawnictwo Instytutu Filozofii i Socjologii PAN. [Russian Religious Renaissance: Attempt at Synthesis].
McGinn B. (1994) *Antichrist: Two Thousand Years of the Human Fascination with Evil*. San Francisco: HarperSanFrancisco
McNeill W. (1986). Mythistory, or Truth, Myth, History and Historians. *The American Historical Review*, 91 (1): 1-10.
Menzel B. (2012). Introduction. In: Menzel B., Hagemeister M. and Rosenthal B.G. (Ed.): *The New Age of Russia: Occult and Esoteric Dimensions*. München: Otto Sagner: 11-27.
Merezhkovsky D. (2000) [1914] *Ne Mir No Mech*. Moskva: Izdatelstvo AST. [Not Peace, But a Sword].
Minjust.ru. *Federalnyj Spisok Ekstremictitskikh Materialov*. Available at: http://minjust.ru/ru/extremist-materials [Accessed 31 August 2020]. [The Federal List of Extremist Materials].
Mitrofanova A. (2005). *The Politicization of Russian Orthodoxy: Actors and Ideas*. Stuttgart: ibidem-Verlag.
Mørch A. J. (2008). In Search of the Grand: Pavel Krusanov. In: Lindbladh J. (Ed).: *The Poetics of Memory in Post Totalitarian Narration*. Lund: The Centre for European Studies: 127-137.
Moss V. (2014). Alexander Dugin and the Meaning of Russian History. Available at: http://www.orthodoxchristianbooks.com/articles/517/alexander-dugin-meaning-russian-history/ [Accessed 31 August 2020].
Mouffe C. (1993). *The Return of the Political*. London; New York: Verso.
Murav H. (1993). A Curse on Russia: Gorenstein's Anti-"Psalom" and the Critics. *Russian Review*, 52 (2): 213-227.
Murawska S. (2017). Paranoja a Technologia. O Teorii spiskowej w Kontekście Technofobii i Postępu Technologicznego. *Studia Etnologiczne i Antropologiczne*, 16: 33-43. [Paranoia and Technology. On Conspiracy Theories in the Context of Technophobia and Technological Progress].
Neumann I. (1996). *Russia and the Idea of Europe: a Study in Identity and International Relations*. London, New York: Routledge.
Neumann I. (1999). *Uses of the Other: "The East" in European Identity Formation*, Minneapolis: University of Minnesota Press.
Noordenbos B. (2016). *Post-Soviet Literature and the Search For Russian Identity*. New York: Palgrave Macmillian.
Nöth W. (2004). Semiotics of Ideology, *Semiotica*, 148 (1-4): 11-21.

O'Connor K. (2006). *Intellectuals and Apparatchiks: Russian Nationalism and the Gorbachev Revolution*. Lanham: Lexington Books.
Oushakine S. (2009). *The Patriotism of Despair: Nation, War, and Loss in Russia*. New York: Cornell University Press.
Panchenko A. (2001). Eschatological Expectations in a Changing World: Narratives about the End of the World in Present Day Russian Folk Culture. *SEEFA Journal* 1(1): 10-25.
Panchenko A. (2004). New Religious Movements and the Study of Folklore: The Russian Case. *Electronic Journal of Folklore*, 28: 111-128.
Panchenko A. (2016). The Computer Called the Beast: Eschatology and Conspiracy Theory in Modern Religious Cultures. *Forum for Anthropology and Culture*. № 12: 186-200.
Panchenko A. (2018). Plan Dallesa: Sovetskaya Literatura, Teorii Zagavora i Moralnye Paniki v Rossii Rubezha XX i XXI Vekov. *Russkaya Literatura*, № 2: 118-136. [The Dulles' Plan: Soviet Literature, Conspiracy Theories, and Moral Panics in Russia on the Verge of the Twentieth and Twenty-First Centuries].
Petrov A. (2007). *Mify Russkoy Idei (Mif Kak Problema v Tvorchestve Russkikh Religyoznykh Filosofov "Serebryanogo Veka"*. Available at: http://www.bestreferat.ru/referat-88805.html [Accessed 31 August 2020]. [Myths of the Russian Idea (Myth as a Problem in the Works of Russian Religious Philosophers of the "Silver Age"].
Piirsalu J. and Panchenko A. (2017). Dulles' Plan as a Diagnosis for Russian Society, *International Centre for Defense and Security*. Available at: https://www.diplomaatia.ee/en/article/dulles-plan-as-a-diagnosis-for-russian-society [Accessed 31 August 2020].
Popper K. (1967). *The Open Society and Its Enemies*. New York: Harper & Row.
Pospielovsky D. (1984). *The Russian Church Under the Soviet regime 1917-1982*. New York: St. Vladimir's Seminary Press.
Przybył E. (1999). *W Cieniu Antychrysta: Idee Staroobrzędowców w XVII w*. Kraków: Zakład Wydawniczy Nomos. [In the Shadow of Antichrist: The Ideas of Old Believers in the 17th Century].
Pyman A. (2011). *History of Russian Symbolism*. Cambridge: Cambridge University Press.
Riasanovsky N. (1985). *The Image of Peter the Great in Russian History and Thought*. New York: Oxford University Press.
Rivkin N. (2017). Russia's Thorny Relationship with Democracy. *New Eastern Europe*. Available at: https://neweasterneurope.eu/2017/05/31/russia-s-thorny-relationship-with-democracy/ [31 August 2020].
Robbins T. (1999). Apocalypse, Persecution, and Self-Immolation: Mass Suicides Among Old-Believers in Late-17th-Century Russia. In: Wessinger C. (Ed.): *Millennialism, Persecution, and Violence: Historical Cases*. New York: Syracuse University Press: 205-219.
Rousselet K. (2015). Religiya i Sovremennye Tekhnologii, ili Protivorechivoe Mirovozrenie Pravoslavnykh Khristian. In: Komina J., Panchneko A. and Shtyrkov S. (Ed.), *Izobretenie Religii: Desekuliarizatsiya v Postsovetskom Kontekste*, St. Peterburg: Izd-vo Evrop. Un-ta v Sankt-Peterburge: 46-62.
Runions E. (2009). Detranscendentalizing Decisionism: Political Theology After Gayatri Spivak. *Journal of Feminist Studies in Religion*, 25 (3): 67 85.
Ryan W. (1999). *The Bathhouse at Midnight: an Historical Survey of Magic an Divination in Russia*. Stroud: Sutton.
Sadowski J., Przybył-Sadowska E., and Urbanek D. (2014). *Rosja: Przestrzeń, Czas i Znaki*. Kraków: Wydawnictwo LIBRON. [Russia: Space, Time, and Signs].

Sanders P. (2013). Under Western Eyes. How Meta-Narrative Shapes our Perception of Russia -and Why it is Time for a Qualitative Shift. *Institute for Human Sciences.* Available at: http://www.iwm.at/read-listen-watch/transit-online/under-western-eyes/ [Accessed 25 February 2020].
Schmitt C. (1963). *The Concept of the Political.* Chicago: University of Chicago Press.
Schmitt C. (2005) [1985]. *Political Theology: Four Chapters on the Concept of Sovereignty.* Cambridge: MIT Press.
Schmitt C. (2008). *The Leviathan in the State Theory of Thomas Hobbes: Meaning and Failure of a Political Symbol.* Chicago, London: University of Chicago.
Schöpfin G. (1997). The Functions of Myth and Taxonomy of Myths. In: Segal R. (Ed.) *Myth. Critical Concepts in Literary and Cultural Studies*, Vol. I, Routledge: New York: 205-220.
Sheiko K. and Brown S. (2014). *History as Therapy: Alternative History and Nationalist Imaginings in Russia, 1991-2014.* Stuttgart: Ibidem.
Shekhovtsov A. (2018) *Russia and the Western Far Right: Tango Noir.* London: Routledge.
Shermer M. (1997). *Why People Believe Weird Things: Pseudoscience, Superstition, and Other Confusions of Our Time.* New York: W.H. Freeman.
Shevtsova L. (2007). Anti-Westernism is the New National Idea. *The Moscow Times.* Available at: https://carnegie.ru/2007/08/07/anti-westernism-is-new-national-idea-pub-19480 [Accessed 31 August 2020].
Shnirelman V. (2012). Khazariya, Apokalipsis i "Mirovaya Zakulisa": Kak Prepodavatelnitsa Frantsuzskogo Brosila Vyzov Zapadu. *Forum Noveyshey Vostochnoevropeyskoy Istorii i Kultury*, № 2. Available at: http://www1.ku-eichstaett.de/ZIMOS/forum/docs/forumruss18/04Shnirelman.pdf [Accessed 31 August 2020]. [Khazaria, Apocalypse and "World's Backstage": How a French Teacher Throw a Challenge to the West].
Shnirelman V. (2016). Alexander Dugin: Building a Bridge between Eschatology and Conspiracy. *State, Religion and Church in Russia and Worldwide*, 34 (4): 194-221.
Shnirelman V. (2017). *Koleno Danogo. Eskhatologiya i Antisemitizm v Sovremennoy Rossii.* Moskva: Izdatelstvo BBI. [The Tribe of Dan. Eschatology and Antisemitism in Contemporary Russia].
Slesaryeva D. O. (2013). Genezis Konspirologicheskogo Romana. *Istoricheskaya i Sotsialno-Obrazovatelnaya Mysl*, 6 (22): 192-196.
Solovyov V. (1954) [1900]. *Tri Razgavora.* New York: Izd-vo im. Chekhova. [Three Conversations].
Storchak V. (2003). *Tema Rossiyskogo Messianizma v Obshchestvenno-Politicheskoy i Filosofskoi Mysli Rossii.* Moskva: RAGS. [The Theme of the Russian Messianism in Russian Socio-Political and Philosophical Thought].
Sulikowska A. (2014). Znaki Antychrysta. Miniatury Starowierskiej „Komentowanej Apokalipsy" z Kolekcji Biblioteki Narodowej. *Rocznik Biblioteki Narodowej*, 45: 79-96. Available at: http://archiv.ub.uni-heidelberg.de/artdok/3878/1/Sulikowska_Znaki_Antychrysta_2014.pdf [Accessed 31 August 2020]. [Signs of Antichrist. Miniatures from the Old Believer's Apocalypse from the National Library of Poland Collection].
Suslov M. (2013). "Sviataya Rus": Geopoliticheskoe Voobrazhenye v Sovremennoy Russkoy Pravoslavnoy Tserkvi. *Forum Noveyshey Vostochnoyevropeyskoy Istorii i Kultury*, 10 (2): 311-327. Available at: http://www1.ku-eichstaett.de/ZIMOS/forum/inhaltruss20.html [Accessed 31 August 2020]. [The "Holy Rus'': Geopolitical Imagination in the Contemporary Russian Orthodox Church].

Suslov M. (2016a). The Genealogy Of The Idea Of Monarchy In The Post-Soviet Political Discourse Of The Russian Orthodox Church, *State, Religion, and Church*, 3 (1): 27-62.
Suslov M. (2016b). Of Planets and Trenches: Imperial Science Fiction in Contemporary Russia. *The Russian Review*, 75(4): 562-578.
The Holy Bible: English Standard Version Containing the Old and the New Testaments (2002) Wheaton: Crossway Bibles.
Tolstanova M. (2008). The Janus-faced Empire Distorting Orientalist Discourses: Gender, Race and Religion in the Russian/(post)Soviet Constructions of the "Orient". *Worlds of Knowledges Otherwise*, 2(2): 2-11.
Tolz V. (2011). *Russia's Own Orient: the Politics of Identity and Oriental Studies in the Late Imperial and Early Soviet Periods*. Oxford: Oxford University Press.
Trenin D. (2002). *The End of Eurasia: Russia on the Border Between Geopolitics and Globalization*. Washington: Carnegie Endowment for International Peace.
Trenin D. (2007). Russia Re-defines Itself and Its Relation with the West. *The Washington Quarterly*, 30 (2): 95-105.
Trepanier L. (2015). Putin's Russia: Power and Postmodernity. *Voegelin View*. Available at: https://voegelinview.com/putins-russia-power-and-postmodernity/ [Accessed 31 August 2020].
Tyutchev F. (2006) [1866]. "Umom Rossiyu Ne Ponyat...". Available at: http://www.ruthenia.ru/tiutcheviana/publications/trans/umomrossiju.html [Accessed 31 August 2020]. [Russia Cannot Be Grasped by Mind].
Umland A. (2007). *Post-Soviet 'Uncivil Society' and the Rise of Aleksandr Dugin: A Case Study of the Extraparliamentary Radical Right in Contemporary Russia*. Cambridge: University of Cambridge.
Uspensky B. and Zhivov V. (2018) *"Tsar and God" and Other Essays in Russian Cultural Semiotics*. Boston: Acadmic Studies Press.
Van Binsbergen W. (2009) Rupture and Fusion in the Approach to Myth: Situation Myth Analysis Between Philosophy, Poetics and Long-Range Historical Reconstruction. *Religion Compass*, 3: 1-34.
Van Prooijen J. (2018). *Psychology of Conspiracy Theories*. New York: Routledge.
Veraksa A. (2013). Symbol as a Cognitive Tool. *Psychology in Russia: State of the Art*, 6 (1): 57-65.
Verkhovsky A. (2004). Who is the Enemy Now? Islamophobia and Antisemitism Among Russian Orthodox Nationalists Before and After September 11. *Patterns of Prejudice*, 38 (2): 127-143.
Viola L. (1990). The Peasant Nightmare: Visions of Apocalypse in Soviet Countryside. *Journal of Modern History*, 62 (4): 747-770.
Wachtel A. (2006). *Remaining Relevant After Communism: the Role of the Writers in Eastern Europe*. Chicago: University of Chicago Press.
Walicki A. (1979). *A History of Russian Thought: From the Enlightenment to Marxism*. Stanford: Stanford University Press.
Williams R. (1999). *Russia Imagined: Art, Culture and National Identity*. New York: P. Lang.
Wodziński C. (2000). *Św. Idiota: Projekt Antropologii Apofatycznej*. Gdańsk: Słowo/obraz/terytoria. [St. Idiot: The Project of Apophatic Anthropology].
Wodziński C. (2005). *Trans, Dostojewski, Rosja, czyli o Filozofowaniu Siekierą*. Gdańsk: Słowo/Obraz/Terytoria. [Trans, Dostoyevsky and Philosophizing with an Axe].

Wolff L. (1994). *Inventing Eastern Europe: The Map of Civilization on the Mind of the Enlightenment.* Stanford: Stanford University Press.
Wöll A. and Wydra H. (2008). *Democracy and Myth in Russia and Eastern Europe.* London; New York: Routledge.
Yablokov I. (2015). Conspiracy Theories as a Russian Public Diplomacy Tool: The Case of Russia Today (RT). *Politics,* 34 (3-4): 301-315.
Yablokov I. (2018). *Fortress Russia: Conspiracy Theories in Post-Soviet Russia.* Cambridge: Polity Press.
Yerofeyev V. (1999). *Entsiklopediya Russkoy Dushi.* St. Petersburg: Azbuka. [Encyclopedia of the Russian Soul].
Yurchak A. (2005). *Everything Was Forever, Until it Was no More: The Last Soviet Generation.* Princeton: Princeton University Press.
Yurchak A. (2011). A Parasite from Outer Space: How Sergei Kurekhin Proved That Lenin Was a Mushroom. *Slavic Review,* 70(2): 307-333.
Zamaleev A. (2010). *Samosoznanye Rossii: Issledovaniya po Russkoy Filosofii, Politologii i Kulture.* Sankt-Petersburg: Nauka. [Russian Self-Cognition: Research on Russian Philosophy, Political Science, and Culture].
Zelinsky B. (2008). *Das Böse in der Russischen Kultur.* Köln: Böhlau Verlag. [Evil in Russian Culture].
Zenkovskiy S. (1970). *Russkoye Staroobriadchestvo: Dukhovnye Dvizheniya Semnadtsatogo Veka.* München: W. Fink. [Russian Old Believers: Spiritual Movements of the 17th Century].

Literatur und Kultur im mittleren und östlichen Europa

herausgegeben von Reinhard Ibler

ISSN 2195-1497

1 *Elisa-Maria Hiemer*
   Generationenkonflikt und Gedächtnistradierung
   Die Aufarbeitung des Holocaust in der polnischen Erzählprosa des 21.
   Jahrhunderts
   ISBN 978-3-8382-0394-2

2 *Adam Jarosz*
   Przybyszewski und Japan
   Bezüge und Annäherungen
   Mit einem Vorwort von Hanna Ratuszna und Quellentexten in Erstübertragung
   ISBN 978-3-8382-0436-9

3 *Adam Jarosz*
   Das Todesmotiv im Drama von Stanisław Przybyszewski
   ISBN 978-3-8382-0496-3

4 *Valentina Kaptayn*
   Zwischen Tabu und Trauma
   Kateřina Tučkovás Roman *Vyhnání Gerty Schnirch* im Kontext der
   tschechischen Literatur über die Vertreibung der Deutschen
   ISBN 978-3-8382-0482-6

5 *Reinhard Ibler (Hg.)*
   Der Holocaust in den mitteleuropäischen
   Literaturen und Kulturen seit 1989
   The Holocaust in the Central European Literatures and Cultures since 1989
   ISBN 978-3-8382-0512-0

6 *Iris Bauer*
   Schreiben über den Holocaust
   Zur literarischen Kommunikation in Marian Pankowskis Erzählung *Nie ma Żydówki*
   ISBN 978-3-8382-0587-8

7 *Olga Zitová*
   Thomas Mann und Ivan Olbracht
   Der Einfluss von Manns Mythoskonzeption auf die karpatoukrainische Prosa
   des tschechischen Schriftstellers
   ISBN 978-3-8382-0633-2

8   *Trixi Jansen*
    Der Tod und das Mädchen
    Eine Analyse des Paradigmas aus Tod und Weiblichkeit in ausgewählten
    Erzählungen I.S. Turgenev
    ISBN 978-3-8382-0627-1

9   *Olena Sivuda*
    "Aber plötzlich war mir, als drohe das Haus über mir
    zusammenzubrechen."
    Komparative Analyse des Heimkehrermotivs in der deutschen und russischen
    Prosa nach dem Zweiten Weltkrieg
    ISBN 978-3-8382-0779-7

10 *Victoria Oldenburger*
    Keine Menschen, sondern ganz besondere Wesen ...
    Die Frau als Objekt unkonventioneller Faszination in Ivan A. Bunins Erzählband
    Temnye allei (1937–1949)
    ISBN 978-3-8382-0777-3

11 *Andrea Meyer-Fraatz, Thomas Schmidt (Hg.)*
    „Ich kann es nicht fassen,
    dass dies Menschen möglich ist"
    Zur Rolle des Emotionalen in der polnischen Literatur
    über den Holocaust
    ISBN 978-3-8382-0859-6

12 *Julia Friedmann*
    Von der Gorbimanie zur Putinphobie?
    Ursachen und Folgen medialer Politisierung
    ISBN 978-3-8382-0936-4

13 *Reinhard Ibler (Hg.)*
    Der Holocaust in den mitteleuropäischen Literaturen und Kulturen:
    Probleme der Politisierung und Ästhetisierung
    The Holocaust in the Central European Literatures and Cultures:
    Problems of Poetization and Aestheticization
    ISBN 978-3-8382-0952-4

14 *Alexander Lell*
    Studien zum erzählerischen Schaffen Vsevolod M. Garšins
    Zur Betrachtung des Unrechts in seinen Werken aus der Willensperspektive
    Arthur Schopenhauers
    ISBN 978-3-8382-1042-1

15 Dmitry Shlapentokh
    The Mongol Conquests in the Novels of Vasily Yan
    An Intellectual Biography
    ISBN 978-3-8382-1017-9

16 Katharina Bauer
    Liebe – Glaube – Russland:
    Russlandkonzeptionen im Schaffen Aleksej N. Tolstojs
    ISBN 978-3-8382-1182-4

17 Magdalena Baran-Szołtys, Monika Glosowitz,
    Aleksandra Konarzewska (eds.)
    Imagined Geographies
    Central European Spatial Narratives between 1984 and 2014
    ISBN 978-3-8382-1225-8

18 Adam Jarosz
    Der Spiegel und die Spiegelungen
    Über Geschlecht und Seele im Werk von Stanisław Przybyszewski
    ISBN 978-3-8382-1246-3

19 Šárka Sladovníková
    The Holocaust in Czechoslovak
    and Czech Feature Films
    ISBN 978-3-8382-1196-1

20 Julia Spanberger
    Grenzen und Grenzerfahrungen in den Texten Viktor Pelevins
    Eine Analyse seiner frühen Prosa
    ISBN 978-3-8382-1460-3

21 Magda Dolińska-Rydzek
    The Antichrist in Post-Soviet Russia: Transformations of an Ideomyth
    ISBN 978-3-8382-1545-7

ibidem.eu